Am I Cured Yet?
My Wonderful Life with Panic Disorder and PTSD
by Jim Blackwood, Jr.

Copyright © 2019 by Jim Blackwood, Jr.

All rights reserved.

Cover art: Natalie Sept

Cover layout/design: Sue Campbell

Editing/interior layout: Jami Carpenter

No part of this book may be reproduced in any form or by any electronic or mechanical means including information storage and retrieval systems, without permission in writing from the author. The only exception is by a reviewer, who may quote short excerpts in a review.

This book is not intended as a substitute for the medical advice of physicians. The reader should regularly consult a physician in matters relating to his/her health and particularly with respect to any symptoms that may require diagnosis or medical attention.

This is a work of nonfiction. The names of some of the people have been changed.

No Clock Books
Portland, Oregon 97215
www.jimblackwoodjr.com

ISBN 978-0-578-54943-9

ISBN 978-0-578-54944-6 (ebook)

First Edition

Dedication
For Sally

Even the most serene face can conceal an ever-changing puzzle of troubled memories.

Contents

Dedication iii

Chapter 1: Making the Invisible … Visible 7

Chapter 2: Just a Nervous Child 11

Chapter 3: It's the Little Things 19

Chapter 4: Smart Kid in a Dangerous World 25

Chapter 5: Showed Me Something 33

Chapter 6: I Guess I Am On My Own 41

Chapter 7: The Freshman Train Wreck 53

Chapter 8: Love, Drugs and Rock & Roll 61

Chapter 9: Crushed Car and Blown Mind 71

Chapter 10: Lost on the Willamette River 85

Chapter 11: Only Ten Blocks from the Senate 99

Chapter 12: Bad Night in a Chinese Restaurant 113

Chapter 13: Fear Gets a Name 125

Chapter 14: Goodbye to the Dream 133

Chapter 15: Arrivals and Departures 145

Chapter 16: A Man and his Dog 157

Chapter 17: Lone Wolf Mode 167

Chapter 18: Where Is That Damned Cure? 177

Chapter 19: Putting Down Roots 187

Chapter 20: I Have Two Best Friends? 195

Chapter 21: I Once Knew a Punk 205

Chapter 22: Poets and Frisbees? 217

Chapter 23: Sally Wakes the Knucklehead 229

Chapter 24: Back in the Left Field Box Seats 239

Chapter 25: How Work Really Worked 245

Chapter 26: What Goes Up 253

Chapter 27: So That's What It Is 265

Chapter 28: Wings of Desire 275

Chapter 29: Getting Back 289

Chapter 30: It's Okay to Close the Door 299

Chapter 31: It Feels Like Home 309

Chapter 32: Bold Moves and Second Chapters 321

Chapter 33: Too Much Loss 335

Chapter 34: Finding My Higher Purpose 339

Chapter 35: Knowing When 351

Chapter 36: The Good Work is Never Done 359

Chapter 37: My Cure 369

Resources 375

Acknowledgments 377

About the Author 379

Chapter 1

Making the Invisible ... Visible

I HAVE LIVED WITH MENTAL ILLNESS my entire life. Several members of my family have also suffered from mental illness. Not all of them made it through the storm. What I inherited genetically shaped my life experience in some awful ways. For decades, my illness was mostly undiagnosed. Lord knows I tried to get someone, anyone, to tell me what was happening to me. Psychologists and doctors treated me with what they knew at the time. By the time science had caught up with my symptoms, my lifestyle revolved around my illness.

For those who live with panic disorder and PTSD, and those who love them, I offer my intimate view of how mental illness arises and evolves over a lifetime. The paths through mental illness often share common elements and solutions. My many years seeking a cure are a critique of what worked and what didn't. And for those readers with children, perhaps my story will offer clues that can lead to early intervention and effective treatment.

Like many PTSD sufferers, my illness can only vaguely be linked to a single incident. It developed over time as a reaction to a number of difficult moments in my life. Bullying is at the core of my trauma. Early on, my mind was wired to misinterpret the world around me as a hostile place. My panic disorder, for all its devastating impact on my life, was a misunderstood clue that something deeper was going on. Traumas, big and small, created fertile ground for my anxiety. The roots of my mental illness spread in many directions. When my PTSD finally did clearly manifest itself, I was shocked. I had no idea.

When I have been honest with friends and strangers about my mental illness, sometimes something wonderful happens. People pull me aside. Often whispering, they tell me that they, too, have a secret. Mental illness has touched them or someone they love. I am often as surprised by what they tell me as they had been when I was honest with them. Mental illness hides in plain sight.

We are the collection of our stories. Story telling runs deep in my family. My people are Scotch-Irish. Poor, insular, loyal, and hardworking, they landed in the back country of Appalachia, then migrated to the Arkansas Ozark mountains. We were hillbillies who finally fled poverty to the new hope of the Southern California desert. We can be a taciturn bunch, most comfortable revealing ourselves by telling stories old and new. Some stories stay locked away. Secret fears. Hidden pleasures. There are the stories we would like to forget but can't. Look away from this page. I bet you are telling yourself a story right now.

The simple catalyst for this memoir was a question from a dear friend: "What happened?" I had a much-repeated supply of stories that I told myself and others. I believed I knew my life story. But memory is tricky. Our memories are not a perfect map of our lives. Sometimes we fill in the gaps with pieces that make us feel more comfortable. Unlike most folks, I have relentlessly recorded my thoughts on every imaginable media. I tossed full notepads, letters, and cards in a pile on my desk and, in moments of clutter fatigue, dumped everything into boxes. Some of those boxes had been sealed for decades. Like an archeologist, I had to open all of those boxes and honestly reconstruct my life. In many ways, it turned out I spent a lifetime preparing to write this book.

I offer this memoir as a reassurance to those who live with mental illness and those who love them. Through all the difficulties and darkness, it is possible to create a life full of joy and passion. You don't have to become what your busy mind tells you to be. You can have a wonderful life.

Chapter 2

Just a Nervous Child

AT WHAT AGE does the word 'bullshit' become part of your vocabulary?

I was eight-years-old when my parents told my brother, Mike, and me that we were taking a day off from school. Who doesn't like a hooky day? We were going to Riverside, the big city 80 miles away. It had freeways, tall buildings, and actual bookstores. Indio had a little library. In Riverside, I could actually buy books.

Whenever I say I grew up in Indio, I know the question is coming. "Where's that?" Same answer every time; "It's near Palm Springs." If Palm Springs in the 1960s was a big white Cadillac with chrome-tipped fins, then Indio was a beat-up 1958 Chevy pick-up with the rear gate hanging open. The kids who grew up in Indio were proud of that. We liked that we weren't Palm Springs and that there were miles of windswept sand dunes between us and them. Endless summer days pumping gas at my paternal Grandfather Blackwood's Texaco, I looked across the street and saw the Indio city limits sign: population 10,260. That's just enough people so you can't know everyone's name but at one time or another you have seen them all.

The biggest surprise of the trip to Riverside was that Dad was driving us during the week. He and my Great Uncle Jake owned a Texaco service station in Palm Desert about halfway between Indio and Palm Springs. My dad worked 12 hours a day, six days a week. Sometimes, a half-day on Sundays. I was happy Dad was going on the surprise trip, but the fact he wasn't at work was confusing.

Mike and I were confined to the vast back seat of the Pontiac. Seatbelts? Pffft ... To keep the peace, an imaginary barrier ran down the middle of the back seat (the precise middle). Violations of the line often required an intervention from the front seats. Not Dad, he was the driver, a near-sacred calling in our family. No, the final authority was my mother: Dorothy, Dot, or Dottie.

Indio once had a place of honor on old Route 99, the two-lane ribbon from the Mexico border up the spine of the west coast to the Canada. A cluster of truck stops, greasy spoons, and charmless court motels were the last stop before the road hooked a left and set out into 90 miles of desert to the Colorado River. Indio's culinary highlights were the competing Denny's and Sambo's. (The remarkably racist legend of 'little black Sambo' was on every menu and, in case you missed it, illustrated in glass tiles on the wall above your head.) Either restaurant was considered a treat for a family meal out.

Eventually, the completion of the interstate freeway shifted the center of gravity of our little town but that day our Pontiac creeped north out of town until it hit the freeway bypass, then Dad 'opened her up.' Nothing sounds like a big old V8 when the second bank of carburetor barrels kicks in and black smoke blasts from the tailpipes. "Good to clean her out," Dad would say as if quoting one of the ten commandments.

There was talk of a big park with trees and water in Riverside. For a desert kid any place that had water was special. Other than when we put the garden hose in the gutter in front of our house and the irrigation canals, moving water was a rare sight. The steep-sided canals were off limits. When people violated the prime directive to stay out, bodies were found floating miles away. As we grew older the roads parallel to those death traps were a playground. Fast cars and motorcycles piloted by stoned or drunk teenagers screamed down the canal roads. Childhood in the desert was a death race. We knew some of us wouldn't make it out alive but chasing away boredom was worth the risk. I knew three kids who didn't survive that chase.

I didn't know the trip to Riverside was about me. My folks were at a loss. Night terrors. The dark was my enemy. I would lay curled up, ears tuned to the slightest noise. Windy nights were the worst. My bedroom window was in the front of the little house with pink stucco walls. Mom planted roses and a bougainvillea in the garden at the front of the house. I hated that bougainvillea. It had long spiky thorns that raked back and forth on the wall outside my room. It sounded like the claws of a creature trying to scratch its way to me. When I could take it no more, I yelled into the dark, "Mommy! Mommy!" until she came. She stayed in my room long enough for me to fall asleep. Mom sometimes told me, "It's just the house settling." My frightened child's mind had no idea what that meant.

Night after night I lay there staring at my door to the hallway. Down that short hallway in the ceiling was the air intake and filters for the central air conditioner. In the desert it could be 100 degrees at midnight. I waited for the little 'tink' of the thermostat followed by the 'clump' of the air filters being sucked upward as the fans spun up. I never knew when this would happen but with all the faith I could muster I knew it would come. Like good guys coming over the hill in an old western, I would be saved by the humming, whooshing sound. I could finally sleep. The worst nights were when I called Mommy, fell asleep, then woke up in terror again. I believed I had used my one-time call into the darkness. With all the will I could summon, muscles tight, adrenaline pumping, I resisted calling out. Even in my child's mind it was embarrassing and weak. Now all I had left was waiting … waiting for that sound of humming fans and moving air. White noise is still my best friend.

In the mid-1960s small town America mental health care did not exist. (I'm not sure how much better it is now.) Family therapists ... nope. Child psychologists ... nope. What we had was our general practitioner. Dr. Wheeler was a man for all ages and ailments. He was the one my parents consulted about little Jimmy's problems.

When we first moved to North Indio, literally the other side of the tracks, I had a friend named Mark. I still have clear memories of playing in the sandy fields before they built the next block of houses behind ours. He and I did experiments on rocks, like putting peanut butter on one and seeing what would happen. Only later did Mom tell me that Mark didn't exist. There were, as yet, no other kids on the block. I invented one. A child's brain that creates monsters also creates friends.

Based on the school calendar, I was only three days from the cutoff to start kindergarten a year later, which meant I was almost always the youngest in my class. In terms of maturation, that is a big deal. My peers were older and bigger. The girls were almost alien creatures. I was precocious, but thankfully my folks said no to my being moved ahead a class when the teachers recommended it.

I didn't want to go to kindergarten. I remember that. I heard later I had to be coaxed and my mom stayed until I settled in. In second grade, I can't recall what happened, but I discovered that in order for me to be in class at all my mom sat in the back of the class.

I don't know how long that went on, but long enough for my folks to be very worried.

Decades later, as part of my trauma therapy, I finally asked my parents what more they could tell me. When I was eight, Mom said, my parents woke up to the sound of pounding. They found me in the bathroom, in the hallway between our rooms, pounding my head against the wall crying, "No! Stop!" and other things they couldn't understand. I woke up not remembering a thing. They admitted that they tried hard to forget that night, which is why I never knew about it until I asked.

Jim and Dot had us young. They weren't far removed from being kids themselves. How confusing it must have been for them to have their oldest boy so afraid. When I was old enough to see my parents as individuals, and cultivate empathy, I thought of my young parents. They tried everything they knew to protect and help me. Something was wrong. There really was no place to take me. There were no books. There was just their friendly doctor who said that Jimmy should have his brain tested. What must they have thought?

Finally, Mom explained the purpose of the special trip. She said, "The doctor said you needed to have a test. It won't hurt at all. Dad and I will be with you the whole time." We pulled in front of an unfamiliar building. A kind woman brought us into the room with glass windows, a tall table with a thin mattress, and a machine, a wondrous machine. My parents had taken me to get an electroencephalogram (EEG). A kid who loved science, I wasn't afraid. I was fascinated. The lady lifted up a bundle of wires. She said they were going to stick little things to my head and plug the other end into the machine. She took the round plug end of the wire and held it against my head. "Like this," she said. She then took the end of the wire that had a little paddle on it and attempted to plug it into the machine. "Well, it works something like this," she said, smiling.

I knew she was wrong. I looked at my folks for reassurance. Surely, they could see the lady was wrong. But they were playing along. For the first time I was afraid. Thank god, someone in a white coat swooped in and corrected the error that so offended me. He flipped the cable and plugged it in the right way. He said I would probably fall asleep while the test was happening. I did. Of course, I did. My folks were right there.

I don't think I was told the results of the EEG, not in any detail anyhow. I remember I got to see the paper with all the little squiggles. I assume my parents were, in part, relieved I didn't have a brain problem. I was a normal kid. What they told me was that I was a 'nervous child' and I would grow out of it. I wasn't buying it. Oh, for that special word … bullshit.

Chapter 3

It's the Little Things

WHAT DO YOU REMEMBER from your childhood? Happy times? Favorite gifts at Christmas? Best friends? Little adventures? As the nervous child, I recalled and relived the times I thought my body had failed me, those moments that confirmed I was not safe in the world.

In elementary school, I was sprouting fast but not putting on weight or muscle. I was very conscious of my body. Dad told me not to worry, I would grow into the long arms and legs. I didn't. I was clumsy and never able to keep up with the athletic boys. Being a skinny, brainy kid, I was an early target for bullying. Being good in class was one thing, but what counted was where you were picked when choosing up sides for kickball or softball. I was always picked last.

By second grade I had glasses. Fourth grade, corrective shoes. Braces for my buck teeth were coming. Oh stop ... The corrective shoes were black leather and oddly shaped, oblong. I had short tendons in my legs and walked on my toes with the gait of a flamingo. The shoes and special exercises I did at night were supposed to help. What I remember is that unlike every other kid in elementary school, I had two pairs of shoes. I wore the bulky leather shoes, then changed to tennis shoes at lunch. The second set of shoes were on a shelf where my classmates could see them.

I began to disappear during school lunch. I was a desert kid who hated the heat. I found ways to sneak into empty classrooms with their air blasting, evaporative swamp coolers, or into the big, dark, air-conditioned multipurpose room. I don't recall anyone coming with me or doing anything while I was in there. I think I just waited, counting the minutes until the bell rang to go back to class.

Fame in a small town is relative. Andrew Jackson Elementary School had a locally famous choir and choir was something I could do. Most importantly, the choir director selected me to blow the pitch-pipe. He handed me the felt case with the shiny, round metal pipe. Every hole had a different key stamped over the opening. I kept a little cheat sheet with the key for every song and at Mr. Rosine's direction, I softly blew the note. Everyone else hummed the note. In my mind, I was the most important kid in the choir.

Mr. Rosine was a talented musician who had his career cut short by polio. Heavy braces on both legs. He could only raise his right hand at the wrist. His limp left arm swung back and forth like an untimed metronome. He directed the choir with one finger. At the end of the song he shifted his weight so that his entire body raised his right hand just a little. Thirty kids stood transfixed by the subtle movements of his finger in a small sphere at his waist.

We practiced endlessly for the Christmas Show. Mr. Rosine taught us discipline in the pursuit of perfection. Parents and kids jammed into the multi-purpose room for our big performance. We stood on risers wearing robes that made the crowded room feel even warmer. In the middle of one of the songs, I felt dizzy. I fought the sensation. Kept singing. I wanted to throw up. I fingered the silver pitch-pipe in my hands. I knew ... knew ... the success of show was dependent on me being able to blow the next note.

I must have looked awful because Mr. Rosine looked straight at me. He came toward me. So did another teacher. I handed the pitch-pipe to his one working hand. I knew he couldn't bring it to his mouth to blow it. He had to give it to someone else. The teacher walked me to the school office, got me out of the robe, and brought me a glass of water. She was reassuring. "Oh honey, you got a little overheated. You might have fainted. But you will be fine." *Fine!?* my nervous child brain yelled. I couldn't trust my body to keep me upright. *Faint?* Holy cow! *Fall down?* I knew I had let everyone down.

Mr. Rosine was kind. I got the pitch-pipe back but from that moment on, as I stood on those risers, I was on high alert, monitoring my body lest it fail me again. Anyone who is anxious understands that 'high alert' is a default state of being. I had no idea then how I had only begun my apprenticeship.

For a nervous child, excitement can be a problem. Think about what your body does when you get excited. Your heart races, you get flushed and warm, your senses all alight. And ... you can get an upset stomach. Sounds like a anxiety attack, doesn't it?

~

Uncle Jake built short track stock cars. On Saturday nights, Dad hitched the race car to the tow truck and the family went racing. The San Bernardino Orange Show Grounds had a quarter-mile track. Under bright lights, smoke and flames burst from the exhausts of the incredibly loud cars as they went round and round the track. My little boy senses were overwhelmed. I loved it. One driver raced in a clown outfit. I loved Bobo. It was a perfect gimmick for a kid, seeing the clown in the car every time he passed the stands. In one main event, lap after lap, Bobo was closing in on the leader. I remember tensing my body to will Bobo into the lead. And then my stomach turned into a knot. I doubled up in pain. My dad took me to the restroom. Nothing happened. I calmed down and felt better. I missed the end of the race.

That seems simple enough. A kid just got overexcited. Happens all the time. However, for the nervous child, this sort of incident was a warning. I began to focus on how to avoid that feeling ever happening again. Eventually, I told people that my nervous system began in my stomach. Now at sporting events, concerts, or even at a comedy shows, when I feel myself getting too excited, I detach from whatever is happening in front of me and focus on my bodily sensations. I take a psychic firehose to the flames of excitement.

The 'nervous child' is the canvas on which the rest of my life was painted. Little incidents, normal occurrences, became life altering, proof that I could not trust my body. Much later in life, when he finally spoke about my anxiety, my dad said I was "... always afraid of the world. I just couldn't understand that."

Chapter 4

Smart Kid in a Dangerous World

IN ELEMENTARY SCHOOL, I always wanted to be the classroom president. Every class. Whenever the teacher asked for nominations I lived in hope. Please, god, someone nominate me. Please. It worked. President, vice-president, secretary. I was that kid. Indoors, I was a leader.

At home, I read both the morning and evening newspapers. My parents invested in the *World Book Encyclopedia*. I read the entire collection in alphabetical order. Straight through. Reading at college level by time I was in sixth grade, I had dinner, watched the news, *Gilligan's Island* or *Batman* or *The Monkeys*, then disappeared to my room to read. My folks had to stop me by turning off the lights.

But for all my verbal skills, I couldn't understand math. One teacher made me stay late to do multiplication on the blackboard. She thought she was helping. Standing at that board writing numbers over and over only felt like punishment. In my reading world, with a near photographic memory, I didn't simply remember what I read, I saw it in my mind. In math, I fell behind. I faked it. One more problem, I can't memorize. One assignment was to recite a poem. I recall my battle with Emma Lazarus' "The New Colossus," the poem on the pedestal of the Statue of Liberty. I watched people buzz through it, but I only recited it with prompting. One day, my inability to memorize would be life changing.

In junior high school, my nervous child gut still plagued me. Our family doctor wrote Mom a prescription. Little Jimmy, meet Donnatal. He said it would help me with my stomach. Google tells me that Donnatal is the combination of belladonna alkaloids and phenobarbital. Yup, mother's little helper was a classic downer. I don't think my folks had any idea what it was; they just wanted to help.

From that point on, in my left front pocket, I had a little tin Bayer aspirin box, which was opened by pressing on the back edge. (Press too hard and you sliced open your finger. What a design!) New, it held eight aspirins. In my case, it held a scrap of tissue wrapped around a single tiny white pill. My personal allocation. In case of emergency, pop open the tin box.

With that little pill box always in my pocket, how could I not think there was something wrong with me. No one seemed to know how to help so I tried to help myself. I set out to find a cure. On one trip to the bookstore in San Bernardino, I came home with a book called *Helping Yourself with Self-hypnosis*. It is hard to imagine what my parents thought when I asked them to pay for that book. Alone in my room, I tried to do self-hypnosis, thinking self-hypnosis would help me not be afraid all the time. It didn't work.

We all took IQ tests. A handful of kids were called into a room and told we did well. For public consumption, we were called more capable learners (MCL). We were the academic alpha predators who had been competing among each other for years. Once a week on Thursday morning a bus pulled up outside the school. The chosen few simply walked out of our classes and got on the bus and were driven to a junior college, College of the Desert (COD). We attended two classes. A real college campus. It was love at first sight. COD had the most wonderful library, as big as I had ever seen. I wanted that place ... badly.

~

In a world before anointed nerds, the science fair was a place where smart kids could compete like the athletes. My seventh-grade science project was based on my idea that certain kinds of light must be able to produce more power from a solar cell. If this was possible, I thought, we could get more energy from each solar cell.

From my earliest memories, Mom and I watched all the NASA spaceship blastoffs. She called me her 'space kid.' One thing that always fascinated me was how they made electricity from the sun. Fearless in my world of words, I sent a letter to the Jet

Propulsion Laboratory asking to know more about solar cells. What came back was a pile of scientific materials, most of which were beyond my comprehension; however, the scientists did send me a place where I could order my own solar cell.

Mom helped me get all of the materials. I bought a millivolt meter and mounted it in the backboard of the project display stand. I got different colored cellophane and mounted it on cardboard like big slides. One by one I measured how the colored light affected the electricity generated. I plotted the differences and displayed my results. That sounds pretty unscientific and simple, but remember, it was Indio in 1967. No one there had actually seen a solar cell. What an edge! Kids kept coming over to my display to see me turn on the lamp and make electricity.

The auditorium, the same room where I was still sometimes hid at lunch, was full of row after row of painted plywood project displays. The judges made their way around the room. After we presented our projects, the judges ushered us outside. The judging dragged on so late that Dad came directly from work. It is strange now to think I was a little embarrassed that he was the only dad there in his green Texaco uniform. Many of the dads wore shirts with their names on the front. I would have several jobs where I wore a uniform. Maybe it was the fact Dad alone was still in his uniform. It must have been near 7 p.m. Tired and hungry, Dad was there for me, smoking cigarettes and waiting.

My heart raced with each prize announcement and I died a little when they didn't call my name. They were done and I hadn't been named. Then the principal reached for the big sweepstakes trophy and pointed at me. It didn't seem possible. I went up to collect the trophy and applause. Looking at Mom and Dad from the stage, I think it was the first time I saw myself as a real person. I had an identity now. Everyone on campus knew me as the science fair guy.

The next year, I won the sweepstakes again. I had attached that solar cell to a little motor to turn the rear wheels of a toy car under the banner, 'Solar Powered Car. Is It Possible?' Aware of the emerging environmental movement, I was making a case for electric cars. I analyzed different types of batteries. The weakness today is still the batteries. They put my picture in the paper.

About the same time, a new guy named Tom walked up to me near the playground and said, "You should run for student body president." Somehow, Tom, son of a long-haul trucker, was plugged into wonderfully strange New York rock scenes. He introduced me the Velvet Underground and New York Dolls music that made us feel like North Indio outlaws. He became my best friend and helped me run my campaign for junior high student body president. I won, beating the first girl I ever held hands with. She lived on my block. Small town. I led the Pledge of Allegiance at every assembly.

With growing independence came new

messages from my parents. Warnings about the world. *Don't go there. Be sure to look around. Know how you are going to get out of there. Be careful. Who is with you? Look what happened to that guy when he wasn't being safe.* We weren't coddled or isolated. I could take my mini bike and BB gun out into the desert alone any time. However, born in the Great Depression, raised during the Second World War, my folks saw the world as a dangerous place. My brother Mike and I had two wildly different reactions to the warnings. I was anxious. He became a deputy sheriff.

For a kid who loved news and politics, the tumult of American in the 60s came to me every day via our newspapers and television. I had stayed up late by myself to watch my first political hero, Bobby Kennedy, win the California primary. I turned off the TV when he walked off the stage. I woke excited to tell my folks that my hero had won. Dad handed me the newspaper with the news he was shot. That seemed to happen all the time in 1968.

One by one, all of the older boys were drafted. I saw them leave for basic training and come home in uniform. I marveled at their transformed bodies. Lean. Strong. One morning, I opened my shutters. Across the street in front of the Villalobos' house was an ambulance. I knew their oldest son was home from the war. He had been wounded. Soon, two men came out their front door with a body in a royal red bag on the gurney. I was confused. Then I realized they had come to take the oldest son's body away. The first dead person I saw was across the street from my house, a casualty from Vietnam.

I am sure my parents wanted to prepare me. My dad had been in the Army during the Korean War. I heard endless tales about Ft. Benning and the south. He loved the discipline and order. They got me a book called, *Through Basic Training*. In captioned pictures, it showed what it was like to be in Army basic training. It horrified me. It was everything I hated about playgrounds and PE. Just more bullies with no escape.

When I did talk to Dad about bullies, he repeated an apocryphal family story, maybe the most important story in Dad's life. During Great Depression, my grandparents moved from the Arkansas Ozark hills to Helena on the Mississippi River. One day, my dad came home crying. He had been beaten up by some bullies. He came into the kitchen seeking comfort from my grandma. She looked at him, walked over to the pile of firewood next to the stove, picked up a piece of stove wood, and handed it to him.

"You go back out and don't you come back crying again. Take care of yourself."

I heard that story many times. My Aunt Jo wrote a poem about Dad that began, "Jimmy, you can put down the stick."

Dad told me, "If they come at you with a stick. You get a bigger stick." He showed me fighting stances. He tried to make me tough like him. He never understood that all I had to defend myself were my wits and words. His story and lessons were pointless.

~

For Christmas, my parents gave me a little yellow nine-inch black and white TV. I love television. Addictively so. That little box was the key to my understanding something big was happening outside of Indio, something I needed. Sitting alone in my room, I was now able to watch things the rest of my family would never watch on our big TV in the living room. I turned on public TV to see a production of Berthold Brecht's *Waiting for Godot*. I was transfixed. I didn't know what was happening, but I could not turn away. It wasn't linear. It was a strange conversation. Sad, lonely, funny. I couldn't believe anything like this existed. I desperately wanted to understand. No Internet. I just had to sit with it, let it soak in. No one thing told me how imperative it was for me to leave Indio as much as that play on my little TV. My family would not understand what I had seen. I wanted more.

Chapter 5

Showed Me Something

ACROSS MY LIFE with mental illness, one advantage I always had was that I learned how to work hard. I have worked, almost continuously, since I was ten-years-old. That is a mark of pride. In my family, working without complaint would garner what is still the highest compliment: "He showed me something." This was the pinnacle. A simple sentence I wore with pride.

At ten-years-old, Dad asked if I would like to go to work with him on Saturdays. The work day was shorter on Saturday. I remember thinking of it as a chance to finally see Dad more. Fifty cents a day, I could save for a telescope from the Sears Catalog, but the chance to be around him was what really counted. My job was to vacuum, then wash the windows inside and out of every car that got an oil change. On a busy day, that could be ten cars. After each job came Dad's inspection.

Sometime around noon, Uncle Jake would step

away from whatever hood he was under to wash his arms and hands. The men in my family had working hands. Proud of their vice-like grips, not even pumice soap could remove the spider web of black lines etched into their fingers. Long sleeves rolled up, a little damp from the sink, he would look at Dad and say it was time for lunch. I washed my hands and jumped into the truck between them.

We always went to the same place, across Highway 111, a small family diner called Keedy's Fountain and Grill. Nods and hellos. As we sat down, the coke for Dad and iced tea for Uncle Jake appeared. I got to order myself. French dip, crisp French fries, and a chocolate milk shake. The restaurant was blissfully air conditioned. Service station lube bays are mostly exposed sheet metal boxes. In the summer, they can hover around 120 degrees. Ever have to peel a windshield wiper off the glass because it had melted? That hot. This moment, in the cool restaurant, between my dad and uncle was the real reason I tolerated everything else. And then, back to work, the blast of heat punching me in the face as I stepped out the door.

I was conscious, even then, that I was giving up being a little boy too soon. My friends played all weekend. They went fishing and rode their bikes. I got to play after church on Sundays. But I longed to make connections in the world of men, especially Dad.

Still, Mom was the anchor. Like almost all of the moms then, she was home with us. She worked hard, too. President of the PTA, forever working on different projects and the keeper of an insanely clean and orderly home. When Mike and I left home, Mom got her real estate license and was successful. I don't think she ever gave herself enough credit for how smart she was, though Dad never hesitated to point that out.

It was Mom who got us anywhere we needed to go. It was Mom who was there when we came home. It was Mom who corralled and encouraged me to work on those science fair projects. And it was Mom who became the backstop for the nervous child. Knowing my mom was there if I needed her was one of the reasons I could ever be brave.

In junior high, I worked at my grandparents' Texaco. It was cross-town from our house, so on Saturday mornings I got a ride from Dad. I was the clean-up guy. Windows, restrooms, shelves. If there was a surface, I cleaned it, and if they got busy, I pumped gas and washed windshields. Tall, with long arms, I had no problem reaching the windshield.

I was lucky to spend so much time with my grandparents. My grandmother worked in the front office doing the books. It was the only part of the station that was air conditioned. She may have been the sweetest woman I ever met. Unlike the rest of the car-obsessed Blackwoods, she didn't drive. She was a recognizable iconoclast in Indio who rode a big tricycle back and forth to work.

Mostly, Grandma was the one person all the regulars had to talk with when they came in. Some folks didn't need anything; they just came by to see

Pearl. Grandpa, known as Blackie, called her Pearly. She had a wicked sense of humor and was likely to give a biting review of the last person in the office. For those in need, she always had a bible verse and a prayer.

The Blackwoods ended up in Indio soon after WWII. Grandad had survived the invasion of the Philippines. Drafted at 35, he was the old guy in his unit. After mustering out, he was part of a wave of soldiers coming home. At a bus station in Arkansas the bus master wasn't honoring the guarantee that soldiers going home rode free. Grandad told me he 'suggested' to all the soldiers gathered there that if the bus was on its side, no one could go anywhere. So, all the soldiers tipped the bus on its side and Grandad told the bus master that if the soldiers were the first aboard, they would be glad to put it back on its wheels. Great negotiator, my granddad.

Soon after he made it home, the family house burned to the ground. With five working cylinders in their six-cylinder car, they took what they had and drove to California. A later day, *Grapes of Wrath*. By time they got to Indio, the total family worth was $3.69.

I adored my Grandpa Blackwood. He was an Arkansas hill person with a gift for storytelling. He called me 'old man,' which was odd for a kid barely into his teens. There is an Arkie device to begin a tale, the equivalent of 'once upon a time.' "Old man once told me ...." I was conscious that what he called me had that connection.

One of the 'old man told me' stories was about a man who had an auto shop in Arkansas.

Grandpa said, "He was a cantankerous old guy who wanted to be sure his boys were working hard. He would walk in to the shop and say, 'I don't hear anything. Make a noise!'"

'Make a noise' could be a cue to get to work. It also was an encouragement if you were standing at a car and weren't sure what to do. "Make a noise," he would say with a sly smile. Then he might hand you a tool and point, "Start there." When I am staring at a project today, and a little lost, I think well ... *make a noise*.

~

From the time I was 12-years-old until I graduated the university, I worked part time at Blackwood's Texaco. When I was 13-years-old Grandpa said I was old enough to run the place by myself all day Sunday while my grandparents went to church. They were good Baptists; Grandpa was a deacon. At home, they each had a La-Z-Boy recliner in the living room; on the side of each tables were well-worn leather-bound bibles.

The station was open for eight hours on Sundays, just pumping gas and cleaning. I wasn't so sure I could handle the responsibility. I was scared the first few times he handed me the keys.

One of the things I liked about the Sunday job was that it got me out of church. I think I was ten or eleven when the science-loving kid tried to make sense of evolution and the bible. One big day, I screwed my courage and after Sunday school approached the pastor. I proposed that God's seven days were longer and that was how there could be dinosaurs. He looked down at me and said, "No, they are regular days. You just need have faith." In that moment, I was done with Christianity. I had worked hard to meet the religion halfway and got nothing in return.

At some point in my tenure at the station, Grandma began having obsessive thoughts. In the 70s no one had a clue. The same family doctor who sent me for a EEG prescribed a nightmarish assortment of medications for Pearl. She would worry endlessly about her oldest daughter, my Aunt Jo. "Did Jo call? Where is Jo? Is Jo okay?" I would look in the office window and see her talking to herself, writing little notes on a pad … suffering. We all played along and sometimes she emerged from the trap of her mind and was the joyous, sweet soul everyone loved. My grandfather bore this burden with another family aphorism, "You do what you have to do." That one would become very important to me.

The Aunt Jo of Grandma's worries was wacky. I loved her. I first knew her as the aunt just out of the Marines who drove an MGB with her Basset hound, Henry, in the passenger seat. But she was troubled, too. Alcohol, a suicide attempt. She became happier with her second husband, retired from the postal service, and lived a good life. Her sister, my effervescent Aunt Joy, wasn't as mysterious as Jo. I loved her laugh and the way she treated me like I was way older than I was.

She went on to have great success in high-end real estate broker in Carmel, California.

There is something to be said for learning how to work at an early age. It is the one thing no one can take away from you. When I got out into the world, I learned that many people never learned the power of work. I liked making money and paying my own way. In great part, knowing how to work, the discipline and confidence of simply sticking to a plan, putting one foot in front of the other, was essential to my life with mental illness. At times, the simple willingness to keep working was all that kept me from falling off the edge.

Chapter 6

I Guess I Am On My Own

THE ACCIDENT OF GROWING UP in a small town made for strange bedfellows; my best friends were all athletes. The quarterback of the Indio High football team. A varsity swimming and track starter. The all-league football lineman. The championship diver. A couple of the guys were bright, good writers. I was their skinny, brainy childhood friend, the one who drove when they were drunk to keep them alive. Ironically, I always had to find someone not in my circle of friends to go with me to home football games. My buddies were on the field playing.

Near the end of high school some of my buddies wanted to go to the football stadium in the middle of the night, walk out into the middle of the field, and lie in the grass. A stoned lamentation. I was with them because I was their friend, some of them since we learned to walk. I respected what they wanted to do but in so many ways I was not one of them. I just wanted high school to end.

High school unfolded as a series of incidents, errors, and ongoing terrors. As the nervous child I often tried to set the terms of my engagement with the world. By now, I was getting better and better at concealing the nervous part of me. People with mental illness learn early to become actors. We get our acceptance where we can and hide what we may not understand ourselves. Never underestimate the power of faking normal.

I began to construct my life around a series of safety strategies. One day in science class I needed to urinate. A very cute girl sat behind me in class. I could have raised my hand and asked to be excused but I couldn't bear the embarrassment. That girl didn't give a damn about me. As the minutes passed, I was in more and more pain. I felt beads of sweat on my forehead. I barely made it to the end of the class and ran to the restroom. All done now with that little inconvenience? Nope. That's not how a nervous child's mind works. I had a new problem.

To eliminate all the places smokers where could hide between classes and lunch, the school had locked all the boys' restrooms, save for one. From that day in science class, whether I had to urinate or not, I walked, jogged, ran to the restroom between every class ... just in case. It was a hidden, shameful, secret ritual.

~

In high school I shot up to 6' 1," about average height for men in my family. But I never filled in to match that frame. I was 112 pounds, nicknamed among my Spanish speaking friends: flaco, skinny. I had acne and a propensity to get giant boils on my face. Nose ... cheeks ... then nose again. I had upgraded my glasses to gold-framed beauties with photo-gray lenses. My arms were spindles. Legs the same. I never wore shorts. Even in the blistering heat of 110-degree days at school I wore long sleeves. And well into college, I wore a knock-off Member's Only coat. I was all about the physical camouflage.

Almost absurdly, I have a varsity letter in track and field. I was a manager. It was a way to experience being part of a team. Toting bags, loading the bus for away meets, and hauling out anything the track team needed for practice. I even ended up being the stadium PA announcer for home meets. Indio High was undefeated in dual meets. I got to be part of a team that intimidated the competition.

The bus ... that damn bus. Because I was loading the bus, I was always the last one to find a seat for away meets. There was a strict hierarchy. Varsity to the back. Once, I looked and saw the only seat left was next to a black kid named Joe P. I knew instantly this was going to be trouble. He was an incredibly fast sprinter with, as they say, discipline issues.

"No way. No, you aren't sitting next to me. Both these seats are mine," Joe said as I walked back.

"There's no place left; I have to sit here," I pleaded with Joe.

The coach yelled back, "Jim, sit down!"

It was a 90-minute trip and for that entire time, Joe trashed and harassed me. He made fun of my skinny arms, my glasses, the fact I couldn't make the team. Brutal. No one came to my defense. Ever. So, I went silent and looked straight ahead. I wasn't going to let him break me. I knew he wanted to make me cry. Maybe ten minutes from our destination, Joe changed gears.

"Damn, Little Man, you ain't mov'n. You are one tough little son of a bitch."

I looked at him. "Yes, I am."

He laughed and slapped me on the back. "You're alright, Little Man."

Though his attendance was sporadic, and he got kicked off the team, whenever he saw me, he yelled, "Little Man!" He had my back.

Our long-distance runners were physically small, descendants of tribes in Central Mexico. Some of them were not actually American citizens. Nobody cared. It was common. The lanky runners from other teams bolted ahead leaving the stadium. Thirty minutes of desert heat on sandy back roads later, our guys returned in the lead. The best distance runner was Gilbert Rosario.

As the track manager, I dragged the pole vault stands back to a little horror called 'The Cage.' Wire fenced, with a metal roof, facing the afternoon sun, it was where we kept our equipment. The pole vaulters stayed late every day. So did Gilbert. Besides track, he led a local gang, Los Niño's de Indio. They roamed the breezeways in a pack, wearing long black duster coats with the gang's name on the back. Fists and knives were their weapons of choice.

After practice, he came to the cage, screwed down the exercise bike to its hardest setting, and road it to exhaustion. His unbreakable will was part of the reason he could run people down in the desert. We joked. I mangled Spanish with him. When his gang was together, he never talked to me, just nodded slightly my way. He had told me, "You're good. None of my boys will fuck with you."

On the team bus on the way back from a meet in Calexico, near the Mexico border, we came upon a temporary border patrol checkpoint. Usually, the bus was waved through. As the bus slowed, Gilbert ran down the aisle and burrowed into the gym bags tossed in a heap in the back of the bus. He was terrified. As we passed the roadblock and gained speed, some of the guys started to give him shit. I pulled back the gym bags.

"It's okay. You're good. Come on out," I said.

He looked around. "Are they behind us?"

"No man, no one is following us."

"Thanks," he said with a lifted head nod.

My friendships with some of the guys who scared other people was another way for me to feel safe.

Even with all the time I put in with the track team, I still had to take PE. During my junior year that class morphed into 50 minutes of terror.

The Smith boys were from wealthy parents; the name of their family business was on the side of trucks all over the valley. Both boys were big and good athletes. The handsome, charming younger boy was in my class. He ended up with a football scholarship to Harvard. His older brother, face pock-marked with acne, blustering and loud, was a year ahead. He got booted from the football team and ended up in my morning PE class. I became his special project. He started calling me Jiiiiiiiiimy. He would linger on the 'i' in my name and used an imitated girl's voice, over and over again. That was just the start.

Each PE class was an opportunity for him to intimidate me. In the locker room in front of all the other boys, body part by body part, he bullied me every day. Constant shoves and little pushes. Every error I made on the field, every failure, was another chance for him to abuse me.

Let's be clear. His abuse was no secret to the coaches. I would look at them for help and they went blank. "Fuck the skinny kid; he has to learn how to take care of himself." The locker room at Indio High was a social Darwinism experiment. The only problem for the kids like me at the bottom of the food chain was that we stayed alive. It would have been more merciful to be eaten.

The class was at 10:40 in the morning. How do I remember that detail? It was the center of my day. My gut started aching and my palms grew sweaty in the class before PE. I had to take the class to graduate. I never told my parents what was happening at school. To the rest of the world, I was a good kid, smart. I was reliable and worked hard. How could I need help? I wasn't a problem.

This went on for months. A daily bullying I could not escape. I began to rate the times in the presence of Tim on a scale of 'he wasn't so bad today' to 'I don't know how much longer I can take this.'

There were a few days I got some relief. Joe P. — when he came to school — was in that PE class. Joe could fight. He got into fights after school and destroyed guys with his quick hands. Tim knew I was Joe's Little Man. Joe scared Tim. I secretly wished Tim would start something with Joe and that Joe would kill him. That's right, kill him right there in front of me so I could laugh. I fantasized about it. Decades later, my trauma and secret wishes emerged in ways that scared the hell out of me and changed my life.

I had experienced bullying all of my life. This was different. I was having my nervous system slowly rewired. I was the prey. My survival by wit and words weren't working. People in power were indifferent. Nobody else would stand for me. My body still tenses as I write about this. I was being traumatized.

One day, as I was dressing next to my locker, Tim was being especially vicious. He physically pushed me. Everyone else stood there silently. He scared everyone. As I lay prostrate on the ground, he stood over me and began humping me like a dog, laughing. I stood up and kicked him in the shin, yelling, "Fuck you, asshole!" I was sure I would now be killed. Instead, Tim stopped. He looked like someone who had been hypnotized, then awakened. He said nothing, just walked away.

Soon after that Tim disappeared from school. One of his buddies overdosed on heroin at Tim's parents' country club house. Tim took the body and dumped it in the sand dunes. When I read the story in the *Daily News*, I was happy. Fuck him. He was going to jail forever. Well … no. Small towns. Wealth. Power. Tim was given an option: go to trial or enlist in the Army. He enlisted. There was no record of his crime. He and his evil disappeared like motorcycle tracks in the dunes during a sand storm.

The damage was done. It took a few more years for the extent of that damage to be evident, but the nervous child, the one who was alert at all times to be safe in his world, had more evidence he was not safe.

~

At 16, having saved my earnings for years, I bought a muscle car. Now, I could drive those canal roads and do what my friends had been doing for years … get high. The Mexican border was only 90 miles away. Much of the time it was easier to get pot than beer. So began my decade long relationship with my favorite drug. The little pill was still in my pocket but pretty much from the first time I smoked pot there was also a little blue ditty bag hidden under my driver's seat with pot, rolling papers and a little pipe that fit in the palm of my hand. The nervous child had finally found something for his nerves.

My life is full of moments where I think to myself, *Who was that guy?* In the midst of my daily suffering, my political aspirations remained alive. I still wanted to be part of the student government, so I ran for student body vice president. I knew it was a long shot because at Indio High those offices were for cool kids and athletes. I was neither. My best friend Tom was my campaign manager.

I picked up Tom to go to school every day. On the day of the big speeches, I was nervous but knew Tom, my big friend, was going to introduce me. He was funny, cool, and a bit of a character on campus. He always walked out his door when I drove up. That day, no Tom. I went to the door and knocked. No answer. Door locked. I walked around the house to his bedroom window. The room was dark. I was getting a little desperate. At school, still no Tom. I hung back, hid in the restroom, and took my little white pill. I was on my own again.

The small podium faced the full stands in the basketball gym. The laughing and heckling began almost as soon as I stood. My speech was a disaster, a humiliation starting with my telling the assembly Tom was missing. But courage is a strange thing. Anxious people can be courageous every minute of the day just to appear normal. While I was deeply hurt that Tom was too afraid to come out of his house, I took a risk almost no one in that assembly could have taken.

Stubborn, determined, I kept a commitment I made to myself. Tom? Little was said about his disappearance. Any shame he had was his own and we remained friends.

Senior Advanced Placement English was a tough class. I consumed it whole. My mind was on fire with the words. Given the state of my day-to-day existence, I think I was fighting depression. In my essays, that pathos came through clearly. I approached writing about the books we read from angles and perspectives that were different from my classmates. When I turned in my papers, I thought they were too strange for my teacher to like them.

An essay on the *Great Gatsby* gave me hope. After class, Miss Hughes took me aside and told me she thought it was be best she had ever seen. She told me I had a gift. That one compliment, that tiny life moment, has nourished me my entire life.

At the end of the year, the best students and athletes gathered at a ceremony to give out athletic and academic letters. After four years as a track team manager, I had earned a varsity letter. I was embarrassed. And then Miss Hughes stepped up and announced that I was the recipient of the academic letter in English and Literature. I was stunned. How could my strange essays be the best? As I walked up Miss Hughes smiled. I think she knew how desperately I needed that letter; how important it would be well after that moment. And I think she understood that just once in high school I needed to think, *Well, I sure showed them.*

I loved government and politics. I excelled in those classes. At some point, I was learning on my own, beyond my teachers. I was easily bored in classes where they had to teach to the masses. Was I arrogant? Of course. I had run-ins with, of all things, my senior government teacher. I was especially angry, and expressed it to him, about how he failed to prepare our Model United Nations team, leaving us to embarrass ourselves at the regional meeting.

In my last high school class ever, when we took the final, the room buzzed like a hive. Eddie, my quarterback buddy, sat behind me. With five minutes left in school, he kept poking me. I finally turned and whispered, "Knock it off." When I turned around, I saw the teacher thumbing through the stack of finals. He pulled out one and carried it over to my desk. He smirked, tossed it in front of me with a red F in a big circle on the front page. Just another bully, he got his revenge. A parting gift. Yeah, fuck high school.

Chapter 7

The Freshman Train Wreck

I SAW MY HIGH SCHOOL GUIDANCE COUNSELOR once. While there may have been a discussion about going to college, the meeting is only memorable because he handed me the forms needed to register for the draft.

Draft registration put us into the yearly draft lottery. Every day of the year was drawn. First third of that year's draw ... you were screwed, Viet Nam. Second third ... it all depended. Last third ... you won the lottery. I was in the 1974 draft. The draft lottery ended in 1975. I won the lottery. November 27, 1955 was number 316. The only lottery I ever won.

Blue collar kids were at a disadvantage when it came time to apply to college. It was immensely helpful if someone in your family had been to college because they knew how it worked. No one on either side of my family had ever gone to college. On my dad's side of the family, starting with my great grandfather Blackwood (another James), there were five teachers scattered across the generations. But that didn't mean they went to college. These were hill people. My great grandfather put his books in his saddle bags and rode across the hollows to a one-room schoolhouse. I met my great grandfather, still an imposing man at ninety. I imagine that back in those hills the teachers were the intellectuals. When I assembled my family history, that fact was reassuring. I didn't feel like such an outlier. Truth be told, I was surrounded by smart people in my family. A generation on, several would have been college bound.

When other kids were applying to college, I was baffled, shockingly so. I had good SAT scores — well, verbal scores at least — a 3.7 GPA, and could have applied to many schools. I didn't know how. Friends were going to universities. Mike, my buddy down the street, got into the University of Redlands, a tough liberal arts school 60 miles up road. But his parents were teachers, so they knew the tricks. Some of my best buddies made one-year boomerang trips to odd little schools to play sports. Academic wash-outs.

I had earned some small scholarships from local service organizations like the Rotary Club. I had no clue what to do with the money.

By default, I went to a junior college, College of the Desert (jokingly referred to by students there as College of the Desperate). I was a 17-year-old freshman. The campus was a cluster of buildings surrounded by acres of alfalfa fields. For my practical parents, it made sense to take all the basic classes there, then transfer to a four-year school. (I wonder what they thought the basic classes in college were.) That saved them a pile of money. But I'm pretty sure the real reason was that I simply didn't know how to go to a university. For the nervous child, COD was a safe choice.

With my friends scattered, or in instant blue-collar jobs, I was often alone. I decided I could do all the intro classes in two semesters. It was a blindingly insane decision. I was taking 20 and 19 units a semester. A crushing workload for anyone. Then there was work. I drove to school in the morning, took my classes back to back, then drove to Indio to close my grandfather's service station each weekday evening. On Saturdays, I worked a nine-hour day, then turned around and opened the station early Sunday. When did I study? What was I thinking?

All across America, people have to do exactly what I did to get a college education. It is tough. Part of me is proud of my ability, my will, to push myself that hard. But even as I was doing it, I knew it was a mistake. I wanted to tell others it was a mistake, but they wouldn't have understood. Even at a community college, the academic demands are entirely unlike high school. I was adrift. I didn't know how to use a library to do research. My typing was awful, but every paper had to be typed. I faked my way through science classes that required my elusive mathematics. I was an A student in high school who was suddenly struggling to get Cs and Bs.

Socially, I was isolated. I went to basketball games, sometimes drove to beer parties to briefly hang with strangers, but mostly, I drove around and got stoned. I had one date the entire year. Near the end of the first semester I got a cold. The cold became a nagging cough. This went on for weeks. I was coughing up yellow stuff in classes and at work. Finally, one morning in class I started coughing and couldn't stop. My ribs were on fire. I left the class and somehow drove the ten miles home. My mom said I needed steam to 'break it loose.' I went into the bathroom and turned on the shower full hot. I sat on the toilet hoping for relief and instead started coughing up blood. Walking pneumonia. I got drugs, finished my finals, and still went to work.

When I think of that story, I wonder why no one looked at me and said, "Maybe you are doing too much." But here's the deal. In my blue-collar family, school work isn't real work. It is sitting and talking and writing and reading. You don't get paid. All through my undergraduate days, this misunderstanding of what it takes to excel academically was a gap in my family's understanding of who I was. Make no mistake, they were damn proud of me. They never questioned paying for my time in school as long I worked every vacation and holiday. But what I was doing and how hard it was remained a mystery to them.

I fell into dark moods. Depression. I was working hard and not doing well in school. A perfectionist who couldn't achieve average grades. I didn't have a group of friends and the guys I did talk to on campus were outcasts of a different kind. Somehow, I connected with the Vietnam vets; I was interested, respectful, and knew when to ask a question and when to back away.

The vets seemed way older. Not so much in years as in life. I actually looked younger than my seventeen years. They looked hard, distant. Most had long hair and beards. Invariably, the vets wore remnants of their military uniforms. Army jackets, insignia on their leather or Levi jackets, tattoos of military units, names of places in-country, and jungle boots. The guys seemed sad and were sometimes stoned in class. This social bubble surrounded them read 'don't fuck with us.' Maybe it was my own isolation or sadness that pierced that bubble. Maybe I looked like who I was, a lost kid. But between classes and during lunch, sometimes at parties, those were the guys who accepted and talked to me. Getting high was something we shared. Decades later, marijuana is used by some for PTSD. Maybe we were onto something.

The vets usually didn't usually talk about their time in the war. But they crossed that threshold with me. I heard about some purely evil shit they lived for a year. I worked at the service station with Beto who survived the Tet Offensive in 1968 by dragging bodies out from in front of twin 40 MM guns. They had to clear the bodies to be able to keep firing. Beto, like the others, wore his jungle boots until they actually rotted off his feet.

Waiting for class to begin, one of the vets was crouched against the wall.

"What are you doing here?" he asked, barely looking up.

I knew what he meant. I looked like a junior high kid in the wrong place.

"I wish I fucking knew," I responded.

He laughed and shook his head.

~

In my family driving is therapy. My Grandpa Blackwood would say, "I need to go for a bowl of soup," and disappear on a long drive. When the depression felt like a boulder on my chest, I had a cure. I drove my muscle car fast and to the edge. Literally, to the edge. Leaving the desert is a two-lane road called the Palm to Pines Highway, Highway 74, that heads toward the mountains and climbs steeply up an ancient alluvial fan. Eons of flash floods created a rapidly rising porch. The road then claws its way up the steep mountain in miles of sharp switchbacks, gaining a few thousand feet of altitude in no time. The road is tricky, no guard rails. Cars go off into the deep canyons. Dad used to pull wrecked cars out of the canyons with his tow truck.

When I could stand it no more, I would aim my car for that road. It took all my concentration to control my car at high speed as I roared up the mountain, tires squealing. Those cars weren't meant to turn well. They liked speed in a straight line. As I went up the mountain, the dark cloud would lift a little. I had no time for reflection or self-pity. What I was doing was dangerous and that was what I needed.

At about 3000 feet up was a viewpoint carved into the mountain. I pulled off. The desert was all there in front of me. On most days the clear desert air let me see all the way to the blue Salton Sea. I would sit on a rock and look at the desert. It was enormous and brown with very few populated splashes of green until the agricultural fields of the lower valley. Below sea level Indio was a green and brown splotch. I called that moment, 'making myself small.' As I shrunk into the world before my eyes, my depression got smaller, too. And when it was small, I could deal with it. I sat on that rock until I could feel again. Then I made a much slower, safer trip down the mountain. That mad drive up the mountain was a trip I repeated many times that year.

By the middle of that year, I knew where I wanted to go to school. My friend Mike came home with tales of life in Merriam Hall. Water to a thirsty man. I picked him up to go to the giant rock festival California Jam and crashed in his dorm room. I was sold. I made one application. I didn't know about 'safety schools.' I didn't even understand that I was picking a small, highly selective and expensive private liberal arts school. I only knew I wanted to be at the University of Redlands. They said yes.

Chapter 8

Love, Drugs and Rock & Roll

MY DEPARTURE from my family's little pink stucco house was strange. With no fanfare, I loaded up my car and drove away. Poof. Gone. Later, in the midst of finals my family moved across town to a new house. I came back to a place that would never be my home. Maybe it's better that way. The home of my youth will always be just that. My childhood and coming-of-age are contained in a near sacred place uncontaminated with the excitement and pain of adulthood. The little house is my own time capsule sealed by the simple act of backing out of the driveway.

The dorm was nothing like those ivy encrusted halls on television. It seemed like an afterthought on a beautiful campus. Merriam Hall was tucked away on the edge of the campus. Built in the 60s, the squat, sick green, two-story brick building seemed more like the best of Soviet era architecture. Men and women were on separate wings of the two-story building. One communal bathroom on each wing. One shared phone in the hall. People got 'buzzed' in their rooms to go the phone for calls. For a virgin, with no prospects, the idea that there were girls where I lived was intoxicating.

Redlands is 60 miles from Indio. For me it may have as well been Antarctica. Once in Redlands, I didn't go home until they threw me out of the dorm. The first night I was in Merriam, there was a party … there were lots of parties. I met new people who did something that had rarely happened in my life. They hugged me. My family isn't anti-affection, but no one hugged. Girls I didn't know gave me a hug. Good lord.

My second night, I saw my old friend Mike kissing a girl. She had hair below her shoulders, a creamy complexion, great body, and expressive hazel eyes. I had no idea who she was, but I was instantly jealous. *Why*, I wondered. A new emotion. I barely knew what it meant. But I also realized I was a blank slate. Mike knew me. For everyone else, I was simply another new guy. Having escaped the smothering familiarity of a small town, I realized I could be anyone.

And this new Jim? Well, he walked right up to the girl as she backed away from Mike and said. "Hi, I'm Jim."

"Yeah," Mike said, "this is my friend from Indio. He just moved in."

"Hello," she said, "I'm Megan."

I had never heard the name before and asked her to spell it. My confusion was in the way she pronounced the first 'e' almost as an 'a.' In a world now clogged with Megans, I have yet to hear it that way from any of the next wave of her namesakes.

There was always pot available in the dorm. Eventually, I had connections for any drug. My rule was not to take anything that someone could make in their bath tub. I kept to that rule ... mostly. I have a low tolerance for any sort of psychoactive. While the self-medicating with pot started in high school, it was in full swing in college. Study. Get high to relax. Go to a party. Get high to come out my shell. Go on a trip. Get high to not focus on how far I was from the dorm. Medication can be fun.

Redlands unglued me. First, it was the people. I used to be the smart one. At Redlands, I was another smart guy who didn't have any of the skills that the students from private schools had. When those kids told me what they read and showed me what they wrote, I was stunned. Though off-balance, I actually loved the challenge of being surrounded by wicked smart, creative people. My small-town boredom plague was shredded. And it seemed like they were all widely travelled. I hadn't been on a vacation since our last family trip to Arkansas when I was twelve. More fundamentally, I discovered that people showered in the morning. All of my people worked with their hands so the logical time to shower was at night. I switched to morning showers.

In a verbal joust, I could more than hold my own. I could be witty and ruthless ... well, sometimes an asshole ... especially in contemporary politics and history. I absorbed material quickly. College in the 70s was very political. We had just seen Watergate; the Vietnam War was winding down but still lethal, and the second wave of the women's movement was boiling over all around us. But academically, I knew I was in a deep hole, not so much one of my making as just the nature of my entry into what seemed like the big leagues.

As a new sophomore, life was coming at me fast. Most of my dorm friends were freshman. Only ever cool and witty Mike, and another guy, Carl, from the desert town of Blythe, were in our second year. Our dorm was home to the debate teams. In the academic world these were the storm troopers. Redlands was a national powerhouse in college debate. Two national championship teams would spring from our dorm. Almost all the debaters became successful lawyers. Mac, one of the best, became a close friend. He had the face of a child but was an intellectual ninja. He typed 110 wpm and had his own IBM Executive typewriter in his room, serviced by a technician in a white coat. Almost blind in one eye, he synthesized depth perception to dominate the dorm table tennis tournament. I was the evil influence for a good Catholic boy. I introduced him to pot and David Bowie.

In some ways, my nervous child was on holiday during that first year at Redlands. I went on all sorts of short trips, deep sea fishing and camping. My usual nervousness about any travel and avoidance was relatively under control ... well ... maybe a little medicated. Redlands had a semester — interim — semester system. The winter interim was a chance to spend a month on one topic, sometimes travel. I was a political science major and the premier interim trip was a tour of five European capitals in 21 days. Meetings were scheduled with politicians in The Netherlands, West Germany, Belgium, Switzerland, and England, with a day for meetings at NATO headquarters in Brussels. I knew my parents were already stretched but I sent them a letter. Mom said it was the best sales job I had ever done. She saved the letter.

~

My first jet trip was from LA to New York to Amsterdam. For most of my peers it was just another jet ride. For me, it was all new ... every bit of it. I needed my first down jacket, my first wool sweater, my first real suit, my first luggage ... on and on. In Europe, one part of the nervous child was a constant: my stomach. I lived on a steady stream of antacids. I had never experienced jet lag. When the 20 of us went out for our first restaurant meal in Amsterdam, I had what I would later know as a panic attack. I became sweaty and anxious. My heart was pounding. I had to get out of there. I made an excuse about an unhappy gut and left.

It was late at night. I was alone and lost among the canals and 400-year-old buildings. I was looking for food but had no idea how to find it. Where was the

McDonald's? I only had a vague notion how to get back to our hotel. So American in my puffy down jacket, I was afraid but curiously free, roaming my first big city alone. Someone appeared from a doorway offering me hashish. No thanks. I knew the name of the museum close to our hotel and asked which way. He pointed a direction. Everyone else was already back at the hotel. I bought food from a vending machine, and to my amazement, a can of Heineken (My big trip goal? Twenty different beers in 21 days) from another machine. Someone had bought some hashish. We did a little 'hash under glass' (look it up if you must).

I had to go to restaurants. Not Denny's anymore. I heard one of my companions order a cappuccino. I had never seen one and asked her to explain what it was. I took trains and buses and cabs. I got lost in some of the great cities of the world. When it came to the meetings with politicians and government officials, I felt at home, almost fearless. I asked questions in every meeting. Good ones, I could see from the eyes of the officials and the looks from Dr. Morlan, the head of the political science department. I felt as if I belonged. I was sure this type of trip would be my first in a lifetime of travel.

Still early in our relationship, Megan sent letters to me at every stop, but I had a little travel crush on another woman on the trip. Blond, curly hair, radical feminist, kind of a waif, I had talked to her a few times. She was part of our drinking crew. Ed oozed the type of sophistication that left me in awe. Rich kid from West Los Angeles, she had been around the rock scene in LA since her early teens. She was out of my league. The next to the last night in London, she found me in the hotel bar, approached with a newspaper and a proposition. I was gob smacked. Somehow, she said she saw me as a kindred spirit. "You up for doing something wild? Just the two of us. I'm kind of sick of the rest of these people." She pointed to the ad for a production of *The Rocky Horror Show* at its original theater in Chelsea. A David Bowie and Mott the Hoople fanatic, I knew Chelsea was the center of the glitter rock universe.

Map of the Underground in hand, we set out. No notice to the others, we just split. In many ways, I was now in Ed's hands. I had no idea where we were going, so I followed her lead. Up from the underground, Chelsea was another world. People passed in glitter rock regalia. I was in a place I had only dreamt about. We found the theater. It was old, a dark mahogany bar in the lobby. The show was wonderful. At intermission, everyone went out into the lobby. Ed smiled when I turned and said, "They serve alcohol during the intermission?"

She didn't make me feel like the bumpkin I was. She just said, "Let's get a drink."

After the show, we were a little lost. I was feeling nervous, creeping up on frightened. It was late and London is huge. I had only ever driven around LA. Ed picked a direction and said, "Come on." I had never been out like that with a woman friend. I may have hoped to kiss her but she was way ahead of me. She had seen the blue airmail letters from Meg and even commented that it was sweet. Hell, she probably knew I was hopelessly in love before I did. We hugged and headed for our rooms.

One day left in London, I woke up with a cold, bought some sort of cough syrup at a little shop, and set out. I talked to Londoners on the street. Took pictures from London Bridge. Even sick, I had a good time alone in the city. I had a fever on the flight back that broke over the Atlantic. My folks came to pick me up at LAX. They asked questions. I didn't know how to explain what had just happened. Mostly, I was sad to be back. What I didn't know was that I would not return to Europe.

Both virgins, at the age of 19 Meg and I became lovers. She is two days older than me. I always conceded her greater wisdom based on that. What we shared as much as anything was a wide-eyed small-town innocence. We would be together for almost seven years. In the midst of the sexual revolution around us, we became the solid couple, the monogamous pair. Our coupling gave me an entree into the world of women. The front first floor wing was dominated by a very close group of Meg's friends. For them, at times, my relationship with Meg made me almost invisible. Beyond the classrooms, this was where I got my real education. I wasn't booted from the room when women discussed their love lives, the relative value of men as sex partners as opposed to a favored vibrator. I felt like the happiest spy on earth. Almost all of these women friends went on to advanced degrees, and in keeping with the time, none of them changed their last names when they married.

I was still this guy from Indio, a blue-collar kid sometimes lost in the speed of the changes. I was in my second semester Sociology 101 class when the professor began a discussion of feminism by asking, "How many of you consider yourselves feminists?"

I wasn't sure. The word itself was still fraught with some confusion for men. I was pondering what to do when I felt an intense pain on the back of my head. One of my women friends had just hammered me with her pencil. I turned around, rubbing my head. "Hey, why did you do that?"

Lea Anne gave me a piercing look and said, "Because you are a feminist, you idiot." Enlightened by a whack on my head I raised my hand.

~

I kept a calendar on my desk, but I didn't see it the same way as my friends. For me, it was always a painful countdown to the day they would close the dorm. Because most of my school friends came from distances away, almost as soon as school started, they talked about what they were doing for Thanksgiving or Christmas. I hated that. For me it was unimaginable that what we were doing at school wasn't something they would want to have go on forever. When I went home for holidays, or the summer, my life was all about work. I suppose that was another reason I hated people talking about vacations. I never got to take one.

While my anxiety was self-medicated and

manageable, my depression was not. I call it depression now, but truly I didn't know what it was then. There were times when I began to feel hollow inside. I would disappear. Sometimes I got in my car and drove. Other times I walked to the lonely edges of the campus and sat staring out into space. There was a difference now. Meg knew. She sometimes tracked me down and held me. For the first time I cried to another person. I had a place to let go of my sadness.

Academically, I was overmatched. I made every mistake of a confused freshman, only I did it as a sophomore. I cobbled together a C average. To be sure, becoming a new person, falling in love, and traveling the world had something to do with my academic collapse. But really, I simply didn't know how to study at this new level.

At the end of that first year at Redlands, I crashed. The exhaustion was emotional as much as physical. I was deeply sad to have to leave the dorm, my friends, and especially Megan. When I got home my folks didn't understood why I was so burnt out. They had no frame of reference. Before I had recovered, they pushed me to stop being lazy and get to work. And for the entire summer that's what I did. Three jobs, 13 hours a day, almost around the clock.

I lived for the letters and care packages from Megan. Her girlfriend game was amazing. A thousand miles away in Walla Walla, she, too, was working all summer. I spent the summer counting down the days until I could get back in the dorm.

Chapter 9

Crushed Car and Blown Mind

ALL SUMMER, I lived for what was going to happen the week before school started. I was driving north to pick up Megan and camp our way back down the coast along Highway 1. I bought the camping supplies, all downsized to fit in half of the trunk of my car.

I decided to upgrade my car's eight-track sound system from two to four speakers. (That's right, eight-track.) A couple of weeks before the trip, I stayed up late to install the new door speakers. They sounded great. The next morning, a quiet Sunday, I drove to my newspaper delivery job. I crossed a double intersection with Black Sabbath cranked up. As I began to cross the highway, out of the corner of my eye I saw that a big old Buick wasn't going to stop. I gunned my car and turned hard right hoping the Buick would turn left. It didn't. It hit me in the driver's door. My car buckled and spun. I watched my hands on the steering wheel go up and to the right. The metal and plastic wrapped around me. When my car stopped, I turned and looked at his stoplight. Yeah, his was red.

My wonderful, hot car and quick reflexes probably saved my life. But the car was totaled. I crawled out of the passenger window. The other guy? He drove away.

I walked to the gas station on the corner and called my dad.

"Are you okay? Cars can be replaced," he said.

My only injury? A huge bruise on my left leg where the speaker I had put in hours before popped out and hit me. Rock and roll indeed.

What happened next tells a certain tale of Blackwoods and work. When Dad got there, I was sitting on the curb. I was pretty shook-up. He looked over at me and the car and said, "Okay, I will have this towed to your granddad's station. You go on to work."

Yup, I walked across the highway to work. I was physically okay and had a job to do. Physically okay.

Meg sounded frightened when I told her the story, but the trip was still on. I couldn't let that dream slip away with my crushed car. In a blur, my car was replaced with a new, but sad, plain white Toyota Corolla Deluxe. My dad had pushed me toward the cheaper car. Now it was just transportation. I pulled the stereo system out of the orange and white Pontiac and put it in the Toyota. The speakers rattled in the cheap, thin doors.

~

I had never been to the Pacific Northwest. Looking at a map, the route that looked shortest to Walla Walla, Washington was Oregon Highway 395. Big mistake. East of the Cascade Range, Oregon is dry and endless. It reminded me of the desert only with wave after wave of steep mountains. Up one mountain and back down for 19 hours. I was always reaching for lower gears to climb in the woefully underpowered little car. I longed for my dear departed Pontiac.

The last six hours of the drive, I was of two minds: I must be getting close and I don't think I can drive anymore. When I got to Walla Walla, spaced out by the road and very nervous to meet Meg's family, I pulled into a store for a six-pack of beer. Before following her directions, I drank a beer in the parking lot.

Megan ran out to greet me. Her home was unlike any I had known. Strangely multi-leveled, cozy with curious nooks everywhere. Her oldest sister was married and gone. Her brother, Kevin, lived in town. Meg's room was part of a basement with a fireplace. Growing up in 60s tract housing, fireplaces are exotic. Finally, a feature that to a desert kid seemed like a miracle, a spring emerged from under their house to feed a brook that ran through the Whitman College campus. When no one was looking, I kept sneaking out to stare at the water emerging from the ground. I couldn't explain to them how mindboggling that was.

I slept for half a day. Sometimes, under stress, I purposely lengthen my sleep to avoid what waking will bring. Safe for a few minutes more. Meg had slipped into the bed during the night for few hours, then left. Cuddling and kisses only in her parents' home. I was awakened with a scratchy sensation in my face.

"Hi, I'm Kevin, Megan's brother." He had dipped his long beard in my face to wake me.

The dining room was up three short sets of stairs from the basement. On the walls were cartoons done by a famous neighbor. Meg's dad was the dean of students. I learned that her block and those surrounding the university were full of professors and administrators. It was as if the school had put out runners like a raspberry and the same fruit was everywhere. Meg had told me about her childhood, but I hadn't really understood. Whitman was the beating cultural heart of the little town. It made the town seem infinitely bigger.

Dinner was a revelation. After an actual cocktail hour with real martinis, a couple of friends, a professor and his wife came over. Kevin appeared. Kevin often appeared like a desert whirl wind, kicked up dust, and just as quickly disappeared. Dinners in my home were for eating. Words were sparse and informative. There were no challenges to surmount.

As this meal progressed, my brain was one exclamation after another, *Holy shit! Are you fucking kidding me? They do THIS all the time?!* Dinner conversation bounded and leaped from literature to politics to art to science. Big Scrib, Meg's dad, and

Ginny, her mom, held court, moved the conversations along, making me feel like a natural part of the scene. Some moments I was desperately fearful that I would make a fool of myself. Others, I jumped right in. Wit was the coin of this realm. I recall turning to Meg with wide eyes.

With Meg's luggage, the little car was at its limit. The trip down the coast was close to perfect. We pitched my little tent on the roots of redwoods one night, on the pad at a KOA (with a loudspeaker announcing bingo) the next, and on a point of land jutting out into the Pacific where deer strolled through our camp. Our final landing was below Hearst Castle, an isolated and desolate strip of California coastline. The waves glowed with phosphorescent algae and we made love as downslope wind gusts tried to rip the tent from underneath us.

~

Back at school, I had a new roommate, Mark, another desert guy. Mark was cool in ways I could only imagine. He was athletic, with long blond hair parted in the middle that made him look like a surfer. He rode a Honda 750 chopper that he had built himself. While others lazily unpacked, Mark and I were in agreement that we would completely build our room first. No socializing. Posters up, beds made, tapestries deployed, stereo wired and cranked up. When we were done, we both took bong hits and laid on our beds admiring our work. People came in to see us. We didn't move. Mostly, we looked at them and said, "What?"

Desert kids. We had the air condition cranked when it was hot and kept our room sauna warm during what passed for winter on the outskirts of LA.

My last two years at Redlands, I realized that in order to buy some peace with my folks I had to declare that, beyond political science, the money they were spending would have a payoff. I used to get speeches from Dad about having a backup plan ... get a teaching certificate ... whatever that meant. Many of my fellow political science majors were aiming toward law school. Okay, I thought, I can do that. My new story was that I was going to law school. Honestly, I had no idea what that meant, or ultimately, how completely mismatched my skills were for that goal.

I was in an academic hole and was determined to dig out. I now knew how to play the game and how hard I needed to work. Every weekday night, I ate dinner and then went right to the library. I would be there for at least four hours a night. I came back to relax, which meant a couple of bong hits and a beer. Now in the groove, my grades came up on a wave of A's and A-'s. I was both relieved and proud of myself for proving I could play at this level. I know how to work hard.

~

It would be hard to find two brothers who looked so much alike and were so different. School was hard for Mike. Only later did we discover that he had been fighting a case of undiagnosed dyslexia. I was conscious that we would be taking vastly different paths in life. I grew concerned that if I didn't take action while I was still nearby in school the life gap between us would become a wall. I invited Mike up to stay in the dorm. First, to hang out and meet my friends. The liberated women's pack lavished him with attention. I can't imagine what he thought. He told me he was really taken by Deb. It was obvious. Deb and I agreed there was no need to break the spell by telling Mike she was gay.

I was able to score tickets for three big shows: Elton John, The Who, and The Rolling Stones. My brother was the designated driver for the shows. Not a big drug user, he got to haul around a crew who, depending on what could be found, did peyote, pot, acid, and mushrooms for those shows. Bras of my friends stuffed with drugs, we went through security. Mike had a good time. A natural caretaker, I think he liked that he was in charge of getting us there and back safely. Mostly, I think my making that connection when I did kept us from drifting completely apart.

Carl was the residence assistant in Merriam our senior year. With flowing long hair and endless energy, he set direction and we followed. Whip smart, a good writer, with a deeply soulful side, Carl was my social battering ram. If I stayed in his wake, I knew I was going to have fun. But given the right combination of loud music and intoxicants, I could emerge from his shadow. I had a notorious stoned act where I stood on assorted furniture and sang along with David Bowie, copying his every stage movement. My impersonation peaked on Halloween when my women friends dressed me from their closets, did my make-up, then drew the Ziggy Stardust lightning bolt across my face. I loved escaping me. Still, I was just as likely to fall back and tend to my introversion.

Carl, like all of my men friends, was crazy about Meg. I'm pretty sure my standing in the dorm was raised by being with her. She was the natural gentle counter to my bundle of blue-collar rough edges, darkness, bubbling anger, and intellectual aggressiveness. For the next few years, Carl and Megan would be on the front lines of my descent into mental illness.

The end of my law school charade came with a law school admission test prep course. Turns out becoming a lawyer is all about memorization, a skill I didn't have. Here's where being the blue-collar kid bit me hard. Some of my friends were moving on to graduate school. I love academics and would gladly have lived in the world of political science, religion, and history forever. What I didn't know was that there was work to be had in those academic areas. People made a living teaching and writing, even consulting. You simply don't know what you don't know. I didn't understand what questions to ask. My law school lie, with its money at the end of the rainbow, resulted in a tunnel vision that blocked another view of my future.

As school moved inextricably toward graduation day my anxiety increased. I had to navigate a series of events. The graduation. The celebrations. The goodbyes. Then they kicked me out of the dorm forever. And now I had to integrate my family into my new world. I wasn't prepared for that.

Traditionally, graduates, friends, and family departed after the ceremony to some sort of catered hall or restaurant. I had to do something about that. My ability to manipulate people and events was ready. Only a handful of us in the dorm were graduating in 1977. I came up with a scheme to have our celebration in our dorm, where there was a large lobby, a kitchen, patio, and lawn. I made the case that this dorm had been our home. This is what our parents had paid for. We could make it so cool ... and even sneak up to our mostly packed rooms to get high on demand. I prevailed. It was all bullshit. I was taking care of myself, my anxiety, and bringing everyone else along for the ride.

A couple of days before the ceremony, my parents decided to exert their rights as both my parents and my funders. Suddenly, they a had need to control the final days. Being the first of my family to graduate college, all my nearby family members were coming to celebrate. Of course ... of course ... they loved me and were astoundingly, button-bustingly proud. What they didn't understand was how hard this day would be for me. They had no clue about the sadness or the sense of loss that was burying me shovel full after shovel full. They didn't understand my exhaustion or how it felt to be once again parting from the woman I loved. My new created family was breaking up and it hurt.

The only way to have a private phone conversation was in one of two lovely wooden phone booths in the dorm lobby. I was in a booth when what my folks didn't understand collided violently with their expectations. There was yelling, both parents on the phone, and an abruptly ended call. I ran up to my room. Fuck it. I was done. As I had done in the past, I needed to just go, drive somewhere. The coast maybe. North certainly. They could have this graduation without me. I was tossing stuff into a pile to go to my car when Megan appeared.

Meg understood. In that moment, she knew the lasting damage I was about to do. She held me. I cried, but I was determined. I was out of there. Fuck it all. Then in the midst of this rage and sadness, my room buzzer rang twice. It was my signal for someone on the phone. I didn't want to walk into the hall and pick up the phone. Megan went to answer the phone. She quickly returned.

"What?" I asked.

"They're here," she said.

"Who?"

"Your parents. They're downstairs, right now."

I suppose it was the one time that only being 60 miles away was helpful. My folks made a high-speed run to Redlands. I didn't want to see them. Dad wanted us to go for a ride. Cars have great power in my family. Asked to go for ride, I could not refuse.

Mom had been crying. Dad looked uncertain. We drove up the mountain to the apple and cherry groves. I told them I wanted to go, just leave, but Meg talked me out of it. I explained what I could. They understood what they could. We came to an accommodation. The clincher was that my Grandparents Blackwood would be there the next day. There was a myriad of people on the planet I could ultimately live with disappointing ... not them. Back at the dorm, Megan had been waiting in the lobby. I said goodbye to my folks and told them I'd see them the following day. Meg took me in her arms. I was exhausted. We disappeared for a time, then joined the parties that went well into the night. Only Meg really knows how close I was to not being at my own graduation.

The next day flew by. People put messages on their mortarboards. Carl and I had agreed that mine would say SMOKE and his POT. He cut out the letters. On the day, I thought of my grandparents and couldn't do it. I rolled a joint and when we sat down I tied it into my tassel. Not visible from the parents' stands, in solidarity with my friend nonetheless. We were supposed to sit in alphabetical order. B isn't next to R. He saw how shaky I was and said, "Fuck it, sit next to me." Our family now had its first college graduate.

Our dads gave Carl and me the same curious graduation gift, a brand new $100 bill. Carl spent his $100, I still have mine in the little box in the basement. There were a few times when having that $100 bill was my backstop, how I would feed myself, buy food for the dog or buy gas for my car. Funny how the tiniest safety net can help you get by.

After the dorm lobby celebration, there was one more event. Always the instigator and organizer, Carl had arranged a drunken, stoned river float on the Colorado River near where he'd grown up the day after graduation. Most of our friends made travel arrangements that allowed them to go. I couldn't join them. I hated the heat and was afraid to float to someplace I didn't know. I couldn't manipulate this adventure to feel safe.

My illness has kept me from many life moments. I made excuses. Endless bullshit excuses. I think Megan knew. Everyone else was disappointed but not unkind. On their return, they came by Indio. There in front of my parents' house were all those sunburned people I loved. We hugged and said goodbye.

Among the musty, mold smelling boxes in my basement I found a farewell that I wrote my last day in Merriam Hall. In a corner of that page was a list of 17 names, my closest friends in the dorm.

In part, was this:

There is a decided emptiness when you realize your life has moved from one place to another. In many respects the shock is unmitigated by the overwhelming sense of anticipation that accompanies a beginning. But I can never quite escape the nagging internal tragedy of an end. The quiet panic of realization falls upon me in the moments of thoughtful solitude. Inescapably, my mind returns to places that will never echo emotions I've felt and people I've loved. At that moment no amount of newness and no degree of anticipation can restrain the longing for a moment of those past joys. Even the worst days seem better than the emptiness I feel.

That poor empty building, how does it survive the ghosts of a thousand emotions and a thousand memories? For me, it will always be empty.

Chapter 10

Lost on the Willamette River

I HAD NO IDEA what to do next. Not a fucking clue. I just knew I was now back in Indio in a house that was never my home, broke and demoralized. For a week or so, I lay in the sun and I hate laying in the sun. My body was wrung out. I was a new species of lizard out there in the sun. I could feel my parents' eyes on me. *Why doesn't he move?* They wondered if this was the big payoff for all that education. Carl was in the same boat. He was recovering a few miles away under his parents' roof. We met and compared our pathetic notes. We also drank and got high. Little lifeboats came to me in the mail, letters from Megan and my college friends.

Mom said her good friends who owned a paint store needed help. *Why not*, I thought, *I need money if I am ever going to get out of here.* The Haynes paint store was in the heart of decaying downtown Indio. I wore an actual pocket protector for my box cutter and pens. Carl got a job driving a big water truck at a subdivision construction site. Fill the truck at a fire hydrant, turn on the sprayer, drive up and down the site to keep it wet and repeat. College grads.

Fall came. My friends and Meg were an hour away at school. I went up to see her on weekends. One day, my brother picked up Megan and our friend Deb to bring them to get me at the paint store. Mike saw Kimm, the owners' daughter. Meg, Deb, and I saw it immediately. My brother and Kimm were, to use an old word, besot. The result of that chance meeting is my two nieces and a nephew.

California was in the midst of one of its periodic real estate bubbles. Carl and I were both pressured to get our real estate licenses. For 600 bucks each, we could go to real estate night classes and appease our parents. What our folks didn't know was that Carl and I would meet before class in the parking lot, smoke a joint and sit, glazed, in the class. It worked out fine for us and our parents were happy. Carl and I talked about moving to San Francisco. I sometimes wonder about that path untaken. But in his senior year Carl had been an intern for the National Association of Manufacturers in Washington, DC. His 'connection' said he could get a job there. He left for the east coast. Even more depressed, I kept going to the silly real estate classes.

Where was my friend, the nervous child? In my free time I was mostly alone. I drove around a lot. If I needed to self-medicate, there was pot. In general, I now felt safe in the desert. It was dull but predictable.

As they arose, episodes of darkness were held at bay by driving up to see Megan and my friends.

In November of 1977, I got a postcard from Lea Anne. A 4-foot, 11-inch, powerhouse, she had moved to Salem, Oregon to go to graduate school in public administration at Willamette University. Another blue-collar kid, Lea Anne was on a mission toward prosperity. She said that I should consider her school. She put my name in as a prospective student. She said Oregon was beautiful and in a small note on the front, "Come see me. I miss you."

I looked up Salem; a small town, but still bigger than Indio. Stradling the Willamette River, it is the state capitol. Salem is like of a lot of state capitols, historically important but not the center of that state's universe. The concrete capitol building looks like a giant mausoleum with a gold statue on top. Startlingly ugly in a beautiful place. I had a BA in political science and had interned one semester for a California state senator. Pulling my flaming jet out of its death spiral, I suddenly had a goal. I was moving to Salem, not because I had a plan but because it wasn't Indio. What amazes me now is that I took no notice of the idea of going to graduate school. I think I already felt I was wasting an expensive education and there was no way my parents would support yet more school. There was pressure to make what I had pay off.

Lea Anne let me crash at her apartment. It worked out that Megan was in Salem for the apartment hunt. We had … mostly … decided that we were going to live together. She was sweating telling her folks. Mine didn't care. We scored a cheap, furnished apartment down the street from the capitol building.

That May, Megan and all my friends of the class of '78 graduated. Lea Anne and I drove down straight through in 19 hours. Dropping her in San Bernardino, I rolled into Redlands just after dawn. Like a peeping Tom, I tapped on Meg's window to wake her and get into the dorm. A few hours of sleep later, I was awakened by the kisses of the covey of my women friends. What could be better? Carl came back from DC. The old crew was assembled. Celebrations, embraces, and the final sad parting.

~

I had enough money to live for several months and figure out how to break into Oregon politics. I made some furtive attempts. I got a line on some of the local lobbyists. I had an awful resume, but wrote good letters seeking informational interviews. I made cold calls. Out of the blue, one my targets invited me to his office at the end of his work day.

I had an uncomfortable suit that didn't work in the real world. I put it on, then took it off. With no clue what business casual looked like, I put on cords and a clean shirt. On the edge of being overwhelmed by my nerves, I knew I was self-sabotaging. I went to his office and walked round and round the block trying to work up the courage to go in. Finally, late to the meeting, I went up the elevator. His look told me I was now annoying him. Rightly so. I asked some questions.

He got ready to go home. He gave me some names, mostly to get rid of me. I calmed down in his presence, but it was too late. I had no idea how to sell myself in this new world. I embarrassed myself.

Salem was fun when Meg got there. We spent summer days swimming and sunning on the Willamette River. We made cherry vodka and went to movies at the old theater downtown. Lea Anne's boyfriend, Mark, rebuilt old Porsches. I went driving and fishing with him. We even went up to Portland to see Muddy Waters play at a club I would visit many years later. Megan found a job as a waitress in a pub. I would show up at closing time to drink beer in coffee cups after hours. I was almost out of money. A guy down the hall got me a job at a 24-hour service station on Interstate 5. The family business again. I took books to read on graveyard shift.

Graveyard shift scared the shit out of me. People traveling on the freeway at those hours are a different breed. I'd watch the hookers and drunks close up shop at the bar next door. The cash drawer was just inside the front door. We had been robbed before. Even in the cold, I left a lube bay door up just high enough so I could slide out and run if trouble came. I spent the night on high alert. One night, a car parked just beyond the canopy lights with two guys in the car. I watched the passenger get out and slide a knife up into his coat sleeve. He came quickly toward the front door. I had one shot. As he got to the door, I shoved it and him and made my way to the outer island of gas pumps. He stayed near the door and kept asking me for things to get me back inside.

"I need a can of oil." "Can I use your phone?" "I need some change."

I said no and kept him and his buddy in sight. He was frustrated and nervous.

Finally, I said, "I know what you are doing here. I am not going inside. I will stay out here all night if I have to."

His buddy crept the car forward. It was taking too long. They gave up and sped off. I was outside, in the cold, watching the streets for almost an hour before someone else came in for gas.

The state penitentiary is in Salem. The station owner had two locations, one downtown and one by the freeway. Texas John was on parole, work release. The owner wanted me to train him. John and I talked, not much else to do. I told him service stations were my family's business and that my people were from the Ozarks. Like I had with my gang friends growing up, I knew how to talk to John. I instinctively saw that John's edginess and clear ability to turn violent wasn't my problem but would be for anyone who crossed him. Once again, a dangerous soul made me feel safe.

A man and his girlfriend got into a beef in the little lobby next to the soda machines. The guy hit the woman. I saw John go for the door. There is a fluid southern man code about violence toward women. I grew up with it. I know men like John could hit a woman in the right circumstance, but I also knew he would not tolerate watching it happen. By time I came into the lobby, John had the smaller man by the throat suspending him in the air against a soda machine. He would kill him if I let him. I talked to John, slowly and clearly.

"John, he's a piece of shit." John turned slightly toward me.

"Put him down, John. He isn't worth it. John, listen to me. Let him down. You don't need this shit right now."

John relaxed and let the man regain his feet. He looked at me and said, "Okay."

I said to the man, "I just saved your life. Get the fuck out of here. Now!"

His lady was cowering in the opposite corner. They ran for the door and got into their car. I looked at John.

"You okay, man?"

He said, "I won't let anyone do that." His shoulders dropped as the adrenaline let go.

"I know. Neither would I but you just got out man. I didn't want that fucker to be your mistake."

Hand offered. "Thanks, man."

John transferred to the downtown station. I missed having him around. One night, a couple of weeks later, he pulled up in a beater car.

"Hey man, you got a car," I yelled as he got out.

"Yeah, it's a piece of shit, but it runs okay. I just wanted to come by and tell you I was leaving."

He put out his hand. We shook.

"Thank you, man, for everything."

"Your parole?" I asked.

"Yeah, I have to get back to Texas. This place isn't working for me."

"Okay, I understand," I said.

"I'm out of here."

"Safe trip, man."

With that, Texas John was gone. He had taken the money from the downtown station. He was a felon on the run who had stopped to say goodbye to a buddy. He may have considered the money in my till but there are some things you just don't do to a friend.

To Meg's chagrin, I was living the Oregon stoner lifestyle. I carved out a section of our bedroom with cardboard and foil in a little marijuana grow room. I wanted a crop to harvest so I could take home some reefer for Christmas. Megan played along and gave me a leather-bound cigarette case for my joints. Growing pot … felony … tucking a cigarette case full of joints in my pocket as I boarded the plane … federal felony. Not my brightest move but Carl was flying in from DC for Christmas, too. My old college roommate, Mark, and Carl met me at the Ontario Airport. I knew having my own homegrown would impress them. We smoked my awful pot all the way to the desert.

I got word that some of my college friends were gathering a couple of days before Christmas in Newport Beach at a pretty swanky condo on the bay owned by one of Megan's friends from the dorm. I borrowed my dad's truck, picked up Mac and Mark, and headed to LA. Carl stayed home with his parents, though he later regretted missing the east LA part of the trip. After partying all night with some of the old crew from the dorm, we crashed on the floor in sleeping bags.

When my friends graduated, I had missed saying goodbye to Robert Gomez in the dorm. He left me a lovely note that ended, "If you ever need anything, I am there for you." He meant it. Robert took his degree and went back to his community to help — Bell Gardens — one of those jigsaw pieces in the puzzle of cities that radiate out from central Los Angeles. Cute rows of houses with invisible gang turf markers street by street.

On Christmas Eve, we went to see Robert. Part of me is never happier than when I am around Latino culture. The sound of spoken Spanish just feels like home. When we walked into his home the men were watching a football game. They all stood to greet us. This was a huge deal; Robert's friends from college came to their home. Our visit, especially on that day, meant we were honoring Robert, thus them. The men offered their chairs. His dad pointed me to his chair. Robert's uncle offered his chair to Mac. I didn't hesitate and sat down. Mac started to demure and I shot him a bullet look. It would have been an insult not to accept the offer. He sat down. The women brought out beers and tamales. We stood to greet them. I made a big deal about the meal they were preparing and how Robert was going to get fat but made the factual excuse that we still had to make it home to our own families.

Before we could go, Robert insisted we say hello to cousins a few blocks away. We had met some of them when they showed up at the dorm. Great guys, some with obvious gang affiliations. The front door of the neat little ranch style home opened to a cloud of marijuana smoke. Robert's 'cousins' sat in a circle of chairs in the living room, bongs and joints circling. Robert said, "My friends from college." It was a magic day pass to a different world. It was so tempting to hang with them. Already late afternoon, I knew if we sat down in that circle we were screwed. I put my arm around Robert, took one hit off a joint to respect the offer, and told everyone how much I missed him and how happy we were to meet his family. Handshakes all around. Never refuse the extended hand of a hillbilly or a Latino.

Driving back to the desert, I dropped off the guys along the way. Alone again, I knew I had just had my best Christmas Eve. That's a tough thought. I also knew I was in deep shit with my own family. I had chosen to trade my own family for my new family. Back home, I tried to explain the unique experience but the damage was done. It was a price I couldn't justify but was willing to pay for just a little more time with my college family.

~

Mike and Kimm got married in April of 79. I was part of the wedding party. I bought a pint of whiskey and paper cups for a toast in a side room of the church before the ceremony. I have pictures of me in a rented brown tux with the redneck yellow Caterpillar tractor hat I wore all the time. I have no idea how I got from Salem to Indio. None. My brother told me I flew down on my own. What was most clear in his memory was that I got stoned in Portland to fly down and scored some pot when I arrived. Evidently, I was high for four days. Self-medication again.

Carl had landed a job in DC as an assistant press secretary for Senator Hayakawa from California. He told me I really had to check out DC. So early that May I made the 11-hour trip there. Portland to Seattle to St. Louis to Atlanta to National Airport DC. Layovers and switched jets. I still marvel at that version of Jim who was able to make the trip. Who was that guy? He couldn't get stoned on a multi-leg trip.

I was exhausted when I got to Atlanta. No one was at the gate so I treated myself to the *Atlanta Constitution* newspaper, sprawled in the chair, and fell sound asleep with the newspaper over my face. When I woke up and pulled off the paper, I was sitting in the middle of an assemblage of 70s post-hippie looking dudes. The black guy across from me had a cast on his foot. He was talking to the longhaired guy next to him about how he was going to play the bass drum with a foot cast. Seems he had tried skydiving and it didn't work out. Listening to them talk my brain suddenly clicked back on. *Drums? A band? Did that guy just call him Jai?* I knew that name. He was Jaimoe, a drummer for the Allman Brothers Band. The guy offering to tape

Jaimoe's foot to the bass drum pedal was, of course, Dickey Betts. I had woken up in the middle of the Allman Brothers Band. As my befuddled brain thought, *Where's Gregg?* I looked to my left and there he was in the signature leather coat with sheep skin trim. He sat down by me. I was invisible to them. I realized that moment was not going to get any better if I said something.

Carl met me at the airport and laughed when he saw I was wearing a wool sweater. I stripped down on the way to his truck. Parked under his window air conditioner on a couch I slept for the first 15 hours. Like my deep sleep after the long trip to pick up Megan, there was a point where I actually caught up on sleep but was holding reality at bay. The old excitement versus anxiety dilemma. Finally, Carl rousted me and we headed out into a whirlwind of activity. Washington, DC was wondrous. Carl's group house was on the House of Representatives side, three blocks from the Capitol. The first night Carl took me to a famous White House staff hangout bar. On the way back, still jet lagged and a little drunk, I turned to my right and there was the White House, the postcard view.

Carl's wild friends all had unimaginable job titles. Deputy press secretary. Legislative assistant. Office manager. Each one with the name of a senator or congressman after the title. Carl, ever my front man, got me set up with a tour of the White House. It was a long walk down the National Mall from his house to the White House. There they all were, the Smithsonian museums. I was filled with giddy reverence.

Before I left Oregon, a neighbor had loaded me up on hallucinogenic mushrooms called liberty caps. I took a small dose and set off across the Mall to the Natural History Museum, one of my childhood dreams. The mushrooms hit as I walked in the door of the museum and saw hanging above me a full-sized model of a blue whale. I have no idea how long I stood in the entryway staring at that whale. Yes, I perverted my childhood dream. Or did I enhance it?

Carl and his friends were baseball fanatics. Carl, his black Irish friend, Dennis, and I crammed into his little Toyota pick-up and set out for Baltimore for an Orioles game. Dennis had a power I have always admired. Within seconds of meeting him, you were his friend. He wrapped you in his humor and charm like a long-time conspirator. Halfway to Baltimore, we got caught in a downpour, checked the radio, and the game was postponed. I was so disappointed. Then Dennis looked at his watch and said, "Hey, let's go to the Cap Center and catch the NBA playoff game. We can scalp cheap tickets."

Sure, let's do that, I thought, dumbfounded that such things were possible in this mystical place. Once seated in the arena Carl saw that we were sitting behind a senator from Arizona and some staff he knew. They smiled and waved at Carl. *Does this happen all the time?*

As he drove me to the airport, Carl said. "You need to be here."

Chapter 11

Only Ten Blocks from the Senate

CARL CALLED.

"I can get you an interview for a job on Hayakawa's staff if you can be here in a week. Everyone begs for these jobs to get their foot in the door. No guarantees but you have to come here now."

Megan and I could make it work. There was nothing to hold us in Salem. She would wrap up the apartment and meet me in DC later. I'm sure we must have talked about moving to DC, but now I wonder. I was scared but more terrified of my mounting malaise. Fear as motivator. I took a couple of days to pull together my stuff, say goodbye, and headed east.

When I think about that trip now I'm almost sure someone else did it. Given how small my world became, this sort of bold trip to the other side of the country by myself with no guarantee of a job or place to stay seems impossible.

In a four-day trip across country, I never ate in a restaurant. It wasn't because I was cheap. It was because I was the nervous child with a deep fear that unless I controlled my food something would happen to my gut. Every night I pulled out my little propane camp stove and put it on the desk in the hotel room. At night I made soup or stew from a can. In the morning, I made eggs and some toast. Lunch? Of course, ham sandwiches and chips.

The ham sandwich on white bread with Miracle Whip was my signature food. There was nothing between the bread but one, maybe two, slices of Oscar Meyer ham. If I went wild, I might squirt on a little French's mustard. I could find all these components for a meal anywhere in America. This is the sandwich my mom made for me as a kid. No embellishments. Lettuce? *Are you kidding me?* It was my most safe food. With little nutritional value, it filled me up, and most importantly, never bothered my stomach. Safe.

It was the heart of the gas crisis. There was a national 55 mph speed limit. The miles droned by. Every American should drive across the country at least once. There's no other way to understand the true American scale. You feel the Rocky Mountains rise and fall in a day. Driving the flat, agricultural expanse of Nebraska is hypnotic. So much so that at one exhausted point I thought I saw cows on the freeway. I pulled over for the night in Oglala, Nebraska. The next morning, I woke up in a panic because I couldn't remember where I was. Thank god they still put hotel matchbooks in the ashtrays. Ahhh … Nebraska …

okay. And then ... crossing the Missouri River into Iowa the palpable relief I felt when I saw the welcoming texture of rolling hills.

At the outer edge of DC, I pulled over to check my map. By early afternoon all my belongings were parked behind the three-story Civil War era group townhouse. No one was home to let me in. I remembered how to get to Pennsylvania Avenue, so I walked up to the Tune Inn for a burger and a beer. Yeah, a meal out. All sorts of barriers broken.

When Carl came home, he told me I had an interview the next day. The ... next ... day. After disjointed sleep, I woke up and pulled my sad suit out of the still-packed Toyota. I walked across the east front of the Capitol. The surreal quality of the walk made me less nervous. Nothing about what I was doing made any sense, so I just put one foot in front of the other. I stopped for a moment on the sidewalk and looked up. All I could think was, *the fucking Supreme Court?* Here I can quote from a typewritten journal entry made later that day:

I have spent a lot of time considering what a D.C. interview would be like. In my imagination I felt it would be very stuffy and quite rigorous. As it has turned out my first encounter with the interviewers of Washington was almost too benign to be believed. There was no reference to my background or GPA. I was just sort of led to a little hallway and someone told me about the job. I had to fight hard just to tell them I was there at all.

Carl, the salesman, had paved the way. I suspect

Steve, my interviewer, only needed to see that I had bathed, knew how to tie a tie, and wasn't drooling on myself. I was too exhausted and time zoned for the early morning interview to be very anxious. The job was in the mail room. They wanted me to start the next day. Overwhelmed, I didn't immediately say yes. I did say, "Could you at least let me unpack my car and then call you back?" Steve was confused but said okay. I called Carl, who said I was an idiot. "Say yes now. People walk the streets here for months to get a job in a Senate mailroom." Thirty-six hours after arriving in Washington, DC, I was a Senate staffer.

On Friday, June 8, 1979, I called my folks, then Megan. I had thought about making that call to my parents, the one where there was proof that college means something. I suppose all kids want to reassure their folks that their faith and hard work was warranted. Dad was surprised and elated. He said he would tell the grandparents. My grandma Pearl had been praying for me. She was one person who if she said you were in her prayers, she was not kidding. Meg was happy, but we were already missing each other. The job started the next Monday.

A roommate had just cleared out of Carl's house, so I instantly had a third-floor room. I'm pretty sure this was his plan all along. How can you not love a guy who thinks of his friends like that? From getting me through graduation to setting me up in DC. The Merriam Hall politicos were reforming in DC. Christine, who lived across the hall from Megan in the dorm now lived just down the block. A job, a home, an instant support group. I was beyond lucky, and for a time, the nervous child took a little vacation. I was newly emboldened to strike out.

The day after I got the job, we went to Baltimore for the first of 32 Orioles games I would see that season. A baseball fanatic's dream, I saw all the home 1979 World Series games including a Game 7. Carl's friends had formed an association they called 'Inebrius Tours' with the slogan, 'The Ride You Won't Remember in the Morning.' Carl put together bus rides from Capitol Hill to Memorial Stadium. Add a keg of beer that was gone by time we hit Baltimore, and ... well ... you get the picture. One of the rules of the group was that at anytime, anywhere, if someone started to sing "Taaaaaaaaaake ..." everyone had to join in and sing "Take Me Out to the Ballgame." On the bus, in the ballpark, in restaurants, theaters, bars, on the street ... we had to sing. I loved it.

In Senator Hayakawa's mailroom, my co-workers were an Ivy League MA and a couple of guys from top line east coast schools. Getting the first job on Capitol Hill was the thing. The Hill is a train station. Everyone is constantly on the move. In the pre-polarization world, we didn't have to share an ideology with our elected official. We were professional staff. One of the conceits was that we didn't refer to our senator or representative by name, we just said 'my boss.' The other thing we quickly learned was 'no awe.' At least, no outward awe. The first time I stepped on an elevator with Ted Kennedy, it took all of my concentration not to gape or gasp and just say, blank faced, "Good Morning, Senator."

I quickly moved from the mailroom to something called Robo. Located across a street in the old immigration headquarters building, we handled the massive constituent correspondence for a senator from California. The job, getting out responses, maintaining the constituent response databases, and running the automatic signature machine could be repetitive and dull. Correspondence was in the early stages of computerization. The legislative correspondents (LC) wrote paragraphs on topics. Each topic was given a number and constituent letters were then answered by a sequence of numbers equaling paragraphs. The human touch. It turns out I had an essential skill. I could look at each of the paragraphs from different authors in draft form and edit them to all sound like Senator SI Hayakawa. That part of the job was challenging and fun.

Not everyone gets to live out their dream. For a kid from the desert who loved and immersed himself in American politics, I woke up every day feeling the heartbeat of the city. I was living in the middle of places that were pictures in those childhood encyclopedias.

In creating a new me in a new place, I wasn't just a fish out of water; I was a fish on the grill. Nothing had prepared me for living in DC. The city was about 80 percent black and poor. If I walked in a straight-line east from the Supreme Court I would be in block after block of run-down federal style row houses all occupied by black families. To be sure, there were wealthy neighborhoods in the opposite direction beyond the White House but those weren't low level staffer territory. While as yet it didn't have a name, I became part of an early wave of gentrification that would ripple in all directions from the Capitol.

For the nervous child, DC felt dangerous. The signs were everywhere. In the blocks around my home not just banks had ballistic glass to protect the tellers; liquor stores, fast food joints, anyplace that had ready cash. In one store, customers pointed at the booze on the shelf, which was given over in a rotating turret. We jokingly called it 'bullet proof liquor.' I'm sure that from my first day in my new home my naturally heightened state of alertness had begun to wear on my psyche. Friends were robbed on the street at gun point. People were paired up when they left a party at night, so they didn't have to find their car alone. Prudent caution was a way of life.

Honestly, street radar meant profiling young black men on the sidewalks around you. It wasn't racism as much as it was simply rational. As a young white guy in a coat and tie, I was conscious of my visibility and vulnerability. There will always be tension when poverty collides with even the perception of wealth. Most Hill staffers simply gave up on DC, got on the train to the suburbs after work, and stayed out of the city at night. After I time, I began to think of the National Mall with all of its museums and attractions as 'white people's Disneyland.' At night, I wondered, where did they all go?

Having that little senate staff ID on the Hill created a caste system. Swarming with visitors, we took special elevators, ate in exclusive dining rooms, and had access to places strictly off limits to tourists. We dressed differently and moved quickly. If we needed to talk to someone about our paycheck? Well, that office was a set of double doors across the hall from the ornate original Senate chambers. I would stand in line there and imagine Daniel Webster delivering a speech. Even as a low-level staffer I was still on the inside. Before it closed, I even got a haircut in the Senate barbershop. On one wall, in lovely niches, the senators' shaving mugs. Heady stuff for a small-town kid.

The group house on New Jersey Avenue was on its last legs. Megan, Carl, and I planned on becoming roommates in a new place after she arrived. I was conflicted about Megan coming to join me. Here I was, the new Jim. A young man with possibilities in the big city. Drinks in storied bars at night. Live music. Theater. Baseball. Was I still in love? Would she like it here? How would we be as a couple, living together in this new place? This seemed like very adult stuff compared to Salem.

When Meg arrived, we were still us. I was relieved. The three of us went house hunting. Even with three salaries, our paychecks were quickly overwhelmed by the rapidly inflating DC rental prices. We were committed to staying on the Hill. Most of our close friends lived there and for Carl and me, walking to work was a requirement. We were aware that to live on the Hill we would have to decide how much safety to trade for location. At the time, people said, "How far out on the urban frontier are you going?" Others said they could never live *there*. Sounds racist and elitist. It was. But it was 80s DC reality.

We landed in a newly remodeled townhouse just off the corner of 8th and F Northeast. It was one of just a few remodeled houses on the block. F Street runs straight down to Union Station and the Senate office buildings. H Street was a major thoroughfare. Most of the storefronts were still burned out and empty from the riots after the murder of Martin Luther King. That fact was sobering. Kitty-corner from us was a little store run by a Korean family. The seeming success of these new immigrants was a tension point in the black community.

Several nights a week, Carl went for a run down by the Senate office buildings, to the National Mall, by all the Smithsonian museums, around the Washington Monument and back. About 3 miles. Sipping a beer, sitting on our stoop, I met him one night. He liked to cool down and stretch using the handrails of our steps. Three little boys walked up.

"What you doin'?" asked the boldest of the trio.

"Just stretching my muscles after my run," answered Carl.

"Where you run?"

"I go down the Mall, around the Washington Monument and back."

"What's that monument? Where that?"

Carl and I looked at each other. I shook my head at him and mouthed, "No."

"The big monument, " Carl said, "The one that goes way up in the sky. You know. You can see it from the Capitol."

"Never seen it," the oldest boy said as they walked away.

Carl and I looked at each other, mouths agape. But there it was. DC was a thousand little worlds, each a few blocks square. For those kids, probably natives of the city, the international symbol of our democracy may as well have been on another planet, because it was.

Across the street from our new house was a single-story building that served as a distribution point for the *Washington Post*. Men and boys lined up there before dawn. A daylight basement below us was occupied by a woman who worked at a federal agency. The house on the corner next to us was a small church. The city was awash in storefront churches. On Sunday mornings, the sound of people singing vibrated through our living room wall. I recognized some of the songs from the Southern Baptist Church of my youth. And ... most importantly ... every window below the second floor and every exterior door had heavy steel bars covering them. Truth was, if the black families could afford them, they had those barred doors, too. They were victims of crime far more than us.

On the ten-block morning walk to work, grandmas and the grandpas were often sitting out in front of their homes. I made a point to greet them with a smile and a "Good morning." I was trying to be a good neighbor. As often as not, I'd get a smile back from the same elderly woman who'd say, "Good morning, baby." I liked that. It always made me think of my own grandma.

Meg and I discovered another feature of our new house. Sitting on the couch, watching TV, and eating dinner, a huge rat ran in front of us and under the couch. Freaked out? Uh … yeah! Meg grabbed a broom. I got a handful of full beer cans. We opened the front gate, absurdly thinking we would herd the rat outside. I began bowling cans under the couch. The rat came out, rose on its hind legs to screech at Meg, then ran into the kitchen. We knew the bar where Carl was so we called him. He was drunk.

"Carl, there's a huge rat in the house. What do we do?" I said.

He reported what I had said to the crowd of friends. In the background I heard helpful advice.

"Make him pay rent! Sublet! Kill the rat! Kill the rat! Kill the rat!"

I hung up. But for reasons that escape me Carl decided to dial 911. He gave our address and behind him the operator heard, "Kill the rat! Kill the rat! Kill the rat!"

Megan and I were standing on two chairs near the kitchen with brooms and mops in our hands when several DC police cars arrived. Moments later, all of our drunk friends came running up to the house. The cops had expected a riot, not two idiots on chairs with cleaning implements.

~

We eased into the pattern of living and work. Meg found a job as a secretary. I was beginning to expand my network of professional acquaintances. In those less partisan days I had friends on both sides of the aisle. One side benefit was that the Republicans always had the best pot. Knowing I was a historical political junkie, one new pal told me I should stop by her work to see the paper shredder in her boss's office. It was the shredder from John Mitchell's office at the Nixon Committee to Re-elect the President. Yeah, that one.

For Christmas Meg flew to Walla Walla, Carl and me to the desert.

Mom and Dad had moved to a condo subdivision in Palm Desert. Mom was selling real estate and at some point, they would flip the condo. After the grit of DC, the home and little subdivision felt sterile. My folks looked like they were hanging out at an extended stay hotel. I had trouble placing them there, though they both loved that the community was safe, neat, and clean. They had a little Christmas party. I was the chief exhibit. I even wore my blue blazer to impress. In the desert, it doesn't take much to impress. I totally got it. Who I had become was a huge deal and my folks had surely earned some bragging rights. Eventually, exhausted by my own stories and everyone in the room getting some facetime with me, I slipped out and walked the empty streets to smoke a joint.

Driving the few miles to Indio to see my grandparents immediately brought me back to earth. I went for some beer at a 7-11 convenience store. Out front was Johnny Ruiz in a long black duster coat. I had grown up with Johnny. Somewhere there is a picture of him with a group of little boys at one of my birthday parties. He was an amazing athlete, but he flamed out and mostly disappeared into the chaos of his family, gangs, crime, and drugs.

"Jimmy! I heard you did good."

"Yeah, Johnny. It's good to see you, man. How are you?"

"Good. You know." His eyes were a little glazed. I didn't know what drug, but he was high.

I said, "I came home for Christmas to see my folks."

After a few more words, we both went into the store. I got my six-pack and came back outside. I waited to tell Johnny good bye. He led me to the side of the store and reached under his coat to hand me a stolen bottle of cheap wine.

"This is for you ... and Christmas ..." I didn't hesitate and took the bottle from him.

"Thank you, Johnny. That's very nice of you. Man, you take good care of yourself."

"Yeah," was all he said and walked away.

I needed some better clothes and my dad

wanted to help. You can only get so far with one blue blazer. In Indio, that meant Sears. I couldn't find a decent sport coat, but I did see the girl who had crushed my one act of high school dating bravery by refusing to go to the prom with me. I had psyched up for weeks to ask her. She was now a clerk there and had seen the pictures of me in the local paper with the senator. How could I not savor that moment? It was every skinny nerd's fantasy.

Farewells said, family hugged, Carl and I played DC big shots and avoided the drive from the desert to LAX by taking a little prop commuter plane to LA. When we landed at Dulles it was bitter cold. There was no way for me to know that would be my last time on a jet for over twenty years.

Chapter 12

Bad Night in a Chinese Restaurant

I WAS JOURNALING, scribbling scenes and even submitting short stories while in DC. Always the guy leaning back against the wall, observation is my thing. It was clear in my notes that my sense of danger in the city was rising. The daily reminder of bars on the windows and doors didn't help. Bit by bit my nervous child ramped up his protections to dangers seen and unseen.

I drove to a men's store in Alexandria to find a winter coat. I had never imagined owning a long dress coat, but now it was a necessity. I found a wool grey monster that had been made in eastern Europe.

Walking home from work on a dark winter evening, a few blocks from my house a young black man approached me. He asked me what time it was. My radar went off. This was a classic street hustle to get you to stop. I had already abandoned watches on my wrist and put them in my pocket as a safety measure. I was about to say I didn't have a watch when his arm came up under his sweater. Was I facing a gun or his finger? He demanded my money. I held out my flimsy Velcro closed wallet. Without taking it, he looked me up and down and said he wanted the coat, too. Hands up, I glanced around. Of course, the street was empty. I said that was crazy. He took my wallet and ran.

Up to that point, I had been hassled a few times on the street, ducked into stores when it looked like someone was following me, but this was different. It had happened in sight of my home. A not uncommon occurrence in DC, but I still wasn't prepared for how deeply it shook me. At home, I called the police. I was shaking but trying to be cool. They were detached and professional. Just another guy robbed on the street in DC. Probably not a gun. You did the right thing. Your coat, too? That's a new one.

After the robbery, I carried my cash in my left front pocket. Still do. No money clip, just folded bills. I had a theory that the next time I would pull out the cash and hope they ran with it. A few weeks later, I almost got to test my theory. Three young men were standing in the street not far from my house. "Hey, you got a watch? What time is it?" Same dodge. They were between me and my house. I just raised my empty wrist and started walking faster. I moved to the middle of the street, coming at them, then zagged quickly by them, not making eye contact, just mumbling, "Don't even own a watch." Once in front of my house I bolted for the door and the other side of the metal bars.

Very quickly, those ten blocks from my house to the Senate side of The Hill became an issue. In winter, the cold mornings were okay. Lots of people on the move. The dark evenings were different. Everyone came home at different times. I never made a thing about this with my roommates or anyone else. Like my daily terror in high school, I was going to deal with this alone. Lots of people get robbed in DC. My experience wasn't violent. Silly to make a big deal out of it.

One night, I walked out of the office and I was afraid. My heart was beating fast and I felt hot. Just as I was trying to figure out what was wrong a cab came down the avenue. I flagged it. I felt better in the cab and just fine when I got home. The next day I drove to work. Just ten blocks. No big deal, except I was building a new safe zone and defining new avoidance patterns.

This began a lifelong parking ballet. In that moment, I didn't consider it a big deal. I was just taking care of myself so I could go to work more comfortably. In a city where there was a subway and busses everywhere, I stopped using all public transportation.

Parking on The Hill was the pursuit of scarcity. The ability to squeeze a car into the smallest possible space was considered an art form. Every morning, like vultures circling carrion, suburban car commuters moved slowly around blocks, timing their moves to be on the right block of free parking starting at 9 a.m. I joined the parking samba line. I got very good at the game. It took months and some bullshit stories about physical limitations, but eventually, I got a much-coveted reserved parking slot near my office.

A couple blocks from our offices was one of our favorite hangouts, a Chinese restaurant called Hunan. We went there after work for happy hour. Crowded into the huge booths, we drank and ate and laughed. Nattily dressed women and men in suit coats, ties dangling loose from our necks, making complete fools of ourselves like pseudo-masters of the universe.

I liked happy hour because a drink came quickly to calm me. One evening, for some reason, we went back into the dining room at a big round table. The dinner service was slow, as was the delivery of the drinks. I started to feel hot and further loosened my tie. I wasn't sure what was going on. I was a little nauseous and my heart was beating fast. My face felt like it was on fire. I thought I was going to throw up. I glued on a smile and told myself, *Easy, Jim. Take a breath. Hang in there.* Nothing worked. I leaned toward Megan and said, "I'll be right back."

I locked myself in a restroom stall and tried to slow my breathing. I shook my head like a dog, trying to shake it off. I thought I would pass out. My checkbook was in my shirt pocket. When I leaned over to grab my knees, the checkbook fell into the toilet. I plucked it out and tried to dry it with toilet paper, then put it into my pants pocket so no one could see that it was all wet. I'm not sure how long I was in there, but when I came out my friends were looking at me. Just what I wanted to avoid. It felt like my head would explode. I had to get out. I had to get home. I had to get to safety.

I said, "I'm not feeling great. I need to go home now."

Not waiting for a reaction, I grabbed my overcoat and headed out the door. It was dark. I was unsteady on my feet. I held myself up on parked cars on the way home. Rushing, not quite running, I realized how vulnerable I looked, which just made the sensations worse. Finally, I got to the door, locked myself in the house, and lay down on the couch. My heart began to slow. I didn't understand what had just happened. The only thing I wanted was to somehow make sure it never happened again.

I had had my first full-blown panic attack. My life had just changed. A confluence of my biology and life events had come together in a single powerful flow. I felt it. If I'd been paying close attention, I could have seen it. Still, life moved on, as it always does.

My parents came to visit. We did all the usual tourist things. The Mall, Smithsonian, Tomb of the Unknown Soldier. We even took my parents on the first Inebrius tour of the year to Baltimore for an Orioles game. This tour was especially debauched. We rented a London transit double decker bus and put a keg on each level. Mistakes were made. After the game, the driver, barraged by endless unhelpful suggestions, got lost in parts of Baltimore where the sight of a load of drunk white people in a double decker must have seemed like Martians landing. No matter, we were out of beer, so after a collection, we stopped at a corner store and emptied their beer cooler. Here's the essential miscalculation; a double decker bus does not have a restroom. Of course, a stop was ordered at the side of the parkway halfway to DC. Men and women piled out to the tree-line. My folks? Couldn't have had a better time. Total gamers.

Carl cooked up a way for my folks not to just meet Senator Hayakawa but for all of us to have lunch in the inner sanctum of the senator's private dining room. This was really showing off for my parents. I was shaky but hid it pretty well. I think.

Our boss had a nickname: Sleepy Sam. He earned that when seen falling asleep at a meeting in the White House. Carl called me right after it happened.

"Holy shit, Sam just fell asleep at the White House. What's that sleeping disease? We have to find a way to cover for him."

"You mean narcolepsy?"

"Yeah, that's it!"

"Sam doesn't have that. He was just out late partying. But it might work. We could say he just missed his drugs today?"

"Perfect!" I said.

An hour later, that's just what the press release said. Problem solvers.

Standing in the hall, introductions were made. Next to the senator, as my parents chatted with him, was a tall blond, a real looker in an over-painted sort of way. I looked at Carl and raised an eyebrow. He edged me to the side.

"Geez, Jim, she's a dancer he was out with last night and he insists she come to lunch. I can't get rid of her. Here's the deal, I arranged for the official photographer to take a picture of us at the table. When he shows up, help me make sure she is on the outside edge of the photo."

"Got it ... seriously ... a dancer? Holy shit."

"Yeah, I can have her cropped out of the picture so your mom and dad can have a picture without her in it."

"Nice."

I was a mess. I shoved food around on my plate, faking eating. I kept looking at the dark mahogany double exit doors. I tried to make idle chit chat. Here I was at a once-in-a-lifetime lunch surrounded DC heavyweights and I could barely focus. I just wanted it to end. When the photographer came, Carl and I made our move. It worked perfectly. The boss, the blond, and my folks never knew about our scheme. Later when Dad asked about the blond, we had a good laugh. It was wonderful picture of Senator Hayakawa, the Blackwoods, and the two young senate staffers from the desert. It appeared in all the local papers. Never saw the blond again.

~

I didn't know what was happening to me. I just wanted to feel normal. I spent more and more time thinking about how I could avoid situations where I felt afraid. Bodily sensations, old and new, seemed to come out of nowhere. A sudden feeling of unsteadiness at the grocery store. Sweaty palms and tight chest waiting in the lunch line. The rushing feeling of blood in my chest, ears, and face sitting in a theater. The fear of another panic attack became its own tyranny.

Meg's parents came to visit that summer. Having made all the rounds of DC with my parents, it was reasonable to demure and let Megan just hang out with hers. I was already scamming to feel safe. One day trip haunts me still. I'm a huge Civil War buff. I love to read Civil War histories. Earlier, Meg and I had gone to several battlefields in Virginia, but the big deal was Gettysburg. Meg's dad wanted to take a trip up to Pennsylvania to tour the battlefield. I desperately wanted to go. Meg knew that. But I was too afraid of the 90-minute car ride and the day in the park. When I thought of leaving with them, I flashed back to the Chinese restaurant and I started to ramp up the same physical symptoms. I didn't want to stay at home alone, but I just couldn't go with them. I broke down crying as they drove away.

What I couldn't know in that moment was that I had just acted out an internal drama I would repeat hundreds of times in my life in ways big and small. That day, in spite of every appearance, I had lost DC. When I had first gotten there, I used to walk from my office to the Mall to eat lunch in the Picasso sculpture garden or under the Calder mobiles. After Gettysburg, I was like Lee, in full retreat from Washington, DC. I didn't again enter one of the museums. I never went to see Ford's Theater. I stopped fishing off the river wall. I didn't walk off by myself exploring brick carriage tracks and houses in the little alleys around my neighborhood. Oh, I did some social things, but always with Megan or a close friend at my elbow. But that wasn't the worst of it.

~

I am infatuated with baseball. I love everything about the game. I get misty-eyed when I see the green field of a ballpark for the first time. I saw my first major league game at ten-years-old at Dodger Stadium. As a kid, I became a lifelong San Francisco Giants fan in Dodger country because I saw my heroes Willie Mays and Willie McCovey in a spring training game in Palm Springs. The baseball fans in DC were my tribe.

In late July, Inebrius had a tour to see the much-hated NY Yankees. The previous season we had gone to a Yankees game and got seats in the perfect location to heckle Reggie Jackson. Being with this crew on a bus was a little slice of heaven for me. Drinking, storytelling, singing long dirges of Warren Zevon songs and repeated choruses of "Take Me Out to The Ballgame." This time, I gathered all of my courage to get on the bus. A big part of me wanted to run but I held it together and got that first beer down. It helped, but not like in the past.

It was hot … humid … very hot. Our seats were first-base side, upper deck in the blistering sunshine. We sat down. My seat was in the middle of our three rows. I didn't like that. As soon as I sat, I felt hemmed in, unable to escape. Aisle seats remain an obsession. The National Anthem ... the first pitch ... the heat ... the heat. I felt dizzy. Without a word to Megan or anyone else, I barged down the aisle and down the stairs. I had to get to the shade. I had to cool off. I had to leave.

I worked my way down to the bowels of Memorial Stadium. Somehow, down a hallway, somewhere below the press boxes, I found a small unoccupied single restroom. I went in and locked the door. Cool air was coming from the ceiling vent. I stood there and breathed it in. Muffled sounds of the game rose and fell. Inning after inning. I don't know why no one else wanted that restroom. I wasn't really sure where I was. I just knew I had to find some way to survive until the end of the game. Finally, I came out and worked my way up the zigzag stairs until I could see about a third of the field. The mound, home plate, and right side of the infield. No one seemed to mind, so I stayed there in the shade. I just couldn't go back out in that sun. I couldn't bear to answer the questions from my friends. I was frightened and ashamed. I was alone.

Before the last pitch, I made my way down to the bus parking lot. The driver had started the bus to cool it down. I went to the very back of the bus, next to the restroom, and sat there counting the minutes until my friends returned. When they came back, they were relieved. Megan was a little frantic that I had disappeared with no word. I talked to my friends about the heat and having stomach issues and needing to cool off. Megan knew I wasn't telling the whole story. They were kind and boisterous, but I could see they were trying to figure out the mystery of Jim leaving. No one pushed the issue.

That Yankees versus Orioles game was in July of 1980. I would not see another MLB game for over 20 years. I hadn't just lost DC. Now, I had lost major league baseball.

Something was seriously wrong. I didn't know what. I needed help.

Chapter 13

Fear Gets a Name

HIS HOME OFFICE was way up in northwest DC. Nice neighborhood. Megan had to drive. I sat in the passenger seat, both hands firmly holding the armrest. I kept telling Meg that I couldn't do this. "Please take me home." We both knew I had to go but I had no will and was utterly dependent on hers. Hers was an awful burden born of love, soon only to increase. She found the address and pulled up in front of the house. I sat frozen in the car. Meg went to the door and talked to a man who came out and kneeled by the passenger door. He talked to me through the window. I have no idea what he said but soon I was in his office. That is how I met Dr. W.

Dr. W was recommended by a friend. I'm not sure what kind of recommendation it was. I think we may have only had one friend who we knew had been to a psychotherapist. In some ways, we were not much more knowledgeable than my parents years before.

The sensations and thoughts I experienced were not new, but they were qualitatively and quantitatively different. In the past, I found ways to cope and do pretty much anything I wanted to do. But now what I conjured was life altering. What I wanted most in the world was a cure. I didn't want to have those sensations again.

Megan and I each told our versions of my story. I did some tests. He showed me the Rorschach cards. I could quickly construct elaborate stories for each of the black and white images. In the end, he seemed reassuring enough that we arranged to meet regularly. He sent me home with a big sheet of paper on which I was to do a multigenerational family tree with notes about their mental health. That version of the family tree had a couple of boxes where mental health issues were known to me. My Grandma Blackwood and her obsessions. Her daughter, Aunt Jo, who I heard had tried to commit suicide. There was a mysterious tale of a Blackwood generations back who hung himself in a barn. I had no idea when. I have that yellowed 'family map' with me still.

~

Among my basement papers are two sheets with the heading 'Phobia Program of Washington.' One sheet is a phobia/fear questionnaire. The other is the phobia diagnostic assessment. I now know that one of the earliest centers for phobia therapy was just outside of DC in Rockville, Maryland. The forms are clearly something Dr. W borrowed from that facility.

The phobia diagnostic assessment had a big winner: agoraphobia. I love the actual text:

Patient is considered to have a phobia and should be treated if: b. The combined score for any single column is 10 or more.

Knowing what I know now, I would have scored myself much higher. Even then, I scored a twenty for agoraphobia. My problem had a name. I was actually dealing with a mental illness. I'm a problem solver. I can cure this. Just tell me what to do. Except, that isn't what happened.

The Phobia Program of Washington was just four miles from our house. You would think Dr. W would have drawn me a map and made me an appointment with one of his more experienced colleagues? Nope. We began talk therapy. Worse yet, we eventually ended up doing couples therapy.

In that same little stack of papers he gave me was a half-sheet of paper with a short bibliography of nine books. He put stars next to two of those books: *Peace From Nervous Suffering,* 1972 and *Simple, Effective Treatment of Agoraphobia,* 1976. Both were written by an Australian doctor named Claire Weekes. That's all I got. Given a diagnosis of agoraphobia, I was told the best option was to order two books.

What followed was essentially my attempt to cure myself by trial and error. Thirty-eight years after buying those books, I looked at them again. I was baffled. Why didn't I have more success? Then, in *Simple, Effective Treatment of Agoraphobia,* I found this:

Far from being dependent types, many nervously ill people show courage and independence fighting their fears, often with little help from their family and unfortunately without adequate understanding from their therapists.

So much depends on the therapist's ability to explain the nuances of this strange illness: for example, to explain why, when the patient is feeling better, setbacks can come for no apparent reason and be as devastating as if no progress had been made; to explain why symptoms thought forgotten can return acutely after months, even years of absence; while all the symptoms can then so quickly appear; why such demoralizing exhaustion can so rapidly follow the return of symptoms; why, despite the right attitude, sensitization may sometimes linger for such an unconscionably long time; why, when the agoraphobic returns home after being successful, it may seem that no success has been achieved and going out the next day is a difficult as ever. The whys seem countless.

Unless the therapist has special understanding, a pessimistic attitude toward curing agoraphobia is to be expected.

Surely, I must have read this. Why didn't it serve as a warning? Dr. W was my first therapist. He was the expert to whom both Megan and I deferred. Why didn't he know this? Could it be Dr. W hadn't read the books he recommended?

Initially, Meg drove me to the therapy sessions. After a while, I was able to drive myself. With no meaningful therapy for my illness, we focused on the stress my illness created. We tackled bigger issues, like why after so long together Megan and I weren't talking about marriage. Worthy topics, but as I was busy building avoidance behaviors, mostly irrelevant. I was creating a new lifestyle around my mental illness.

To be sure, the impact of illness on Megan and me was an issue. In terms of the state of the science and treatment in 1980, it was as if we had been tossed into a stormy sea before the invention of the lifeboat. Meg began to evolve from lover and friend to my 'safe person.' And because she loved me and was supportive by nature, Meg shifted willingly into that role. I felt safe going places if she went. That was never going to be a cure.

Among my correspondence are a couple of letters from Dr. W almost three years later. Even then, his reaction to my continuing struggles is telling:

I'd be interested in learning what you're doing to maintain your ability to deal successfully with your fears. Do you continue to read Weekes or anyone like her? Do you meditate? Do you practice being in the present? What do you, so obviously successfully, to take such good care of yourself?

Seeing his letter reminded me that I was more of an experiment than a patient. I had no treatment plan but how I was living with mental illness was still useful information in his work. I was angry. It seems like we could have done more. While the nervous child was always inside me, it turns out the appearance of this illness was classic. Most sufferers of agoraphobia and anxiety manifest in their mid-twenties. I was twenty-five ... right on schedule. Unique in that I was a male sufferer, I was now part of an estimated six million America living with this disease.

The world around me kept telling me I wasn't safe. Before a baseball game on TV, Megan and I went across the street to the Korean quick mart for beer and chips. Long line at the checkout, there was a commotion at the front of store. Mr. Hung, the owner, confronted a young black man who was stealing something. The man dropped a bottle of orange soda out of his sleeve, swung hard and hit Mr. Hung full in the face. Glass and blood, orange and red everywhere.

The owner's brother ran out with a meat cleaver to chase the man down the street. I pushed people out of the way to help Mr. Hung. His wife, at the cash register, was frozen in shock. In the midst of the chaos, the people in the checkout line did not move. I got my car and took Mr. Hung down 8th Street to the Capitol Hill Hospital. Meg stayed to close the store and bring Mrs. Hung to meet us. By the time we got home, the game was over. I rarely went to that store after that, partly because of the minor hero status I now had with the family. The owner's kids, college students who worked there on weekends, said I would never pay for beer there again.

Meg and I made one more trip that summer. Relatively nearby, in Harper's Ferry, West Virginia, is a famous hotel called the Hilltop House a favorite of Mark Twain. Nestled in the junction between the Potomac and Susquehanna rivers, I was intrigued with

Harper's Ferry because that was the location of John Brown's rebellion and one of the places Lee's army camped on their retreat from Gettysburg.

My illness intervened in strange a new way. Now I didn't trust my little Toyota. I don't remember why. I decided that to go sixty miles we needed a rental car. Meg played along and walked down to Union Station to pick up a car.

I loved that trip even though for short spells it seemed like I was just hanging on by my fingertips. I balked the first night at eating in the dining room. We went to the historical sites, but even there I created a new 'safe' bubble and limited how far I would walk from the hotel. Just beyond my imaginary safety bubble, we took the car. I could see Meg was just glad to have escaped the city. The relative success of that weekend made us feel like I was making progress.

It was an illusion.

Chapter 14

Goodbye to the Dream

IN SEPTEMBER OF 1980, our lease was up. We found a different federal style row house farther out from the Capitol. It was just down the street from a Metro station on Pennsylvania Avenue but that didn't matter, I wouldn't ride the Metro. Without guidance, I was doing everything wrong. I was making my illness my life. I have never seen New York City or Boston. In my time on the east coast, I expected to visit those places. I only made it to North Carolina, Virginia, West Virginia, Maryland, and Pennsylvania.

Soon after we moved into our new home, Meg and I planned a trip to see the fall colors in New England. We were going to take ten days and vagabond about, as my dad says, 'following my nose.' After the trip to West Virginia, this seemed the next logical step in reclaiming space. I was once again okay with using my car. The first day was an easy run up to Harrisburg, Pennsylvania. When we checked into the hotel I became conscious that the next day's driving would put us beyond an easy one-day drive home. Home was safety. I couldn't stop thinking about being more than a day from home.

I had learned the value of a glass of Scotch as a tranquilizer. Dewar's White Label. I have no idea how I settled on that brand. A stiff drink settled my nerves. Still, there was that distance thing. I couldn't get it out of my head. The next morning, I was adrift in my own world of conjured fears. My mind darted about from one imaginary disaster to another. I couldn't get my thoughts under control. Nothing in my limited bag of tricks made any difference.

Weekes' technique could be summarized in a repeatable acronym.

FAFL

Face - do not run away.

Accept - do not fight.

Float - do not tense.

Let time pass - do not be impatient with time.

But as I would learn many years later, while those ideas can be fundamental to the management of anxiety illnesses, they are merely a framework. Without a mentor, the system was just an empty set of instructions. As much as the reasoning part of my brain believed the system, my lizard self-preservation amygdala told me I was in danger so … run!

Meg's positive coaching wasn't making any difference. She was crushed. I was having panic attacks and depression was creeping in. Meg had to drive us home. I just stared out the passenger window ... defeated.

Back home, Carl was confused. I tried to explain but mostly went up to the bedroom, pulled the shades, and slept. I was humiliated. I asked Carl and Megan not to tell anyone we were home. I just wanted to be invisible for the rest of our 'vacation.' I didn't leave the house for days, living a shadow existence in my own life. I was mortified that I had disappointed Megan, but my fear was more powerful than my love.

I got back into the cycle of work and safe things with Meg and our friends. I created workarounds at my job to avoid leaving my desk. I had used my staff ID to see the Senate in session from the staff gallery, but in all my time on The Hill, I never made it over to see the House of Representatives chambers. I had the magic pass and simply couldn't use it. I could call for CRS (congressional research service) briefing papers on any topic but I was now too frightened to actually go into the Library of Congress. I never saw the inside.

I received a rare offer. In the interior of the Capitol Rotunda is a narrow staircase and walkway up near the place where the dome meets the building. I was given a chance to have that tour. They say a person standing up there on one side can whisper a conversation to a person directly across from them. The acoustics are that perfect. I will never know.

To people who have never experienced what I then called agoraphobia, it is difficult to understand the tricks your mind plays on you. Over the years, when I have tried to explain what was going on, compassionate people immediately jumped to a moment where they, too, were scared or as they called it, panicked. They described their experience and told me how it felt to have the fight/flight instinct kick in. Rapid heart rate, hyperventilation, sweaty palms, racing thoughts, feeling flushed. Then, they'd look me and say, "I understand." Bless them ... they didn't.

They had experienced a discrete moment of fear with a beginning and an end. The reason for their reaction was clear and manageable. Without a doubt, their safety seeking amygdala did its job. In the middle of the brain is that happy little amygdala, the lizard brain. It is the part of our brain in charge of keeping us alive. It is the alert friend that turns on our endocrine system, filling our muscles with blood, ramping up the heart, tuning up our senses. What they can't imagine is having all of those sensations when combing your hair getting ready for work or sitting on the couch watching a movie. They don't understand that the normal discomfort of digesting a big meal is a sensation that can create a panic attack. They will never know how hard it is to visit a dentist or get a haircut.

My hair grew shaggy in DC. I drove around looking for the 'perfect' barbershop defined as off the beaten path and lacking customers so I didn't have wait. Right on Lincoln Park, not far from our house, I found a two-chair barbershop strangely alone and out of place. The owners were Greek, the last remnants of a former Greek immigrant neighborhood. Circling the block, I stalked the shop from my car. Finally, screwing up my courage, I went in and right to the chair. Eyeing the waste bin where I could throw up, fighting my urge to run away, and jabbing my thumbnail into my palm hard enough to create pain, I distracted myself to get a haircut. Even now, I sometimes do the exact same thing when my muscles start aching to jump out of the chair.

~

The holidays were coming. Everyone ... everyone ... was going home for Christmas. Flying was no longer possible for me. I begged my housemates to stay but they were going home. I was as afraid of being alone as I was of flying ... maybe more.

My family didn't know what had happened to me. After all, just a year before I had flown home the fair-haired child. I think it was Megan who suggested that maybe they would want to come to DC for Christmas. They were not fans of the cold. But I also knew their coming might be the only way I could survive the Christmas holidays. The word 'survive' isn't an exaggeration. I believed I could not take care of myself if I had more panic attacks with no one around. I needed to humble myself on the phone.

I called them and explained my problems. Mom didn't hesitate. Dad was there to problem solve. The thread I didn't understand at the time was that for both of them, I was still the nervous child. Memories of my frightened youth were indelible for them whereas for me what was happening all seemed new. At that time,

I did not know about Mom sitting in my second-grade classes day after day so I could go to school. Conversely, they didn't know that many of my days in high school were spent trying to avoid bullying and humiliation. I can't imagine how their hearts must have sunk when they got that call.

My parents flew into National Airport. I couldn't pick them up. They took a cab. It was record setting cold. We found a little Christmas tree. Mom cooked. I don't recall a lot of touristing, but we did drive down to see the National Christmas Tree and the monuments in their holiday decor. We may have even had a good time. Face to face, I could talk more about what had happened to me. I lied to them and myself. I put a good face on the therapy I was doing and my prognosis. The streets were icy the day they departed. I shuffled with them to the Metro stop at the end of the block. You never stop being your parents' child.

My friends were about to stream back. Still, there was New Year's and they weren't back yet. Out of the blue, my baseball buddy Bob called and said he was coming over for New Year's night with a surprise. He showed up with a bottle of Dom Perignon. Bob passed out about 11 p.m. in a chair in our living room. With his unknowing help I had made it through the holidays.

In the spring, there was growing momentum for Megan and me to leave DC. My ever-present sense of danger in the city was slowly killing me. Megan, on the other hand, was just settling in. She had gotten a job in the office of a foundation doing work she loved. But she was willing to do whatever was needed to help me recover and for us to survive this illness. To that end, she had an offer from a childhood friend to move to a farm on the Columbia River just outside of Longview, Washington. They sent us pictures. It looked idyllic, a cure for urban life. I now had a story I could tell people that seemed like a plausible reason to leave.

About the same time, I got word from my brother that there was trouble at home. The folks were suddenly moving from their condo in the desert to Bakersfield in California's central valley. Dad had been having an affair, had come clean, and in order to make a new start he was selling the service station and the two of them were leaving the desert. One night, very late, I got a call from Dad. They were in a crisis. Mom had been drinking, was suicidal, sitting in the living room with Dad's .32 revolver.

He said, "Just talk to your mom."

Over the next hour or more, I talked and I listened. I tried to gauge how serious she was about suicide and if she meant to kill Dad, too. My bond with Mom was always close. She had a dark side from a difficult childhood with a domineering father. But Mom had a special relationship with her nervous child, probably more than I ever understood. From my earliest memories, I lived to make her proud and most importantly, puncture her darkness and anger with laughter. I could always make her laugh. I remember completely locking in during that phone call. I needed to get the gun out of her hand.

"Mom, I think it would be helpful if you took some notes about what I am telling you. Okay?"

"Alright," she said, "I will get a pencil and paper."

I heard her tell my dad to get what she needed. I improvised, having her make a list of whom she loved and what about her life was still good. While I had her busy taking notes, Dad removed the gun and locked it away.

I was able to turn the corner to conversations about the house they were building and the future. I'm pretty sure I was hard on Dad. I wanted Mom to know she had an ally. Eventually, and I have no idea how we got there beyond our shared muscle memory, Mom and I laughed. Situation diffused, I told them I loved them both, hung up, and called my brother. None of us spoke of that night again. I did get a letter from Mom thanking me and telling me how much she loved me.

Working on The Hill, I had almost reached the pinnacle of my childhood dream. The dream went something like this. I am in the political engine room writing, negotiating, and counting votes for new legislation. There I am on CSPAN sitting behind my member in a committee hearing. I am walking down the hall of the Senate office building with my boss and standing next to him when the Capitol Hill police pull tourists off the subway so he can get to a vote. I have written the speech he is delivering on the floor of the Senate as I sit discreetly in the back of the chamber.

That is why I came to DC but none of those things happened.

I had gotten a heads up that the senator's legislative assistant (LA) for agriculture was unhappy with her legislative correspondent (LC). Being an LC was the gateway to my promised land. Soon after, she fired her LC. I had a good working relationship with Mary, the agriculture LA. We had spoken about language to respond to constituents. I had pushed back on her writing a couple of times and she conceded that my edits made the responses clearer. And as always, my buddy Carl was in her ear.

I got a call from Mary. "Would you like to go to lunch?"

I knew what it was about. She wanted to eyeball me for the LC job. This was how it was done on The Hill. There wasn't going to be a job announcement or a competition. The fix was in. She was doing the final 'fit' conversation. I knew it. And yet ... her question terrified me. She wanted to go to a crowded Hill restaurant for lunch, something that I had stopped doing a year before. I scrambled, looked out my office window, saw the lovely day and counter-offered.

"It's so nice outside; would you like to enjoy lunch in the park?"

Pause ...

"Uh, sure, it would be great to get out of the office for a while."

Yes! The park. Not crowded. No need to look for exit doors or find a seat on the outside of the table.

Exits in every direction. Perfect.

"How's your typing?"

Terror again. "Good. Not as good as yours, I'm sure, but not bad."

"Okay, we can talk about that at lunch."

We set a date for a couple of days out. Megan's reaction was more concern than excitement. She wondered what this would mean for the move. I dodged. She also knew what this meant to me. She would play my hand ... again.

This was it. I had come here to do this. I was sure I could be very good at it. But I had too much time to think. The reality of my illness kept tossing up roadblocks. My heart raced and I broke into a sweat just thinking about it. Every opportunity in the LC job became an impediment. Going to a committee hearing became an opportunity to suddenly panic and bail out. Lunches ... in restaurants. Dinners, too. I couldn't hide out like I was in my current job. Every anxiety avoiding adaptation would be achingly obvious. Where currently I was just eccentric or quirky to some folks, that wouldn't be so easy as an LC. But even in that onslaught, somewhere in the edges of my consciousness was the faint hope that none of that would matter. I could make it work.

We came from different directions, lunch food in hand, and found a spot under a huge tree. I sat down. She was wearing a dress and sat awkwardly. I was suddenly aware just how dumb this workaround really was. But she seemed happy to be outdoors and told me how nice it was.

I was faking it. I knew it. We talked about the job. She was seeing if she could work with me. I had no problem showing my genuine passion for Congress and the work. I was completely aware of what the senator was working on and showed her my time editing the response library meant I was plugged into every issue in the office. We both loosened up. She had a reputation as a hard-ass boss. I thought she seemed fine. Hell, I had worked for my perfectionist father. Lunch went long as the shadows under the trees shifted.

Then it came.

"How would you like to come to work as my legislative correspondent?"

There it was. The dream. Hanging like a cartoon text bubble over her head. I smiled back at her smile. I had done it. And as soon as she finished her sentence, I knew I couldn't do it. Still smiling ... I was devastated. Words tumbled out of my mouth. I was honored, wished my circumstance was different, wished I hadn't made a commitment to my girlfriend to move back to Washington state. It was a word salad where I was doing everything but tell the truth.

My answer would haunt me. Worse yet? The look on her face. She knew what this meant to me. She knew she had in her hand the much-coveted golden key. No one ... *no one* ... turns that down. I don't think she was angry as much as she was confused. I had led her on just to hear the offer hoping that alone would change everything. My illness owned me. I could no longer fool myself. We shook hands. It was done.

I traded the Corolla for a little Toyota pickup. A new life vehicle. We wrapped up our lives in DC, though Megan was so loved by her employer that they kept her on as a consultant. There were going-away parties. Songs … beer … loving embraces. I saw Carl for the last time in DC the night before we left. Carl had been the architect of my dream. There are few things one friend can do for another that are as important. He was disappointed but he had seen my agony and knew I had to get out. We stood in the street and talked, lingered in a way men usually avoid. Eyes red, we both knew it was the end of a chapter and that we would never see each other like this again. We hugged. He left.

The night before departing, Meg, our friend Christine, and I slept on the living room floor in sleeping bags. Our sleep was interrupted over and over by an electronic chirp. None of us knew the sound a dying smoke alarm battery makes.

Chapter 15

Arrivals and Departures

OUR FRIEND CHRISTINE gave us a little toy to stick onto the truck dash. "Press the button every time you cross a state line," she told us; a little bear would swing on strings and dance. I played a mind game on myself. If my safety was home and Megan, then my home was now under a black plastic tarp behind me in the truck and Meg was sitting next to me. Of course, there was nothing healthy about any of that construct, but it was getting me back to the west coast. Shots of Scotch helped, too.

    The artificial safety of my traveling bubble let us do a little touristing. Free glass of ice water at Wall Drug in South Dakota ... sure. I was in history heaven at the Little Big Horn battlefield. Things got weird at Mt. Rushmore. It felt too far from the freeway. I was belligerent when we rolled into the parking lot, fear escaping as anger. Megan got the worst of it. I said it was a waste of a perfectly good mountain. It wouldn't be the last time my anxiety put on a mask and came out as a different emotion.

For the next two years, move after move, I kept looking for the anti-DC safe places. The farm outside Longview fit the definition but from the moment we arrived it was clear we were not meant to be there. Meg's best friend announced she was pregnant. Her husband, of dark Serbian stock, didn't like me on sight. I wanted to be invisible. At night, I disappeared into the basement to blow my marijuana smoke into the exhaust of the wood burning stove. We headed back to Walla Walla (W2).

In W2, we solved our need for cheap lodgings by moving to Megan's family cabin. A dozen miles outside of town, back across the state border to a rut in the road melodically named Kooskooskie, Oregon, the cabin is a multi-room affair with two sleeping lofts. Almost 100 years old, it had been expanded several times by Meg's family. The expansive back deck was just feet away from the tumbling Mill Creek. No place on earth could have been more different from downtown DC. For Meg, the cabin was childhood sacred space; for me, it was a new adventure. My hair went long, I grew my first scraggly beard and acquired a pretentious black beret.

Meg was still making money working remotely for her non-profit. No mean trick in the days before the Internet. I had stashed savings I could stretch for a long time because we were living lean.

W2 is an isolated little diamond of a town

tucked deep into the corner of SW Washington state. The heart of W2 is Whitman College. There is a wonderfully sophisticated intellectual and social life that flows out from the university into the agricultural paradise that is the Palouse. Plays, music, basketball games, film festivals. And then there was her brother, Kevin. Kev was the Internet before the Internet … a one-man network. Kevin's personality precedes him into any room. Orbits of people around him had fascinating dining salons and hippie truck farms with teepee homes. We road his coat tails to create a social life.

Meg's family was generous with their time and space. But always the outsider, I felt like I was just a little out of sync. It's hard to drop into a family and know where to stand. I hadn't even figured that out with my own family.

Megan had a budding career that kept her busy. I was a wanderer with no real clue about what was next. I knew I felt most comfortable with Meg safely in my peripheral vision. A big part of how she loved me was buffering me from the scary bits or explaining my curious behavior to others. That simply wasn't a place one could live in forever.

I wanted a dog. Meg was all in on the idea. But we both had doubts because of the burden a dog would create to find an apartment. One day Kevin took me aside and said, "Jim, would you ever really want to live in a place that didn't allow dogs?" That sealed the deal.

As a small child, my first puppy was a black lab I named Frisky. For my dad, dogs were strictly outside creatures. They could visit indoors but always had to go back out at night. We only had my puppy for a few weeks before he got sick. The vet said it was distemper. I had no idea what that meant. I only knew that one night I got my biggest wish in the world. Frisky slept on the floor next to my bed. I was so happy. I got out of bed and held him in the middle of the night. The solace of holding my dog, the unfiltered, undemanding affection left a deep mark on my heart. I put him back outside before I left for school. When I got home, he was gone.

Meg and I came home from the pound with a black lab puppy. I was on a Humphrey Bogart movie binge. Her full name was Fred C. Dobbs, the Bogart character in *The Treasure of Sierra Madre*. We called her Dobbsie.

The first snow in the forest was beautiful, gentle, and just a few inches deep. It was a warning. The cabin wasn't designed for wintering over. We started to move some of our stuff back down to town. The snow kept coming and we retreated to Meg's folks' house until we found a house to rent. Fully furnished, it was owned by a couple who spent winters in the Rockies skiing. Meg took over the dining room table with her job. I set up my Olympia typewriter in the study.

Meg had to go out of town for a few days for her job. Dobbsie was an energetic early riser. That morning, I didn't get the puppy wake-up. No whining, no jumping, no barking. I woke confused. Next to me on the floor Dobbsie sat motionless, calm and erect. I reached out to pet her, then saw that her eyes were completely crusted over. I tried to help her open them, but the crust was solid. I ran to get a warm washcloth and held it over her eyes to soften the crust and carefully cleaned her eyes open. Able to see me again, she got excited and wagged her tail. I let her out and got her breakfast. By that afternoon I had the diagnosis. Our puppy had distemper. My heart fell through my chest. No. Not again, I kept saying as I hugged her.

By time Meg returned, she just seemed like the same happy puppy. I wasn't willing to give up on her. The vet said a dog could survive distemper with some issues later. Her teeth would stop making enamel and there could be mental issues later, depending on how the disease progressed. I just couldn't repeat my childhood. Meg and I agreed to roll the dice. Her canines were puppy sized her entire life. Her tongue would fall out of her mouth. Sometimes, when she was sleeping, the tip of her tongue completely dried out. I would give it a little tug like a window shade and she would pull it back in. Her flopping tongue certainly wasn't a very dignified look but she didn't care so it was fine by us.

With spring of 1982, the rental was nearly done. Again, our old friend Lea Anne was the catalyst. She and her current boyfriend had visited W2. Lea Anne lobbied us to move to Portland, Oregon. Another possibility was Santa Rosa, just north of San Francisco.

Our other school buddy Christine had moved there for a job. We loaded the red pickup and headed west.

After a night in the burbs with Lea Anne, we headed to downtown Portland for a look. As usual, it was raining. I had driven the freeways through it a few times and had visited from Salem to go to shows, but I didn't know the city. We took the freeway and crossed the Willamette River on the upper deck of a huge bridge. At the top of the bridge, in a rain deluge, I had a panic attack. That was it. I shut down to the idea of living in Portland without really giving it a chance. I don't remember what Meg thought. I probably didn't even ask. She was looking for a place I could feel safe.

Santa Rosa seemed just right. Big enough to have things to do and for me to get a job. For the first time in my life, I was in the television market of my San Francisco Giants. Big upside. Finding a place that would take Dobbsie was a chore. We settled into a four-plex on the edge of the city. We had a couple of beach chairs in the living room with the stereo, my little black and white TV, and we slept on the floor on rolled out sleeping bags. I would wake up with Dobbsie sharing my pillow.

If you are broke, wine country is a mixed blessing. Lovely drives through vineyards and hills, though the only wine we sampled was from a cheap jug. I am still in love with the trip from Santa Rosa down the Russian River to the sea at the looming Goat Rock. That relatively short trip became the equivalent of my mind-clearing trip up the mountain from the desert years before.

Though I was diligent, jobs were rare. Christine was always around to play. She fell in love with Dobbsie, who by this time was reaching her full size and showing signs of hip dysplasia. My big, black dog loved to go for walks in the empty fields just around the corner from the apartment. Short walks because of her hips, but that was okay with me. I had a new invisible safe walking zone that extended just a few blocks in any direction. I never gave much thought to how bad this avoidance behavior was for my mental health. Years later, when I told my therapist about my personal game of creating safe bubbles, she smiled and told me, "Of course you did. You believed, really believed you were in danger, so you did the logical thing to keep yourself safe."

~

Megan loved to travel. I was aware that now I was now little more than a boat anchor. For me, a huge accomplishment was to go down to a family reunion in Carmel, a few hours away, to be part of Blackie and Pearl's 50th anniversary celebration. I was so proud of myself. It was a family occasion I actually enjoyed. On the way back, after suffering a traffic jam panic attack, we drove by Candlestick Park, the home of the Giants. It was the only time I would see 'The Stick,' home of all my childhood heroes. Less than 90 minutes away from Santa Rosa, it would be abandoned with my never having seen a game there.

Meg and her college roommate took a

backpacking trip to Ireland. For me, her departure would be a test. How could I do on my own? I think Meg had the same question. And ... in retrospect, I'm pretty sure Megan had been looking for a place near one of our friends to enable what she had to do next.

I was getting serious about my fiction writing. It was the one thing I had that made me feel productive. I was determined to have either a short story or a poem published. Any time I went out, I took my note pad. Everything around me was fodder for my stories. I found a regular poetry scene in the little hippy town of Sebastopol. I never had the courage to share one of my poems but I liked being around people who did.

Megan came back from Ireland. Things had changed. It hadn't been a good trip for her. Years later, she sent a letter to tell me she just couldn't protect me from the world anymore. But in that moment, that was not the reason she told me she was leaving. Her non-profit in Ohio had offered her a full-time job. She said she needed a break and needed to see if she could make a real go of the job. She knew why she was leaving. I knew why she was leaving. But we still loved each other very much and were, beyond everything, each other's best friends. We were a study in denial.

The day she left, I loaded her suitcases in the truck and took her to the shuttle downtown. A round-trip to the San Francisco airport was out of my reach. In all of our time together, Megan and I had never flown together. I unloaded the truck and we held each other. One more hug for Dobbsie. She cried. I was numb and didn't. I genuinely didn't see this as our final parting. I'm not sure what I thought was going to happen next, but this wasn't the end. Then I left, but I didn't go far. Across the street was a hardware store that sold mattress-sized pieces of foam rubber. I wanted to finally get a bed off the floor. My last sight of Meg was her waving from the van as I loaded a single-sized foam bed into my truck. Single sized ... and still I wasn't sure what had just happened.

Christine and I saw each other often but she still was the only person I knew. She had always been a confidant who was always up for an adventure. I was in regular correspondence with my scattered friends from college. There was a little shock reaction from them as they found out Meg and I had parted. Our relationship had seemed the solid core of our circle of friends. I offered the nebulous message that this wasn't a total break up.

~

Even broke and blue, I still had live music to give me joy. I picked up a couple of tickets to see the Jerry Garcia Band at a little club on the Russian River. Christine was my partner in crime. There was a little bar next to the club and a couple of joints in the truck. The club had a Deadhead crowd, new and old hippies, plenty of pot in the air and no doubt dropped acid here and there. Everyone sat the floor waiting for our prophet, Jerry ... for hours. No one was angry.

An opening act created itself. Someone got up

with a mouth harp, another tapped out rhythm on the front of the stage. A Grateful Dead singalong began. Jerry and the band finally showed up and slipped right into the vibe of the room. Christine, thick long hair like an umbrella, joined the spinning women down front. Jerry jammed until the early morning hours. When we walked out a thick fog had formed along the river. Too altered to be nervous, I aimed the truck out into it. Years later, Christine would recount how I seemed to be one with the fog and how we magically appeared in Santa Rosa that night.

I was depressed. Jugs of cheap wine came and went. But I still had Dobbsie. With her around, I was never completely alone. She and I made trips out the Russian River or over the hill to Calistoga. We were a cheap date. A little gas money, a handful of doggie treats, and a bowl for her water breaks. I was running out of money. In one of my ancient notepads a page was devoted to the math of decline. I figured I had two months of rent left. On the bottom I had estimated what I could get for my stereo if I sold it.

Then Christine came through. Her non-profit boss was a scion of a wealthy family and an early technology adopter. I had some exposure to computers in DC. He had an early desk-sized computer in the office. He wanted to use a first-generation database program called dBase to 'computerize' files full of the grants the non-profit was writing. He needed someone to learn the program and create his database. It was a job that had to be done on a swing shift so as not to disturb the office at day. I had no idea how to do what he wanted … not a fucking clue. But I was smart and could bullshit day and night. Hired!

I read the dBase manual. Still not a clue. I picked up on the idea that every file would need 'keys,' so I went through all the paper records and created a classification system. When you are bullshitting others, it is helpful if they are also ignorant and too arrogant to admit it. I was now a grifter.

At night, alone in their downtown building, I was afraid. My DC street radar clicked on for unseen danger. I heard things that go bump in the night. I roamed the office looking out at the empty streets. I was getting nothing done. I needed Dobbsie. The entire office was full of pet people. They were fine with it. I left her in the truck and brought her in when they left. Dobbs settled in and so did I.

Dobbsie went everywhere with me. She began to see the passenger seat of the truck as her home. If she was there, I felt safer. If I was there, she was home. We now commonly see support dogs for PTSD and other conditions. Fred C. Dobbs was my service dog. I wasn't conscious of what I had done. I just knew I felt better when she was with me.

Even with the small cash infusion from the job, I was sinking fast. I got a call from my brother who was living with his wife and my new niece, Emily, in, of all places, Redlands. He was now in the family paint business. I couldn't hide that I was circling the drain in Santa Rosa. My brother and Kimm threw out a life ring. "Come live with us for a while, work at the paint store in Redlands, and get back on your feet." I accepted this act of love.

I had to try to finish the categorization of files I had begun but I couldn't afford my lease. Christine said I could stay at her apartment. Her roommate was not happy, and the complex didn't allow pets. Dobbs and I slept on the floor in Christine's room and again tried to be invisible.

One morning, Dobbsie was in the living room and I heard choking. I found her on the floor and tried to help her breathe. Her legs started flailing and she snapped at the air. She lost control of her bladder as she went into full convulsions. I was helpless and terrified. After a few minutes she came out of it and tried to run wildly in every direction. I hung onto her collar to keep her from crashing into furniture. Then, just a suddenly, she settled, shook her head and looked at me. Finally, she drank a whole bowl of water and was Dobbs again. I found a veterinarian in the yellow pages.

Dobbsie had had a seizure. She had a lesion on her brain as a result of the distemper. This would be our life now. Daily massive doses of phenobarbital, sometimes valium. Regular seizures. Now I had a support dog who needed me maybe even more than I needed her. We were an inseparable, interdependent team. She was a year old.

Our travels together had just begun.

Chapter 16

A Man and his Dog

THE TRIP to Southern California was the first time I had travelled without Megan since DC. My safe person was gone but Dobbsie was there. It was fall. In the Sonoma wine country, the leaves on grape vines change with all the colors of New England. The startling difference is that the leaf colors are based on the grape variety. Mile after mile, huge blocks of red, orange, and yellow rolled across the valley up into the hills of the coast range. I was nervous but couldn't deny the beauty of this parting gift.

We crossed the Sacramento River delta and jogged east to old Highway 99 in California's central valley. I was getting hungry and Dobbsie needed a break, so I pulled into the lot of a fast food joint, but not to eat, as I was on my traveling diet of ham sandwiches. In a parking lot in Turlock I was suddenly conscious of how alone I was. A panic attack came hard. I tried to fight my hyperventilation and reached into the truck for the Weekes book and its sparse set of tools. It wasn't working. Then I looked at Dobbs who I sometimes called Boss because in so many ways she dictated my life rhythms. She was sitting on the passenger seat, head hanging out of the window staring at me as I paced up and down beside the truck. I stopped, went to her, and stroked her ears; warming my hands melted my fear just enough. I realized I was the only one who could take care of her and love her with her disease. She needed me to get her to somewhere safe. I didn't have a choice. For both our sakes, I needed to keep going. "Okay, Boss, let's go."

Mike and Kimm's place was on a hill on the east side of Redlands. I unloaded again and tried to make the room comfortable. Like my dad, Mike believed no matter how much you loved them, dogs were for the outdoors. When I explained how Dobbs had seizures at night he relented and let her sleep in my room.

The paint store was on the same avenue as the University of Redlands. Working for my brother, never complaining, I was humiliated. I had left Redlands less than five years before to conquer the world. Now I was back, subsistence living, more than a little lost. I also lived in fear that someone in Redlands would recognize me. How would I explain it all?

Emily was two-months-old. I was painfully conscious of what a special time this was for Mike and Kimm. First-time parents, they were just adapting to the rhythms of a newborn. I got to experience many of the things they were learning. I don't have kids and have never figured out how to be with children. It would be years before I would figure out why. But during those months with little Emily, I let myself enjoy her. I watched my brother learning how to be a dad. I got to see him passed out on the couch after work with Em sleeping on his chest. I listened to Kimm's worries about how to be a good mom. Those months in their guest room would be the sum of my experience with a baby. I have never changed a diaper.

Meg and I were still in close touch. Not to bother anyone, I would drive down to the paint store at night and have Meg call me. She mailed me documents that I edited with her over the phone. The denial dance was alive. I took a drawing class because it got me out of the house one night a week. I can't draw anything. I went downtown to see movies so Mike and Kimm could have the house. I saw the German version of *Das Boot* six times. Good movie.

College friends rolled through town to visit. Carl came out for Christmas. He showed up with another buddy, Wild Bill. We got stoned. They wanted to go to the big city of San Bernardino for fun. Using my rapidly advancing people management skills, I directed them down to a biker bar at the bottom of the hill where I sometimes grabbed a beer. They got to see artwork of the Harley Davidson logo slammed into the ceiling with hundreds of beer bottle caps. Funny to think I was more comfortable in a sketchy biker bar because it was closer to where I lived. But that was my life.

Leaving Dobbsie at Mike's house, I went down to the desert to see Carl's sister and enjoy the pool at her parents' house. I got a few miles from her house and had a panic attack at a stop light. I made it to her house and sat in the hot truck trying to recover. Finally, Renee saw me sitting there and came out to see what was wrong. Carl had told her about my illness. She was kind and helped me inside for a beer. I never did swim.

I had moved six times in less than two years, the irony of an agoraphobic in constant motion. I would need two more moves before I found a place that Dobbs and I would call home.

My presence in the home of new parents was wearing thin. Mike and I almost came to blows in an argument about how to weed his gravel driveway. He said spray it with Roundup. I said do it by hand so you didn't track chemicals into the house with a new baby. I had picked up hippie, organic judgement in W2. Blackwoods don't like to be told what to do, especially in their own homes.

Again, my old friend Lea Anne came to the rescue. She and her boyfriend (always a boyfriend) were now living on a houseboat at Jantzen Beach on the Columbia River in Portland. On a postcard, she wrote:

Come to Portland, spend the summer on a houseboat, learn to sail, lots of dogs live on the river, you need to get out of California, don't worry, David and I have great jobs, live rent free until you find a place.

Quite a salesperson that Lea Anne. Well, except

she failed to mention that the Oregon timber economy had just collapsed and the unemployment rate in Portland was hovering around 12 percent. Details ....

I had stashed enough money to head north. I remain grateful to Mike and Kimm for their rescue mission. And I am fortunate to have six months of my eldest niece as a baby in my head.

I knew I hadn't really given Portland a chance. My time in the Pacific Northwest had taught me that it was my real home. Rivers, water, green, and in Portland, urban enough to give me a better chance for a job than Santa Rosa. I had finally shaken off the need not to be in a bigger city.

I again told myself that my entire home was in the pickup truck. Cord cut; I had no fall back. And there was Dobbsie, my charge and best friend, my accidental service dog. Getting Dobbs into the truck required a special trick. Her back legs were weak with dysplasia, but she was always willing. When I opened the door, she hopped her front legs onto the seat, then I reached down and in one motion swept under her back legs and brought them level with the seat. She walked forward and sat down. We were off!

Jantzen Beach on Hayden Island in the Columbia River is inside the city limits of Portland ... barely. The houseboat village, on the south side facing the city, is not the main river channel. It was a strange place to live. There was one Safeway, a locally famous greasy spoon, some condos, and the houseboats. On the west side of the island was a mall with a movie theater and the kinds of stores that attract Washington residents who want buy goods in Oregon, the land of no sales tax. From the deck of the houseboats, I sat sipping a cold beer watching the bumper-to-bumper traffic on the freeway bridge above.

Moving onto a houseboat was a total pain in the ass. Shopping cart by shopping cart I brought all my earthly belongings down a ramp and over a long boardwalk to the houseboat. Being on the end of the pier was kind of cool; the river was my new front yard and in it was Dave's 21-foot San Juan sailboat. My new housemates gave me a cozy room at the back of the houseboat. I grew to enjoy the gentle undulations of the floating home. After I gated off the steps to the outer deck so Dobbsie would not fall into the river when she had a seizure, I could relax being outside.

Almost as soon as I got there, Lea Anne told me she and Dave were breaking up. *Holy shit … really!?* I think part of the reason she wanted me there was to provide Dave with a keeper for the break-up. Just like in Redlands, I would escape their dramatic evenings to the movie theater. I'm pretty sure I saw the awful sequel to *Saturday Night Fever* a half-dozen times. So, there I was, living with a total stranger who was crying and depressed all the time while Lea Anne moved to a swanky apartment downtown on the Willamette River. Dave kicked me out of the cozy little room in the back because he just couldn't sleep in 'their' room. Dobbs and I were back on the floor.

I was highly motivated to get a job and get off

the water. Dave was okay with me not paying rent. He even taught me how to sail. We took drunken runs onto the main river channel at night. I dealt with my anxiety on those escapades with pot and booze. By time I left, I could single hand the sailboat. Quite an accomplishment for a desert kid.

Without a place to set up my typewriter, I wrote a lot of bad poetry on white legal pads. I kept submitting stories from the cache I had accumulated in Santa Rosa. When you aren't anything else, you can still be a writer.

Every day I made a trip to the Oregon Employment Office in Northeast Portland. (I called it the Unemployment Office.) *Every day.* I was fighting a collapsed economy headwind. I felt comfortable in northeast Portland and sometimes would go from the office to the public library there. In the 80s, pre-gentrification, that quadrant of the city was home to a thriving African-American community. I discovered that many white residents considered that part of town sketchy. I didn't get it. I spent my days with other poor people looking for work. After living in DC, northeast just seemed familiar.

I began to look at different neighborhoods in the city. I liked what I saw in inner southeast, just across the Willamette River from downtown. Like DC, the houses were old but the apartments were far cheaper. At that point, I couldn't figure out why no one realized that the neighborhood had low priced, wonderful housing so close to downtown. It took a couple of decades but people figured it out and have flooded the neighborhood in a gentrification tsunami.

I had two visitors. Christine came. On a hot day, she walked out onto the deck, looked at the river, and jumped in for a swim … fully clothed. Lea Anne was out of town and said I could use her apartment anytime she was gone. So Christine and I went to some bars in old town. Christine bought many tequilas and we ended up adding a new dimension to our long friendship. I suppose it was inevitable, but we were both still surprised.

Near the end of summer, Dad came for a visit. He was worried about me. Dad arrived on a Thursday night. The next day, as I always did, I asked him to hang there for a while I went to the Unemployment Office. I had been sending out resumes for almost anything. Still nothing. Funny how little things matter to my old man. Before he left, he told me he was impressed that I was working so hard to find a job. It "showed him something." I guess he had thought I was lounging by the river. He'd also taken an immediate dislike to Dave and said I needed to get out of there as soon as I could. I still had enough money for first and last on an apartment so I turned down a loan.

Before the fall rains, I pushed loaded carts back up the boardwalk. In a 1906 house converted into a triplex I found a furnished upstairs back one bedroom. $145, utilities included. Down the stairs and just left of the landing was a fenced backyard. Dobbsie and I had a home, a lasting home. The vagabond days were over.

She would now know more than me and a truck. And at last I had a place that seemed like a beginning and not a pause.

Chapter 17

Lone Wolf Mode

ON CHRISTMAS EVE in 1983, the downtown Unemployment Office in Portland served free cookies and coffee. I felt sorry for the state employees who had to work that day but happy to munch cookies and chat with a fellow job searcher.

I was alone and broke, but the apartment was cozy, and my brother sent me a little cactus decorated to look like Santa. On Christmas Day, I called my family, sent a couple of letters, and opened presents that had arrived in the mail. The next day I was back to work writing my stories and looking for a job. Dobbsie and I settled into a rhythm that allowed a few luxuries. I had a subscription to *The Oregonian* newspaper and could buy a six pack of Bohemian Beer for $1.69, a beer-like substance. I began to explore my neighborhood and the city looking for free, or dirt cheap, stuff to do.

Portland in the 80s was a wonderfully

depressed, blue collar sort of town. Probably my favorite version of my home. Northwest Portland had a huge warehouse district next to the extensive train yards. Tucked in those cheap, industrial spaces were thriving live music venues and underground theater companies. I found a regular open mic poetry scene at the clubs called The Mediterranean and Cafe Oasis. The 'Med' was great. I met street poets and writers and just plain characters. Presided over by a Greek immigrant, the nights were lively and for 50-cent drafts I could enjoy a night out. Street people would sometimes show up causing a ruckus. The owner would ransom them back outside by handing them a quart of Bohemian in a brown paper bag.

Many people in that scene ended up in Portland film director Gus Van Sant's early movies. His first film, *Mala Noche,* was based on a novella by Walt Curtis, a semi-famous literary icon in Portland. One night, and I only figured this out later, Walt tried to hit on me at a reading. Seems he had a thing for tall skinny guys. I fit the bill. Within a couple of years, that poetry scene moved to the heart of Skid Row to a club called Satyricon. For the next few decades, that rock club would be a west coast punk scene that rivaled New York's CBGB. It was a mandatory stop for touring punk bands and the nursery for such bands as Nirvana and Pearl Jam. To his demise, Kurt Cobain met Cortney Love, a Portland stripper at the time, at Satyricon.

Portland also had, and still has, some of the best second-run movie theaters in America. In the 80s, formerly grand movie houses, assuming you could tolerate the occasional rat, were cheap places to spend an evening. I developed a special affection for these theaters. Before the wrecking ball took some of them, I made a point of seeing movies in every one in the city. I was introduced to art films in the theaters owned by a company called Seven Gables whose lobbies always had a big pot of mint tea. Free tea in hand, I learned the joys of Eric Rohmer and Akira Kurosawa. Little bits of heaven with sub-titles.

I had yet to make any new friends, so I began to call this sort of living 'lone wolf mode.' (I had just read Barry Lopez's beautiful book, *Of Wolves and Men*.) For my nervous system, this independent moving about in the night was perfect. I could become the anonymous observer, most importantly, uncommitted to anything I was doing. I could leave any time. I created elaborate safety structures around everything I did. I had to park my truck as close to the event as possible. When entering a building I first found the exits. In theaters, always an aisle seat. The excuse I used was that I have long legs. Almost every safety adaptation to manage my anxiety comes with a plausible story. The simplest way to avoid all the exhausting work explaining myself to people was to just go into lone wolf mode. Go out alone. It's a pattern I had created as a child, which became an intricate personal lifestyle as an adult.

I had scored a couple of interviews. Meter reader. Records clerk. My resume was confusing. Good academics. Good school. Senate staffer. Then chaos. Most often, my story read 'over qualified' and 'a flight risk.' I kept at it. But now my money was really running out. I had one asset: the truck. I started to look at what I could get for it if I sold it. My folks knew about the economy in Portland and were convinced I was working hard to find work. My dad, always the finance guy, could do the math. When I told him I was looking to sell my truck, he said absolutely not. A few days later, Dad sent me a wonderfully supportive letter and a loan of $500. A fortune.

I have never underestimated how lucky I am to have a loving family who worked hard to create some means. I know that without their help, I could have just as easily been homeless and on the street. Mental illness, bad luck, and the lack of a support system in friends and family are often the underpinnings of homelessness. The solution for so many mentally ill people is often just numbing it out with drugs. My need to remain clear-headed enough to care for myself and manage all my safety systems made me a poor candidate for substance abuse. When I see people on the street, I always think about how easy it would have been for me to be one of them. I harbor no illusions about my life and luck.

Of course, I didn't have any health insurance. If I spent money at all on medical care, it was for Dobbsie. Me? Aspirin, Maalox, and cheap beer. That winter we had a classic Portland ice storm. I went out on the porch for a better look. The ice had blown up on the porch. I took one step on it and went down hard on my side. I tried to catch myself with my right arm. Something popped. Winded, I sat up and my arm was just hanging by my side. Adrenaline rush. I knew no one, had no money, couldn't even get down my iced front steps. I sat there for a few minutes and diagnosed myself has having dislocated my shoulder. I still don't know why I thought it would work, but I leaned forward and then let myself fall back onto the porch on the right side of my back. Pop again. It worked! My arm was functional again. It hurt like a SOB. But I had fixed it. I went back upstairs and took a couple of aspirin. I still don't have full motion in that shoulder.

My neighborhood was on a rise 18 blocks from the river. Every day as I turned my truck onto the street that took me to the Hawthorne Bridge, I would look out at the downtown skyline and yell, "You haven't got me yet, motherfucker!" It was my war cry for the day. The job hunt was made trickier by my need to work in close radius to my home, my safe zone. I had interviewed for a job filing records for Standard Insurance Company. I was turned down. When one of the same jobs appeared, I applied again. The second time, the same supervisor said she was worried I was overqualified but clearly, I was serious about needing the job. In March 1984, I was finally employed. I bought some expensive Budweiser to celebrate. I had done it. After over two years of aimlessness, I had a home and a job for myself and my epileptic companion.

I had a job. Now I had to get there. For almost anyone else this was no brainer. The bus stopped at the end of the block and it was a quick ten-minute ride downtown. I had never commuted on public transportation. There were fairly cheap surface parking lots all over downtown, but I decided I had to take the bus. It felt like I was cutting myself adrift from my safe world. My apartment. Dobbsie. Our truck. Now it would just be me on a bus with my little commuter back pack and a ham sandwich. Heart pounding, that Monday I walked down to the corner to wait for the bus. *Wait* for the bus. Those were such long minutes of anticipatory anxiety. I was fighting the urge to bolt back home the entire time.

The job was as awful as I thought it would be. Records was in the basement of an office tower. A little machine printed out cards. I took a stack of cards, pulled an insurance file, put the card on the file, and dropped it in a cart. Cart loaded; I then went up to the 10th floor. Floor by floor I worked my way back down. Brainless … right?

Here's how it felt to me. Everyone did the cart runs to distribute the pulled files. I had two runs a day. I knew the run times and began anticipating my turn an hour before. Elevators were a problem. My pulse quickened each time I got on one. Next, I had to push the cart around the business floors. I have an ego. I looked away from people in nice business clothes. Again, I wanted to be invisible. Seriously, I dreamed about my invisibility superpower. Elevator ride by elevator ride, by the time I got back to the basement, I was exhausted. I had survived another cart run.

Unseen by my co-workers, I created a new adaptation. I used my little back pack as a safety device. Starting then, and for years to come, I never went anywhere without that little back pack. (It was the same sort of bag used by my hero, Josh, the character on *The West Wing*.) In it was my legal sized note pad, extra Maalox, Pepto Bismol tablets, sometimes a water bottle, and some notes from the Weekes books. I kept it on the lower shelf of a table near the cart. When it was my turn, I leaned down and furtively tossed it on the bottom of the cart.

The back pack meant two things. First, if I needed to throw up, I could just do it in the bag. (Reality check ... I have never thrown up because of anxiety.) Second, if I couldn't take the mounting fear anymore, I could toss it over my shoulder and flee. Lone wolf on the run. Honestly, I have no idea where I thought I was going, just to the safety of home, I guess. Later, when I had medication, I kept pills both in my pocket and in the bag. I'd like to say I got over this bizarre adaptation, but the truth is I had several generations of that back pack. The final one was a nice Timbuk 2 version. It was always there in the office and always slung over my shoulder when I left. I still have a bag I toss in the car. My dad, the nervous observer himself, once remarked that I seemed to always have the bag with me. *Busted, damn it.* When I stopped taking it everywhere, he noticed that, too, and was proud.

I still didn't leave the city without Dobbsie at my side. She and I went for rides to the coast. I loved to see her perk up when she first smelled the salt air of the ocean. We even spent some weekends there in dog-friendly cabins. Because of her rear legs, the beach walks were short, but she would curl up at my feet as I read, wrote, and watched TV.

Portland was a big blues town. I always had an affinity for the bluesy rock bands and began to wonder about their real roots. I set a new goal to see every living delta blues performer who came to town. I joined the Cascade Blues Association and went to monthly meetings. It was perfect for lone wolf mode. I met people I saw regularly but created no new friends while seeing terrific performers.

I lasted on the bus to work until the weather warmed up. On one of the first warm days, I was on the bus heading for home when we got caught by a bridge lift. The bus was warm. I felt flushed; my heart rate went up. I tried deep calming breaths. But there was no stopping the panic attack. I was angry for putting myself in that position. I felt like I was going to puke … pass out. I strained to feel the slightest bit of air coming from the vents. I wanted out. I was considering how to push people aside and get to the door when the bus started moving again.

No rational person would want those sensations again. They are awful. We are all wired to avoid scary situations and pain. Touch the flame once, then never again. What is different about this mental illness is that things that are not really threatening are interpreted as dangerous. Crowded buses were out. Totally out. I didn't take public transportation to work for the next 30 years. Never. On snow days when only the busses were running, I stayed home. The illness is not so much about having panic attacks as the extent to which you will alter your life to avoid them.

I drove to work, parking a few blocks away at a surface parking lot. Next problem. The attendants filled the lot with cars bumper to bumper. For me that meant I couldn't get away quickly. I can be charming, so I made friends with the parking crew. I told them I had a job that might require me to come and go during the middle of the day. More bullshit. "Could you just keep my truck out of the stack for me?" "Did you see the game last night? Yeah, they sucked." "Sure, that spot would be great. Many thanks, sir."

I couldn't really afford the parking on my salary, so I kept drinking the swill beer and buying Dobbsie's food on sale. The extra parking expense was not an option.

My web of avoidance is complex and requires lying and a quick mind. Fortunately, people with this illness are often some of the brightest folks you will ever meet. We can create our own demons almost as fast as we can slay them.

I have never been a morning person so each new day was an opportunity to doubt I could make it to work at all. Some days were worse than others. On those days, even the truck a few blocks away didn't feel safe enough. I would risk it, and park on the street on the block above my office. It meant sneaking out of the office every 90 minutes to feed the meter. I watched the clock all day, timing my breaks with a dash out to the car to plug the meter. I was creating anxiety all day long to avoid anxiety. When I did get a parking ticket, well, that was the cost of doing business. I had to think through the smallest detail in an effort to control the world around me.

I now had health insurance. I set out to find the latest treatment for phobias or agoraphobia or whatever it was I had. Pre-internet, I started with the *Yellow Pages*. I looked for articles on agoraphobia. Finally, I found something … something local.

Let the treatment begin. I needed a cure.

Chapter 18

Where Is That Damned Cure?

I LEFT DC with a rudimentary psychological tool kit. I had my Claire Weekes books and applied what I didn't fully understand in a random way. I had Megan to lean on, a bottle of scotch, and a little pot. I lost Megan and added the unquestioning love of an epileptic black Labrador. I can't say that anyone in my family or among my other friends had any real clue what was going on with me. What they saw was mostly my absence. I left it to them to make up their own stories about what that absence meant. For my family, I was the adult version of the nervous child; for everybody else, I was just an eccentric guy who could be fun right up to the moment he disappeared with no explanation.

I found a couple of therapists who were doing groups with a technique called territorial apprehension (TERRAP). Created in the 70s by a psychologist in San Francisco, TERRAP is a program designed to deal directly with the results of anxiety using behavioral therapy. Explicitly, it isn't talk therapy designed to find out 'how this happened.' I was okay with that. If it cured me, fine.

For my people, the nervous people, the first challenge on that night in 1985 was getting to the group session. I didn't have a 'support person' and this would be one where Dobbsie couldn't help. That first night, I found the place in NW Portland and followed the signs upstairs. Peter and Pat greeted me at the door, handed me a little stack of papers to fill out, a mostly empty red binder, and pointed to a semi-circle of chairs. I recall flashing a half-smile at the folks in the chairs and noticed people were also sitting at the back of the room. Ah, support people, I thought.

I was crawling out of my skin. Every impulse of my lizard brain was telling me, *Get the fuck out of here!* Sweaty palms, flushed, heart racing, and vision a little weird. That last one was especially unsettling because it made me question whether I could still drive. I sat down. Quickly, the rest of the chairs were filled with my people, mostly women. And then it hit me. My god, I am not alone. I kept the half-smile glued to my face and looked at each person. Except for little tells, a sipped water bottle, some deep breaths, a tapping foot, everyone in the room looked ... well ... calm. I knew everyone there was feeling some version of what I was feeling, but to the outside world this gang looked more serene than a cluster of folks waiting for a bus. *Is that what I looked like? Really?* Unbelievable. We look fucking normal. This made no sense whatsoever.

Over the next eight weeks, the personal stories started to roll out. Women who only left home to come to the group with a friend or spouse. Lost jobs. Lost families. Depression. Desperation and confusion. And like me, endless adaptations to a shrinking world. The common fear was of the fear itself. I was with my people.

When I commit to a class, or practice, I am relentless. The core of the training addressed the fact that the symptoms we felt were distressing but not dangerous. We could actually trust our bodies. I was desperate to believe that, but in my case undoing the experience of a lifetime would be hard. I had never really trusted my body to take care of me and seemed to have evidence that it didn't. But I kept at it. TERRAP was an advance over what I had read in the Weekes books. Most importantly, I finally had people guiding me, something that was completely missing in DC. And we were going to practice ... out in the real world.

The course also brought in something new: relaxation. There was a lot of talk about energy in the body and how we could release that energy. That made sense. A panic attack can feel like grabbing a hot electrical wire. They taught us something called bioenergetic grounding. We needed to release that bad energy into the ground. We all stood, breathed in a certain way, and leaned over. I guess I got the point, but never really bought into the method. Still, I practiced over and over.

Cognitive behavior modification is the common

core of anxiety treatments. We did a series of exposures to things we feared. We went outside and walked around the block feeling our symptoms, exposing ourselves. The object was to keep doing the exercises, adding distance or complicating factors to convince our minds and bodies that we were safe in any circumstances. If we did have that panic attack, so much the better. It was a way to prove to ourselves that we could handle it anywhere. I so wanted this to work. But something about that early approach felt more like armoring us to 'fight' off the panic attacks. Underlying 'success' was a lot of will power. I didn't want to live like that. I just wanted a cure. I wanted the awful sensations to just stop.

But as usual, I was a star pupil. So much so that Pat and Peter asked if another class member and I would do a panel on public access television. I still have the VHS tape. There I was on television, wrestling with my symptoms while being questioned. I told my story. I was a fountain of hope and persistence. Except for an unnatural stiffness in the way I sat on the chair and forced earnestness in my answers, I looked kind of normal. For the rest of the class, the two of us were heroes. We had done the impossible. I liked being a hero. I wished I really believed what I was saying.

The graduates, red binders now full of the lessons, swore we would stay in touch and encourage each other. We didn't. And me, I knew I had new tools, but I wasn't cured, not by a long shot. The proof. I asked Peter if I could continue as a one-on-one client … for years.

I was a regular in the self-help section of the world-famous Powell's Books. In science and literature, phobias and agoraphobia were now being called anxiety disorder. The people who have this illness skew toward people who are bright, sensitive, articulate, and high achievers. Nailed it! That also means we are big readers, takers of classes, and buyers of self-help tapes. We are a huge market.

~

Carl called. He was getting married. His fiancé was from Davenport, Iowa, where the wedding would be held. He asked me to be his best man. I was deeply touched. He knew about my struggles, but he was willing to take a risk. I told him how hard I was working to get into the air again. Could he give me some time to make a commitment? He gave me a 'have to know by date' and we left it there.

Across my life, with far-flung friends and family, the inability to fly was becoming a source of my greatest regrets and anguish. Think of all the special life events: marriages, births, deaths, holidays, anniversaries. When you are the one who chose to set off in a direction to make a new life, you are also the one who needs to get to the people you love when the big stuff happens. One by one, my college friends, my second family, were pairing off and getting married. Carl's invitation would not be the last. But the only wedding I ever attended was Lea Anne in Portland.

Around that time, I got a call from my dad. He and Mom were very excited. He said his Christmas present to Mom that year was me. He would pay to fly me to LAX and then drive the two hours down from Bakersfield to pick me up. We talked about dates. I was excited with them on the phone but the notes in my journal tell a very different story. I immediately combined the two invitations from Carl and Dad into unbelievable pressure and opportunities for me to fail.

The hour of the flight to see my folks approached. I was packed and ready to go. I found a kennel to take care of Dobbsie. I had scoped out the airport. I knew where I would park in the economy lot and how to get a bus to the terminal. The day before the flight, an inversion layer dropped down over the Willamette Valley. Fog. I kept looking out my second-floor apartment window and couldn't see across the street. Over and over I called the airline. I tuned to the radio and television news. I called home. Dad was already on his way to LAX. I told Mom I didn't see how they could fly out in this stuff. I had psyched myself up for this flight. I was as ready as I could ever be and then they shut down the airport. Dad got the news when he got to the LAX.

The flight the next morning was canceled, too. My nervous system was being yo-yo'ed in a most cruel way. I could barely eat and slept in fits. The next day the fog lifted. I had an afternoon flight. I called and gave Dad the flight number.

I parked in the economy lot and got on the shuttle bus. It was the first time I had been on any public transportation since I gave up busses to get to work. I was nervous but pretty happy with myself when I had got to the terminal. I was early. My gut was not happy. I paced and went to the restroom several times. I felt like I needed to urinate but couldn't. I felt like I was going to throw up but didn't. I tried my breathing techniques to break the hyperventilation cycle. I pulled my TERRAP notes from my bag and read them over and over.

Our plane arrived and people disembarked. My fellow travelers started lining up. First call. Another trip to the restroom. In the stall, standing there with the door closed, I gave myself a pep talk. "Dad is waiting. You can do this. This is important." But the only thing I saw when I closed my eyes was that jet door closing and me going crazy and running for the door demanding the attendants open it so I could get out. Over and over, for days, that had been the scenario I couldn't shake.

Back out to the gate. Last call. Stragglers were heading down the gangway. The woman at the door now saw me as a person. We looked at each other. I took another deep breath and put my boarding pass in my hand. She had seen people like me before. She tilted her head and gave me a closed-lipped sad smile.

"Everyone is onboard. We have to go now. Can I take your ticket?"

I was frozen in place about ten feet from her. I couldn't move. All of the energy went out of my body. I just lowered my head and shook it no.

"I'm sorry," she said and closed the door.

I stood there. I thought about making a dramatic run to knock on the door, but I was spent and defeated. The lounge was empty. I sat down and heaved in tears. I had failed, and worse yet, I think I knew the entire time that I would not get on the plane. Now I had to deal with the results of my failure. I found a phone and called Mom. We were both crying. I had no real explanation. After waiting out two days of fog, I couldn't do it. It was just too much. She said she wouldn't call Dad at LAX. That was my job. I knew it was.

I went to the counter and they kindly connected me to the counter at LAX. They paged Dad. I grimly squeezed the phone in front of all those people until he came on the line. I told him I was sorry, but I just couldn't do it. He said it was okay. It was the fog. I said yeah, it was the fog. I can't imagine what he thought on that long drive home.

I got back on the bus and went to my truck. For just a moment, I was proud of myself. I had taken a bus. It was a huge accomplishment, but I could never celebrate it with a soul.

I picked up Dobbsie and we disappeared into our little world. I talked to my parents again. They said they would mail my presents. I had forgotten that the next day was Christmas. Completely forgotten. Another Christmas day alone. It was becoming an awful habit and the reason I still don't put any expectations on the holidays. I couldn't bear to make myself that vulnerable again nor could I allow my acts to disappoint anyone else again.

I wrote Carl and told him what happened and said I couldn't come to Iowa. I still didn't have the language to explain what my life was like. I tried to explain how bad it had gotten and what happened with the fog. It didn't really matter. The most important people in my life were now out of reach.

What I had left was a growing life inside my Portland bubble and a stubborn belief that I was still going to beat this illness. I was going to find that cure. For those who often see me as a cynic or some kind of a grouch, I think that hillbilly stubbornness and some tenacious well of optimism has always sustained me. Every failure was another problem to solve.

Chapter 19

Putting Down Roots

FOR THE 24 YEARS I worked at Standard Insurance, I somehow manipulated an entire company to create a career that accommodated my illness. To be clear, none of these jobs were 'make-work.' Each one was needed, only the company didn't know it yet.

A decision was made to replace the records request system. I volunteered to help the programmer and systems analyst as an expert on how the department processes worked. What I didn't know yet was that I actually had an essential and lucrative skill.

I have always been fascinated about how things work. Systems and machines. My innate curiosity, coupled with an obsession with problem solving and my communications skill gave me the ability to be a translator. I could look at how something worked and just see how it could work better. More importantly, I could tell people in Information Technology (IT) about those insights in a way they quickly understood. In a world where computers were about to move to desktops and distributed systems, I had a skill that would be coveted. And to my delight, I discovered that the kinds of people who worked in IT were both smart and eccentric. I had landed in a historical moment, a crease in the intersection between business and technology where who I was and how I thought were important. In other words, I got lucky.

I made myself invaluable. So much so that IT created another work space on their floor so I could work interactively with the analysts and programmers. Today, this sort of relationship is common but in the mid-80s it was remarkable. I was having fun. I no longer had to file paper and I was learning a new world on the fly.

My old pal Lea Anne's executive assistant was part of a book club. I joined that group and began to attend monthly book club meetings. In some ways it was perfect. I could manage my anxiety and come and go as I pleased. There was always beer, so when I arrived, I quickly downed one and relaxed enough to be able to become absorbed in the conversations about the book. The core of the group had all gone to the same high school in a ritzy Portland suburb. The others had grown up in the high-end West Hills of Portland. As usual, I could be funny, sometimes charming, but still the outsider.

I was lonely. Apart from my illness, I'm sort of a ninja level introvert. I really have to push myself to connect with people. Meg and I had been together a long time. I had a little affair with Christine, but she lived in California. At work, there was this beautiful woman who was back after a year off on maternity leave. Around her was a little group of fun people from the Records Department. We hung out as a group, but it was clear there was a vibe between Peg and me. Just friends.

I suppose if you live long enough, and are more than a little self-aware, you can actually watch yourself being stupid. You see the light of the approaching train in the tunnel but are mesmerized by it getting bigger and absolutely confident you will know when to jump out of the way. Hubris is a wicked life coach.

As the systems project was coming to an end, I knew I could not go back to file paper again. I now had advocates from the project team. They said I was a natural analyst and the Administrative Services Department badly needed one. There was no such job, so I drafted a job description and sent it to the assistant vice president, the only woman at that level in a very conservative company. Presto! I was now an administrative systems analyst.

So, here's a secret … don't tell anyone. Systems analyst is a real career with college courses and follow-up training. I had none of that. Once I had the job, I asked to go to a local two-day seminar on systems analysis. In 24 years, I acquired every other skill by reading, watching, asking questions, and frankly, just making it up as I went along. I had a degree in political science and history. Never underestimate the all-powerful liberal arts education.

The ever-ill Dobbsie got an infection in her foot. I almost lost her. I developed a good relationship with the 24-hour doggie hospital. One of my new friends offered his house at the coast to do some writing and for Dobbsie to heal. The first day I didn't let her go far from the front door. She was willing but the legs were still uncertain. Dobbs couldn't climb the stairs to the bedroom, so we camped together in the living room. I left most of my stuff in a bag close to the front door for a quick escape. A fear adaptation I still cling to at times.

The drugs and rest were working. Dobbs had figured out where to find the trail to the beach. She wobbled over to the trailhead and gave me a look. *Okay, if you say so,* I thought. Slowly, we made our way to the high tide beach. She wanted to run, but I kept her close. We walked to the water. I put two fingers in the water and brought them to my lips to taste the salt. It has always been my little ritual to remind me I am part of the ocean.

I was now a guy with a little money. I could afford to go out more often. I got season tickets to Portland Arts and Lectures where I watched writers talk. I also moved more deeply into the underground theater scene. There were terrific small acting companies in makeshift spaces. I was especially in love with a company that was doing the entire cycle of Sam Sheppard's plays. Sheppard was a lone wolf, too.

Awash in rationalization and hormones, I began an affair with Peg. Her marriage was ending. I tried to be the good guy and back away, but her professions of love were irresistible. She separated, then divorced. She had her daughter every other weekend. On the alternate weekends we had a tempestuous, psycho-erotic relationship. The drama became my addiction. I professed to want more, but that wasn't true. As with Megan, one of the issues with Peg was the limits imposed on me by my illness. There were places I would not go and things I could not do. To live my life, I ended up dictating the terms of the relationship. I always looked for safety first.

For other people, my mental illness is inferred by the negative space. *What is missing? Why did he do that? How come he just can't do it anyhow?* Quite naturally, people create their own explanations for my behavior. *He's shy. He doesn't like that. He's just an asshole.* I wasn't very good or open about explaining how I felt or what was going on inside my head. If they wanted to think I was odd or shy or even an asshole, I just went with it. It was easier that way. I would try to punctuate my relationships with overt acts of kindness and in-the-moment attention as a way to compensate for what was missing. I could be warm, then disappear. Unfortunately, for Peg, deeply insecure by nature, she took my efforts to create a safe world around me as something aimed at her.

I was on a fast track at work. A small team had formed to bring the next era of computing into the company. They would use mini computers, new terminals (eventually PCs) and earth-shattering tools like email and spreadsheets. The guru, a startling, quirky genius, was one of the team at Bell Labs who wrote the UNIX operating system. Bill was endlessly patient with the incessant questions from the new guy. The tech team adopted me as their systems analyst. I created yet another position. Another salary bump. There were six of us. I created a new email alias. Of course, I called it SIXPACK.

Late summer, Peg and I drove down to see my family in Southern California. This was the first trip down since I stopped flying. My niece was three and while we were there, my brother announced he and Kimm had another baby on the way. Peg was uncomfortable. My default mode around my family was to be on edge. It was a mess.

We headed back home in the early evening. Though we were not going to stop in LA, Peg had never seen downtown LA and wanted to drive through. Just outside of LA proper is a freeway junction to a different route through the valley, bypassing downtown LA. As we approached the junction, I saw the traffic stacking up going to LA. I looked over at Peg. She had no idea how the freeway system worked. I was getting nervous about the traffic and didn't tell her. I chose to go around downtown … didn't say a word. Eventually, she asked when she would see it and I said she wouldn't because we went another way. She was livid.

Back home, I dropped off Peg and went to the kennel to pick up Dobbsie. She was not happy about our separation. She didn't greet me as usual. She ignored me and walked to the passenger side of the truck. On the ride home she stared straight forward. It was the longest we had been apart. Nobody was happy at the end of that trip. Dobbs finally relented after she had water from *her* bowl and food from *her* dish. At least Dobbsie forgave me.

~

Work kept getting better. We had a terrific boss who loved to just hang out with us in his office after work hours and spin dreams how we could sell our new technical ideas to the business. I again had a unique boss, the first African-American manager at the company, though Nike soon spotted him and stole him away. To solidify my importance to our efforts, he made me a technical project leader. The salary astonished me. Again, a job that hadn't existed. I never took a project management class. I just did it.

My confidence with my unique skillset grew. In long design meetings, heated arguments broke out. I would sit quietly for a long time, taking it in. Then, in a creative leap, I saw how to deliver what everyone had been arguing about. I would get up, walk to the white board, and say something like, "Try this," and in front of everyone sketch out the steps and phases of a rough project plan. I still don't know how I do that. I just see organization and people follow.

As a project leader, and eventually an infrastructure manager, I managed people by not micro-managing. Part of the trick was that I was always worked with highly skilled, self-motivated teams. In other words, people like me. When someone asked me what my management style was, I said, "Make sure everyone knows where we need to go. Get them what they need to succeed. Then get the fuck out of the way."

With increasing responsibility came more stress. One of the things they advised us in the TERRAP training was to get up and move. I discovered that physical exercise calmed me. Big revelation, right? Maybe then it was. I was no longer that skinny kid with the rapid-fire metabolism who could eat a package of Hostess donuts and wash them down with a beer at midnight. But never one to join public exercise because I was embarrassed about my slight frame, I recorded an aerobics workout off local access TV. So there, in my little living room, I danced about working up a sweat several times a week to the same video ... over and over. Exercise became a lifelong habit.

Part of my old TERRAP crew was tackling the biggie: flying. We went out to Portland International Airport and did exposures. We had a tour of the tower. And then, the biggest deal, we boarded a parked passenger jet to sit in the seats and visualize being on a flight. I loved all the insider access and tried hard to do that visualization, but my people are not like other folks who are afraid to fly. There is wonderful bit of dark humor about phobics. People with our flavor of anxiety aren't afraid of crashing; no, we are afraid of the flight attendant closing the jet's door. Deep down I wasn't buying all the practice at the airport. Something was missing. I didn't yet know what.

Chapter 20

I Have Two Best Friends?

MY ENTIRE FAMILY came up for a summer vacation. We rented a couple of rooms in a little courtyard motel on the Oregon coast in Cannon Beach. We flew kites and drank beer and told stories. The first night Mom fixed a big dinner, my favorite: fried chicken and mashed potatoes. The next morning, I woke up anxious. I was obsessing about how far I was from home. I was worried about what would happen if I suddenly had to drive home in the middle of the night. My negative thoughts raced out of control. Fright became flight. I told everyone I had to leave. I was sorry. My family was confused. I just had to go.

I fought the panic symptoms all 90 miles back to Portland. Once in my house, I calmed down but now I was depressed. I had disappointed everyone again. Sitting in my chair, staring out at the tops of trees, I wanted to make it all stop but there was Dobbsie. Then my doorbell rang. It was Mom and Dad. They wanted to know what happened. "Why don't you want to be with all of us?"

"You don't understand," I said crying, "you are my family, of course I want to be with you. Don't you see, everyone is 90 miles away and I can't get to you."

I explained how I had been living since they last saw me and how hard I had been working to get well but my world was getting smaller. Then my dad said, "Well, we want to be with you so we will all come here." My family decamped from the coast and came to Portland for a day. It turned out as good as we could get. Still, not that great.

~

I needed to try something new. In my hours in the self-help section at Powell's Books, I had read that sometimes new drugs were all that was needed to beat anxiety and agoraphobia. By that time, pot had stopped working for me. Ironically, it just made me paranoid. I didn't like the idea of altering my mind with pills but got a referral from my therapist to see a psychiatrist. I was looking for the magic bullet.

Dr. E. seemed optimistic, if humorless. I was doing the right behavioral work and maybe just a little chemical intervention was all I needed. A cure in a bottle. I knew the drugs that alleviate depression can also help with anxiety. And there are truly amazing drugs called benzodiazepines that melt away the fear, but they are highly addictive. He gave me a drug called Buspirone, what he called a 'low side-effect' option.

I'm a medical research nerd. When I go to a

doctor, I know what the treatment options are. Dealing with general practitioners, who don't understand my illness, I have had to educate them. My experience is that there is no reason to ever assume a general practice doctor has a clue how to address mental health issues. When a doctor says "take this pill," I will cut it in half, take it with trepidation, and judge when to increase the dose after I know the side effects. The first medication I got from Dr. E was awful ... *for me*. The biggest side effect was an increase in anxiety. Nope, not doing that one.

Next, he prescribed an old school tricyclic antidepressant: Elavil. I had the array of side effects. Dry mouth, constipation, dry eyes, and this sense of feeling just a little off. These drugs come on slowly, a month or more for benefits, so I hung in and endured. Eventually, I thought the drug had the good effect of making me feel steadier, less reactive to my thoughts. I didn't touch my new benzodiazepine, Ativan. It was as needed. I did not want mix drugs. When I did try it, wildly anxious after a bout of food poisoning, it worked. I had a new lifetime friend. In moderation.

In 1988, my Grandfather Blackwood flew up to visit. I was good about my correspondence with Blackie and Pearl but they missed me. We had been an almost daily presence in each other's lives in my teen years. I grew up on Grandpa's stories. From him I got the idea that we are the collection of our stories. I wanted to get to the airport plenty early to pick him up. My truck wouldn't start. I looked under the hood; battery terminals seemed fine. Nothing worked. I was now getting a little freaked out. I kept checking my watch and realized he must be on the ground. I called the airport and they said the plane was delayed. I asked them to give him a message to call me.

While I was outside tinkering with the truck, his plane arrived. He had called and left me a message. I called the airport and paged him. No luck. I was really ramped up now. I tried to page him again and this time he came to the phone. I apologized and explained what happened. I asked him if he had heard the other page. "No, but an old man once told me that if two people are trying to find each other, one of them had best just sit still, so that is what I did." Imagine an adolescence full of those kinds of lines. He took a cab.

When the cab arrived, Grandpa got in the truck and I pulled out my jumper cables. I tried the key one more time. It started. In my freak-out, I hadn't done what he had taught me years ago at the service station. Clean the terminals and try again. I was embarrassed. He just smiled and said the battery looked old, "So let's just go get a new one." In some way it was perfect that my grandpa and I began our visit in the waiting room of a service station.

We had a wonderful time together. I gave up my bed and slept on the couch. We touristed a bit, but mostly we just talked. One night, a new woman I was sweet on, Sally, came over and had dinner with us. More stories around my little kitchen table and after he said he thought she was special. I noted his approval.

One night he pulled a book down from my shelf

called *Deep Blues* by Robert Palmer. It is a history of the Mississippi Delta blues music. I explained I was spending a lot of my time tracking down and listening to the last of the great black blues artists. As he read the book, he smiled and nodded. He turned to the pictures and whispered to himself, "Oh yeah … yep." Finally, I stopped him and asked him what he was doing.

"Oh, I know these people."

"What? Which people?"

"The people in your book here."

I was stunned … still am. I came over to look over his shoulder.

"You can't tell but this man had the brightest red hair," he said. "We called him Red."

He was pointing to a radio announcer on KFFA in Helena, Arkansas. In the first half of the twentieth century, it was *the* radio station for blues in the delta. The iconic *King Biscuit Time* was a daily blues show that hosted all the greats, especially my favorite harp player, Sonny Boy Williamson.

"Knew him, too. He used to play for pennies on Cherry Street after the radio show."

He was pointing at … I kid you not … Sonny Boy.

I was beside myself. "How in the world did this happen? How is this even possible?"

He said that during the Great Depression he moved the family to Helena to find work. He eventually got a WPA job as a government agricultural agent. He travelled the entire delta by car and had once seen a lynched black man hanging from a tree outside a small town. He got quiet for a bit, looked down, and shook his head.

One of his jobs was to give the morning farm report on KFFA radio. *King Biscuit Time* followed him so he would sometimes linger to hear the music. He would talk to the musicians on the back steps. Stories … always stories.

A couple of decades later, my wife and I went to Seattle and visited a blues exhibit at the Explore Music Project. I rounded a corner and there on the wall was the actual sign from KFFA. On a table in front of the sign was the microphone that my grandpa may have used. A cold wave tumbled through my body. I teared up. Amazing.

Grandpa didn't like my little one-bedroom apartment. It was upstairs in the back. He told me he didn't like being someplace he couldn't escape if it caught fire.

"You need to buy something of your own. Some place on the ground where you can get out of in a hurry."

At the airport, I parked so I could walk him to his flight. So many missed conversations over all those years.

Megan married a friend who was part of our DC Inebrius baseball crew. In one of those strange life flow events, she was now living in Washington, DC, the place I brought her to, and I was living in the Pacific NW, a place I knew first through her. Our effects on each other's lives are indelible. Her wedding, with all our friends there, was in W2 at her family cabin. She was kind in letting me know that it would just be too strange to have me there. I got it. And ... though I didn't say it, I doubted I could get there by myself. Maybe she knew that, too, and was sparing me.

After the wedding, Carl and his new wife drove west to see me in Portland. It was clear that the changes in my life were a shock to him. As chance would have it, they were there on the date of their second anniversary. He wanted to take us all out for a big meal. A cold wave went through my body at the thought. I balked and convinced them I would make dinner. Tacos ... I made fucking tacos. The look on their faces when they departed was somewhere between sadness and pity.

~

Every night after work my highlight was being greeted at the door by Dobbsie. One night, after I let her out to do her business and went back down to get her, she was gone. Unbeknownst to me, someone had left the back gate open. I figured she couldn't get far, so I started walking the neighborhood in wider and wider circles. I switched to the truck to cover more ground. After 2 a.m. I collapsed on my bed. As I lay there, I thought, no, she has never given up on me. I got back in the truck and cringed every time I saw a shadow next to the curb. Finally, almost eight blocks away, I saw her standing in a front yard. I hugged her. We found each other. Back home she just wanted her dinner.

Dobbsie had been slowing down for a while. She was seven-years-old and had outrun distemper. But her hip dysplasia was getting worse. She was still excited to go for a walk, but the slow stroll was now only to the corner and back. She had trouble getting up. She would pump her front legs and kind of pull her back legs up behind her. Sometimes I came over and gave her a little boost.

Friday night, end of a long week, I opened the door and as usual, she was happy to see me. Tail wagging, but her back legs were stuck, so I reached down and gave her a little lift. She fell over. I tried again. Her rear end flopped over again. She was the same happy dog, licking my face, but she could not stand up. She tried to drag herself into the kitchen. I knew this was bad.

I quickly changed clothes and carried her down the two flights of stairs and put her in the back of the pickup. The emergency vet was on the other side of the river. I pulled open the slider window to the camper shell and yelled back to her that it was going to be okay. Once there, I ran inside, and the technicians came out with a doggie stretcher. I stayed close during the exam and X-ray. They said her spine had collapsed. She wasn't in pain but there was nothing they could do. I could consult with a vet who was an expert on spines the next day.

I was in shock. She seemed so normal but just couldn't walk. I knew what was coming, but I wanted her home for the weekend. They put in a catheter and showed me how to reinsert it. I carried her up and put her on her bed at the foot of my bed. I gave her water and food and laid on the ground with her. She so wanted to get up to poop. She knew she wasn't supposed to do that inside and was desperate to go out. I just kept telling her it was okay and cleaned up after her.

The next day the specialist talked about surgery and said it was all up to me. I knew I really didn't have a choice. On Sunday, I had to call Megan. We had gotten her as a couple. I figured she needed to know what happened and what I needed to do. She asked me to hold the phone next to Dobbsie's ear so she could say goodbye to her.

I had tweaked my lower back bringing Dobbs up the stairs. I was pretty sure I couldn't carry her down again. On Monday, I called Peg. She refused to help. Then she said, "Call John. He's your friend."

I had worked and played with John for years, but somehow it had escaped me that he was my friend. I called and all he said was, "When and where do you need me?" No questions, he was there for me. I was surprised. *Why didn't I know this?* He came from work in his dress clothes. He grabbed Dobbs. Halfway down the stairs, her bladder let go. I had screwed up the catheter, and bless her, she was holding it as long as she could. Our shoes were covered with her urine. John wasn't fazed.

I told the vet that the sun was out and I wanted her to feel the sun one last time. He agreed and came out to the grass behind the office. John started to lift the big girl, but I said no, this was my job. I laid her down, took her head in my hands and got close to her. I looked straight in her eyes. I told her she was going to run again. I looked at her until the life fell from her eyes.

John and I were silent on the way back downtown. Then he said, "Dude, no one could have done that any better than you did. I'm glad I could be there with you." He said I needed a good stiff drink so we could toast Dobbsie. We went to a regular haunt. He bought us doubles and we toasted my best friend. Drinking, tears in my eyes, it hit me, I still had a best friend.

Soon after, I told my folks about Dobbs. I got a letter from Dad. Letters from him were a rarity. For some time he had been very worried about what would happen to me when I lost my dog. He said he was proud of me and how I handled it. I was doing what I had to do.

Dobbs needed me. She had saved my life more than once. I owed her.

A few weeks later, I took my new drugs and went out to the coast to spend the night for the first time without Dobbsie. I walked to the waves, touched the water, brought my fingers to my lips to taste the salt.

Chapter 21

I Once Knew a Punk

WHO WAS MY ACCIDENTAL BEST FRIEND? More than two decades on, John seems like my fable. A story I tell to explain wonder and sadness. John had a purple spiked mohawk when I met him. Everyone in the Records Department basement seemed happy to see him. We were a little sensitive about our place at the bottom of the corporate world, yet John was almost completely lacking in judgement. He took everyone as they came. A way of living that I have never been able to master.

Talking with John was like walking into a riddle. I was sure I was in the presence of a mad genius. In his world, everything was possible and the most obscure was just as likely as the obvious. For the life of me, I couldn't understand why he was a clerk in an insurance company. Nothing about him screamed insurance. Once I did know him, I discovered that everyone seemed to know him, from up in the lofty executive suite to the paper shufflers on my floor. With his sparkling eyes and endless enthusiasm for ... well ... everything, John sucked you in with the skill of a con man.

John had escaped high school. Well, maybe he was thrown out. He got his GED, but he was an autodidact with no shortage of ADHD. I'm sure teachers liked him but had no idea what to do with him. He had grown up in Portland and was sort of a city historian, but not a history most people would understand.

Punk rock was John's salvation. He was part of the earliest scene in Portland and told tales of house and basement shows, slam dancing, and getting into fights with the much-detested hippies. The most important part of punk philosophy for John was DIY. Punk bands didn't have record deals or publicists. Recordings were low tech and raw. Music moved across the country from scene to scene in a constant stream of cassette tapes. News was distributed in cut and paste 'zines. For John, this slightly structured improvisation was perfect.

At work we were alike; we both created jobs that hadn't existed before. My skill was an intuitive understanding of organization. John consumed all the latest technology, taught himself how to write scripts, program and administer operating systems. The gravitational pull of the new technology team, the outlaws, brought us together. We both were huge advocates of personal computers. He was a Macintosh guru. I was a PC guy. Personal computers were brand new and more than a little suspect in a conservative company. Most of my computing futurist thinking came from John.

When not spiked, John had jet black hair he slicked back. He was Italian and proud of it. His considerable charm made him very popular with women. In our nighttime travels, I was the natural wingman. He had a circuit of bars and clubs where he seemed to know everyone. He called everyone his friend. He introduced me as his friend, which gave me instant credibility. Pretty women actually talked to me.

On Friday nights, around midnight, we were always at the jammed Veritable Quandary, a narrow, old bar. When John walked in it was like he was Norm on *Cheers*. He chatted up the owner and our drinks came right away. At midnight, the stereo went down and all the wait staff got behind the bar. Then they cranked up Aretha Franklin's "Respect." Standing on the bar now, the waitresses used cards to spell out R E S P E C T as the crowd sang along. Not long after, John would catch my eye, "Dude, let's jet."

In this part of the 80s the word 'Dude' wasn't yet a thing. For some reason John had given me the moniker right away. We passed it back and forth. He was the only one who called me that and that was the only way he ever addressed me. I don't recall him ever calling me Jim.

We usually made our way to a quieter restaurant on the other side of downtown. It was the sort of place that served upscale dinners, then stayed open late for the cocktail types, heavy on couples who were night-capping. There we explored ideas. What did we want to do with tech at work? Or just as easily, John could go on a riff about the Kabala and Jewish mysticism or a story about a homeless person he met who told him some important secrets. With John, I just went with it. Part of the reason I grew to love the guy was that I wanted to see how his mind was going to hyperlink next.

John lived close to downtown and walked everywhere. "See ya, Dude," and he was gone. I knew he wasn't done for the night. But he had figured me out and knew I needed to go home and chill. I always had the feeling he was watching out for me.

John was one the first people to whom I tried to explain everything I knew about my anxiety. Nothing about me fazed him. Others, not so much. Once, I had actually gone to a movie with a woman and revealed a little bit about myself. As we walked back to my truck, she told me I was very dark and she wasn't going to get more involved with me because she would be dragged down into my abyss. One date. She did suddenly appear at my apartment one afternoon for some random sex. The abyss? Just visiting.

Up to that point, I had probably been to over 100 live music shows. So far in Portland, I was mostly into blues and some local bands. Punk rock was a remote curiosity I most often dismissed as 'three chords and a scream.' As we roamed about at night, John educated me on the punk scene, the bands, and especially the DIY ethic. I liked that philosophy ... a lot. He introduced me to his favorite, Black Flag, and their front man, Henry Rollins. Smart, demanding, revolutionary music.

On one of our circuits, we went back to John's high-rise apartment. He had to change clothes. The place was surprisingly bare but in the middle of the living room was a stack of Macintosh computers and modems with multiple phone lines. Turns out John was running one of the most notorious Apple hacker bulletin boards in America. This was that time before Internet when wonderful geeks built dial-up bulletin board systems in their closets and bedrooms.

John and I ran into a much younger woman from work. As such things go, we ended up back at my apartment. John disappeared and our co-worker stayed. Things went as they sometimes do, but it got weird the next morning. She lived in an apartment complex way out in the suburbs and it was assumed I would give her a ride home. Problem was, her home was out of my current safe travel bubble. After an utter bullshit explanation, she called her roommate to pick her up. When she had gone, I realized I had a new relationship requirement. They had to live in the right zip code.

Based on the dramatic end of my relationship with Peg, I wanted a relationship with no drama. Someone smart, focused, and secure. Several days a week at lunch, I would crash for 20 minutes on one of the couches in the employee lounge. A tiny woman with short, black, curly hair sometimes dozed there, too. She was very 80s fashionable. She had a style that set her apart from the other young women. What really caught my eye was her socks. Short, ankle length white socks with fold-over lace. One day, lying on the couch, I opened my eyes to see a black skirt, black pointed toe ankle boots and those socks ... oh my ... those socks. What also caught my eye was the way she moved and the look on her face. Her no-nonsense attitude fell slightly over toward 'don't fuck with me.' I was intrigued. Her name was Sally. She was a clerk who also taught the lunch time aerobics class. I thought about her all the time but was scared to death to contact her.

One of the more sophisticated pick-up scenes was something called Museum After Hours. On Thursday nights the Portland Art Museum opened up with live music, wine, and beer. I had been there before, both on my own and with John. I never talked to anyone. One Thursday night, John and I rounded a corner and there was the tiny, black-haired woman standing in a knot of friends. I nudged John and motioned toward her.

"There she is. The little one in the middle."

"Dude, let's go talk to them."

"Oh no, I can't do that. I'm not ..."

"Take off your top coat and give it to me."

"What?"

"Just do it and watch."

John took my coat and tossed it over his shoulder, holding it with two fingers. He circled back so he could walk in front of the women. In front of them he let go of the coat, and in a routine that would have made Charlie Chaplin proud, he tried to catch the coat and kept fumbling it like it was too hot to handle. Splaying his legs apart and almost falling, he finally got his hand on the coat. As he looked up sheepishly toward the women, they were all laughing at him. He smiled, settled *my* coat on his shoulder again, and began talking to them. He then motioned me over to join them.

"Hey, this is my friend, Jim. We both work at Standard. Have I seen you there?"

Sally said she recognized us from there. I finally spoke up to say I thought she and I had both spent some days napping in the break room. Somehow, we all talked about where we lived. She lived in northwest Portland, downtown, just down the street from both my favorite movie theater and brew pub. I have no idea if I looked remotely cool when I heard this. Still a coward, the next day I sent her an email asking if she would like to meet for drinks at a Mexican bar down from her apartment. She said okay. Turned out she was working to pay for graduate school at Lewis and Clark in psychology and her serious persona was as real as her ability to express genuine delight.

She still has both a copy of the email I sent and the little plastic monkey from her drink. The little plastic monkey looks at us from the sill of our kitchen window. John had introduced me to my future wife.

Sally and I began dating. I was smitten. She was cautious. The first time I leaned in to kiss her at her door, she leaned back and slid away, all in the most graceful and disconcerting way. Her clear power in the small package was even more of a turn on. As things progressed, she was capable of big surprises. On my birthday, she got us tickets for an Ibsen play preceded by an hour soak at one of those hot tub places. Who else puts that combination together?

Not long after I began my relationship with Sal, I awoke to a vivid dream of someone breaking glasses on the sidewalk below my window. In a half-conscious state of annoyance, I realized I smelled smoke. I looked out the bedroom window and below me I could see the sidewalk covered with broken window glass. Smoke was rising from below. The adrenaline hit. Shit ... Grandpa Blackwood was right!

I am always amused when I hear people play the parlor game of 'What would you take with you if your house was on fire?' Let me clear this one up for you. When you know your house is on fire *you take your ass*! I grabbed a dirty t-shirt from the floor, threw it on. As I was pulling up my Levi's I looked at my shoes and then the phone. Shoes? No. Call 911. No ... run!

I felt my door to the upstairs landing. It was cool. Getting low, I slowly opened the door, pounded on the door of the other upstairs apartment, and yelled fire. No response. The guy was often gone. I ducked down, took a deep breath, and leaped down the stairs three at a time. I could feel heat radiating through the wall onto my face. I could tell by the melting paint on the door of the downstairs apartment that it was bad. No way to pound on that door. As I pushed the front door open and stepped onto the big porch the glass in the bay widow behind me blew out and hit my back. I was out.

Smoke was pouring out of the windows. The heat was amazing. Barefoot, I worked my way through the glass to the concrete stairs that led to the sidewalk. It was a cool night, but I didn't feel it yet. I saw the windows were open to the bedroom of my neighbor's house. I yelled and yelled, "*Fire.* Call 911." My neighbor looked out, saw me and the smoke and disappeared. I went out into the street.

My neighbors came out and brought me a jacket. Still barefoot, I stood there listening for the sirens. Other people appeared. The fire truck came down the cross street and turned the wrong way, away from my house. I must have been quite a sight, running down the street barefoot in an oversized coat, yelling, "Motherfuckers! Turn around." Luckily, some guy in shoes, much faster than I, ran and turned them our way.

They knocked down the fire. The entire first floor was destroyed. The fireman said it looked like it started with a cigarette in a couch. It was seconds from flashover and consuming the entire building. It was so hot that glass melted in the 1906 cabinets. Someone brought me some slippers. I was on the porch talking to the firefighters when the guy who lived in that apartment came home with a six pack in his hand. A chain-smoking alcoholic, he immediately started to yell he had lost all his stuff. I grabbed him by the shirt and pushed him into the wall.

"Fuck you ... your stuff ... you almost killed me, you motherfucking asshole. Fuck you. You left a cigarette burning and went for more beer? Fuck you and your stuff, you drunken asshole!"

Two firemen grabbed my arms and pulled me away. They told him to leave. I went down to the sidewalk. The adrenaline was wearing off. Firemen were ripping furniture out of the apartment and tossing into the street. As I stood there, a black woman walked up to me. She was wearing a tight leather dress with high stiletto heels. She put her hand on my shoulder and said, "Honey, if you need a place to stay, come with me." A generous and strange footnote to my night.

As the sun rose, I took a broom and dustpan down to the sidewalk to clean up the broken glass. The kids would be heading to school soon. When Grandpa Blackwood heard, a serious scheme was hatched to get me out of that apartment.

The ultimate hardcore punk band in Portland was called Poison Idea. Front man Jerry A drank an endless supply of an ugly malt liquor called Mickey's Big Mouth. The 450-pound heroin addict lead guitarist was called Pig Champion. John was determined that I see them. Erratic in their line-ups and shows, they finally did a show at one of our favorite clubs. John came to my cubicle and as he often did, ordered me to meet him there.

At the merch table was the most amazing rock t-shirt I have ever seen. It was based on the cover of their infamous EP. On the front of a white t-shirt (all punk t-shirts are black, so being white actually made it more punk) was a picture of Jesus. Underneath was the phrase, 'Pick your King.' That didn't make sense until you saw the back of the shirt, which had a picture of Elvis with the same phrase, 'Pick your King.' Fucking genius. I was laughing when John appeared next to me, pointed at the shirt and yelled, "Buy that!" I did.

John was in full punk regalia. Black t-shirt. Long black skater shorts. Black socks tucked into black Doc Martin boots with red laces. On his head was a blue doo rag tied like a pirate. He showed me how I needed to dance. The circle pit at a hardcore punk show is a whole other beast. Mostly men and boys, and for my money a few of the most amazing women on the planet, move in a violent circle in front of the stage. The dance is called skanking. To skank, you bend low, get your center of gravity down and walk in a circle foot stomping. Most importantly, arms crooked, fists ready, you swing wildly to clear your space in the maelstrom. John showed me the proper technique near the merch table. He was gloriously happy, I think both to be in full punk mode and to be mentoring his friend, Dude. It's a sequence I replay in my head when I want to call up pure joy.

Poison Idea hit the stage. The sound blasted and the pit started spinning. With songs like quick explosions, the music rattled my chest. And then, it happened again. When the show is right, I leave my troubled body. I felt a chill start at the top of my head and roll down to my feet. My fears rattled to the floor around me. I started pogoing up and down. I got to the edge of the pit and helped toss guys back in. Here I was, on the edge of a tribal violence, music ear-bleeding loud and I was calm. I was happy. No, better than happy, I was ecstatic. I usually tamp down excitement because it feels so much like fear. But in that moment, I began laughing. Everything about the show, the crowd, and that moment was simply absurd. John was right. This was the best.

When it seemed like the band had reached a noise crescendo, everything blew up. John had warned me. Jerry A put down the Mickey's and lit a wand, then took a swig from a jar and blew fire out of his mouth and over the heads of the swirling crowd in front of him. The fire came right at us. He repeated the fire trick several times, singeing the heads of people who reacted with pure glee.

I had been initiated. John knew it by looking at me. I was hooked. I'm still hooked. Even in the darkest parts of my life, that setting, that music live and loud is like a reset switch for my nervous system. For the rest of my life, like a religious seeker on a quest, I would seek my punk release.

Chapter 22

Poets and Frisbees?

I STARTED ROAMING inner southeast Portland looking for an affordable house. I found a small, 750 square foot, two-bedroom house in the Mt. Tabor neighborhood. I am lucky in my birth. I know that. My Grandpa Blackwood had sold his service station, but at 80-years-old was still working part time. He called one day and said he "... wanted to get some of his money out of California." My Aunt Joy was a real estate broker. Working with them and Dad, we created a loan with my grandparents so that they could collect monthly retirement income with interest, and I could buy a house. My grandpa got me out of the old apartment that had tried to kill me.

Monthly check-ins with my grandparents became a wonderful connection to them. Inspired or not, I wrote them a monthly update letter. Because I couldn't be with them, the letters became a lifeline. My Grandmother Pearl sent annotated cards of a religious nature. She always said she was praying for me. Sometimes she clipped bible verses from a magazine or the Sunday church program. Every few notes would be a plaintive question, "When are you coming to see me?" Those broke my heart. I never saw her again.

John helped me move. It seemed like John was there whenever I needed him. I tried to return the favors, but he was fiercely independent and more than a little secretive. He loved strange conspiracy theories. We had done the whole 'black helicopters' thing and at one point he became obsessed with the children's show, *Teletubbies*. Seriously. I got daily reports on the episodes where he decoded the messages that were being sent to children.

Sally didn't move in with me right away. She was busy with a mental health services practicum and grad school. When she joined me, we decided it was time to get a dog. I had been without dog energy for far too long. We went to the Humane Society and walked the kennels. Sally was on the other side of the big room. In the back corner in one cage was a small, shaking mess of a black and white dog, a girl on the low side of 30 pounds.

I squatted down and turned my body to the side, a trick for all dogs as it removes the sight of physical confrontation. I lay my hand on the fence, fingers dangling inside. And then, I just talked, low, calm, eyes averted. I'm not sure how long I did that, but the little border collie started to creep toward me. I was thrilled but didn't change my aspect. With little, cautious steps, head held low, she made it to the fence, sniffed my hand, then backed away. Sniffed again and then licked my fingers. What I had been saying over and over to her was, "If you trust me enough to lick my hand, then we are out of here."

Sally came around the corner, saw me and her and said, "Oh no, Jim, not that one."

I said, "I promised her."

I knew very little about border collies, which was good. They are smart enough to be neurotic. I named her after my favorite David Bowie song. Ziggy was now family.

Mt. Tabor Park, a few blocks from our house, is an enormous park that surrounds an ancient cinder cone. For Sal, that time with the sun rising while she is walking our generations of dogs has been restorative. Ziggy was always ready to go. She was built to go. But she was also very afraid. The little yellow house had a tuck garage and a basement, perfect place for a dog while we were at work. But Ziggy wanted in the house and proceeded to rip all the carpet from the basement stairs and chew the moldings from the basement door. Nothing we did seemed to console her. I used chicken wire to block her at the bottom of the stairs. She chewed a hole though the wire and gnawed off the end of the banister.

In my last conversation with Grandpa Blackwood, I told him about her and how she was destroying our house. In his calm way, he said it wouldn't be a problem soon, she would figure us out.

Not long after that call, my brother, now a deputy sheriff, was on patrol early in the morning and saw Blackie's car parked at a 7-11. He went in to say hello and realized Grandpa was ill. Grandpa had dropped by the store to get a 7-Up to 'settle his stomach.' Mike put him in the patrol car and took him to the hospital. He was having a heart attack. I got word and called the hospital. He was in the ICU. They wouldn't let me talk to him, but the nurse said he was looking much better and had a good dinner. I told her to relay a message that was a Blackwood code he would understand. "Tell him I love him and to get with the program."

The next morning, like most, I started the day in our hidden network prototyping lab. I checked my messages and there was a voice mail from Dad. When I called him back he said to sit down. I did. He told me my grandpa had died.

Grandpa Blackwood … Clarence … Blackie had been a constant presence in my life. He was my deep connection to the Ozark hills and its philosophy of steadfastness tempered with a deep Christian faith. His would be a big funeral as he was a deacon of the church and known to so many in Indio. I fought myself for days, trying to find the courage to get on a jet. In the end, I wrote a eulogy and sent it to my family. It was the best I could do. Not nearly enough.

Grandpa was right about Ziggy. When I bought the house, my dad (Jim) and Uncle Jim (at one point there were five Jims alive in my family) loaded all my old boxes of books and junk into a pickup and came to see me. The basement had a big concrete shelf about five feet high that ran its width. I had stacked the boxes there. One day I came home, opened the door from the garage, and there was no Ziggy. Then I saw her little head peeking out from behind the boxes. My barrier to the stairs had not been touched. Of course, I realized, she needed a hideout to feel safe during the day. She had jumped up five feet and solved her own problem. I moved the boxes into sort of a den and put her bed there. She never bothered the stairs again.

For months I had been throwing the frisbee in the back yard. Ziggy pounced it to the ground like a cat. One evening she ran after the disk, jumped, and snapped it out of the air. She landed on all four paws and stood staring at the back of yard, then turned and looked at me. You know the look: *I got this.*

~

My illness weighed heavy on my soul. I began to seek ways to heal that hole. I joined Sally at Unitarian Universalist church services, but it didn't take long for the relentlessly liberal dogma there to alienate me. Nice people ... too nice. As I have never been a joiner, I set out to create my own path. I began to consume writers on the works of Carl Jung and poets who spoke to me and found a Jungian psychologist. If behavioral psychology couldn't rid me of the fear then I would find a cure in the world of the subconscious and soul.

This coincided with the flowering of the men's mythopoetic movement. Of course, Portland was a hotbed of the work. There was much to learn from that movement, which said that in a rapidly moving industrial world men lost track of what it was to be a man. We had forgotten the stories that taught us for thousands of years, across all cultures, how to live as a man who is compassionate, calm, and powerful. Modern living had reinforced the power side of the equation without the heart. That made good sense to me.

I consumed the writings of Robert Bly, Robert L. Moore, Robert Johnson, Joseph Campbell, Michael Meade, and most importantly for me, the poetry of Oregon Poet Laureate William Stafford. I was looking for the wisdom of tribal elders to heal myself. It all sounds a bit goofy now, but it is useful to recall that Bly's book, *Iron John*, spent 62 weeks on the NY Times bestseller list.

My work with a Jungian psychologist I nicknamed Soccer Bob turned out to be a funny waste. There should be a rule that if therapists see they are not helpful to the patient, then they need to toss the patient out of their office. That is rare, especially when they can bill your insurance. Jungian therapy is designed to work with the subconscious using dream analysis. Newsflash! I was on a strong enough dose of a tricyclic antidepressant that I didn't dream, or at least I could not recall them. A little side effect. So, I would sit in his comfy chair and we would just talk. On the rare occasions I recalled a little bit of a dream we would strangle the memory for meaning. I did learn a lot about his daughter's high school soccer career.

There was a three-day workshop with Robert Bly and Michael Meade. It was way out in the suburbs. I used all of my tricks to get there. It was intense. All the myths were told with drumming. It turned out that Bly, a boisterous, booming teller of poems was staying with his friend, William Stafford, who was nothing like Bly. Stafford was a small man who came to the stage and gave his poems quietly. A Stafford poem leads you down a silent path to an explosion of meaning. And lest we not get the full impact, Bly would stand at the side of the room and say, "Again Bill. Again." Bly was right. The ear sometimes does not connect with the mind and heart at the first telling. Again, it was just what we needed.

When he finished his reading, he fumbled around in his — of course — rumpled coat pockets for scraps of paper. "These are new. New to me, too." Stafford, a professor at Lewis and Clark in Portland, wrote every morning. *Every* morning. He called it following the golden thread. Don't ask questions. Just keep following. We then got to hear what his work had been the last few mornings. For me, in his calm he evoked my Grandpa Blackwood. While my time in that movement and at church didn't lead me to my cure, it did open cracks in my psyche and heart that would allow me to recover. I never fully rejected anything I tried to get better. Each one was additive.

~

The first time I told I Sally I loved her was at a BB King show. Well into the show, the music was doing what music does to me, lowering my anxiety and inducing a little ecstasy. I leaned over and told her I loved her. We kissed and held each other for a moment. At the end of the show, BB handed out little gold plastic lapel pins, a replica of his famous Gibson guitar, Lucille. I went forward and thanks to my long arms, received one. Like a good supplicant, I had received my blues communion. The union between Sally and me had been blessed. Think that's weird? When I came back to get her, Sally smiled and shook her head. She knew exactly what I was thinking.

We became a little family in a little house. I had seen my illness kill one great love and I was determined it would not happen again. However, one of most insidious ways my fear inserted itself in my life was my belief that other people kept me safe. I was safe if Sally was there. At work, I felt calmer when John was around. When they weren't around, I developed a little ritual that I fight to this day. I make lists of who is available if I need them.

My mind is constantly constructing little disaster scenarios. My body will somehow fail me, and I will need another person to save me. When Sally went away for a weekend, or John was traveling for business, I would make mental lists of people I could call. Of course, those became actual lists of names and phone numbers that I tucked into my ever-present backpack.

Because of my job and responsibility for teams 24 hours a day, we were some of the earliest adopters of mobile communication. We all were given those early giant cell phones and every belt had a pager. While great for work, my access to technology became a new crutch. Now I could call anyone, anywhere. John especially was, in my mind, always available, since always on call, he had to have that pager on him.

On a Friday, when Sally was out of town for the weekend and I was getting pretty ramped up with anxiety, I let him know. His reaction became a reassuring ritual. He said, "That's cool. I'm on the wire," tapping his pager. Sometimes, without prompting, when he left work on Fridays, he would simply say, "On the wire." Reacting to my revealing that I sometimes had night terrors that woke me up in a full panic attack, he said, "I put my pager in a coffee can of pennies next to my bed so it will always wake me when I'm sleeping." *Who does that?*

Life with this illness is one of endless little adaptations. What I didn't fully understand then was that the adaptations are one of the ways you keep yourself trapped. It's perfectly natural to try to keep yourself safe if you believe you are in danger. But if there isn't actual danger, every little bit of protection acts to tell you the opposite. Danger is everywhere.

While I went to many music shows, don't for a second think that was easy. Anticipatory anxiety kicked in and I had to fight the urge to just stay home and do nothing. Even now, that reflex hasn't changed. I suffer a little bit for everything I love to do. This is a habit of mind I have never been able to shake.

However, once there, I may be the last to leave. I still can't explain that either.

~

On my big deal 40th birthday, I chose to go to my favorite rock club, La Luna, to see the all women group from Minnesota called Babes in Toyland. I have a thing for badass women rockers, especially the Riot Girls of the northwest. I invited everyone. It was the night of a book club meeting with my first group of Portland friends. Sally and I went to book club, then left to go to the show. None of them showed up. Right then, I should have said what it took me another 15 years to say. "It's been fun; have a good life."

But John and Sally's good friend, Holly, came to that show. I mentored Holly at work. She is younger and at that time was in a Goth band. She met us there. For a long time that night, I thought John, too, had abandoned me. I was bummed. Then John came bouncing in and gave me a big hug, told me happy birthday and handed me a pen. *A pen?*

He said, "Dude, open it."

He said he had been heading to the West Hills and saw a car pulled to the side of the road with a flat tire. Being John, he stopped to help. The car had four young Latino men who spoke little English. To thank him for helping them, they gave him a nicely rolled joint. John immediately decided the joint would be my birthday present, but he needed to wrap the present to bring it into the club.

I opened the pen and he had replaced the ink

with the joint. It had been years since I had gotten high. Getting stoned in the club was strictly verboten. But John would not be dissuaded. He put it in my mouth, pulled out a lighter, and lit it. Holly came around the corner and joined us. Sally, not a stoner, watched, sure we would be thrown out. We weren't. It was a wonderful night. The music was insane. I was high and happy and 40, doing one of my favorite things with my best friend who had just saved my birthday.

Chapter 23

Sally Wakes the Knucklehead

I NEVER WANTED TO BE MARRIED. That entire natural progression from couple to marriage to having kids had no resonance for me. Especially the kid part. From a distance, kids are intriguing. But up close, I don't like them. I didn't like kids when I was a kid. If I was ten and there were five-year-olds around, I got away from them as quickly as possible. I wanted to hang out with the adults. Kids were loud, random, and annoying. When my friends had babies, they would thrust the baby into my hands. I had all the responses they expected so as not to offend but in reality, I was on countdown to hand the kid back.

Now I understand what that is all about. My entire life, as a nervous child and anxious adult, I have felt vulnerable. I have always been uncertain that I could take care of myself. I didn't trust that at some critical juncture I would fail a child. If you know, *know*, you can't take care of yourself, then how can you take care of a child? I saw all that small package vulnerability as overwhelming. Rationally, it always seemed safer for the child if I was not the one in charge. I couldn't live with any harm to a child in my charge. The answer was actually pretty simple.

Sally shoved me back against a wall, looked me in the eye, and gave me a deadline. Small but powerful, my Sal. In retrospect, it was a reasonable request. We had been living together for years. Marriage … okay.

Sally didn't want an engagement ring, just a very nice, custom designed wedding ring. But I still needed a symbolic ring if I was going to propose. I went to a department store and bought a simple gold band. But how and when was going to be the tricky part. I had told Sally I loved her the first time at a BB King show. He was coming back to town at a smaller venue. I got good floor tickets.

The day BB and his band came to town, I snuck up a back fire stairs into the venue. I had written a letter explaining what happened at that first show and how I was going to propose that night, and asked the great man to sign the note and send it back to us in the envelope I had provided. I got inside and security nabbed me. I told them the story. The guards loved it. They took me up to the promoter's office. They were annoyed until the women in the office heard my story. (Never underestimate the power of a good story.) They broke protocol and gave me the hotel and room number of the road manager. I went there and left my envelope.

I had the ring in my pocket, but I was so afraid I would drop it in the dark that I took a piece of yarn and tied it around the ring. About halfway into the show, I snuck it out of my pocket and in between songs, I leaned in, reminded her of the first time I said, "I love you" and popped the question. She said yes, so at 42, I was now the engaged guy. Three days later my envelope arrived stamped from the next city of BB King's tour. He had signed the letter with best wishes. (The piece of yarn and letter are in her wedding book.)

~

If I was getting married, I wanted to tackle my anxiety once and for all. Let's call my new therapist 'Gets It.' She was one of my people. She had severe anxiety from childhood and lived a life in recovery. She flew everywhere. For the first time, I could talk about how I lived and have her just smile and nod yes. It was such a relief. She got it.

The new, and at last, more spot-on definition of my illness was panic disorder (PD). The broader definition captures the depth of my anxious world. I wasn't just afraid to leave my *home*, an agoraphobic. I was afraid that my body would fail me, that I would not be able to take care of myself. I feared being afraid.

I can be manically disciplined. I am most happy when I have a plan, something to do. Gets It gave me a workbook, *Mastery of Your Anxiety and Panic II*, by David H. Barlow. It starts with in-depth information on the physiological and psychological structure of a panic attack. For the first time, I really understood what was happening to me when those awful symptoms suddenly appeared. There were clear examples of how PD sufferers begin to obsessively monitor their bodies. The new plan was to demystify my body. The book had exercises and tests as assignments for every chapter.

At last, I felt like there was genuinely something I could do for myself. I read, took notes, marked up the book and came to every session with questions for Gets It. There were charts and graphs to mark my progress, deconstruct every panic attack and tests that Gets It did before and after the work to empirically reveal my progress. I was in PD geek heaven.

Gets It was part of an anxiety disorders clinic. This gave me access to a psychiatric nurse practitioner (PNP). When I started taking Elavil, the nightly anti-depressant, I noticed that mostly what it did was slow down my reactions. Pain in the gut. Oh god ... I'm going to puke. I'm going to die. None of these are rational thoughts, but they are real, nonetheless. The drugs I took basically said ignore your amygdala and give your big brain a pause to weigh in on that instant fright/flight stuff.

However, from the first time I took the medication, I saw it as a weakness, a character flaw, a crutch. The drug also robbed me of some of my wonderfully heightened ability to see and understand the world. *All* anti-depressants have side effects. Messing with the meds is no fun. But I didn't care, I wanted a full cure, one without drugs, or at least with as few drugs as possible. As I was working this new program, I lowered the Elavil as much as I could.

With Gets It guiding me, I was retraining my mind. I needed to modify the self-statements that got me into a panic state and unwind all those adaptations and safety behaviors. With Gets It as my coach, I began to take trips on the MAX, the local light rail. I went to stores and crowded places to expose myself to anxiety, carefully record and monitor myself, then apply my new body and mind management skills.

Eventually, Gets It had me subject myself to exposures without my cell phone. Very hard. The public transportation recovery battle drama was entirely in my head:

Watch your breathing.

Remember the training. Practice your new skills.

Your heart isn't going to burst. Sweating is normal.

Your body will take care of you.

No! I can't do this.

Too far.

I wonder if that person across from me will help if I suddenly faint or go crazy.

Hold it. That's just a thought.

Go back to your skills.

You can control this.

Ah, celebrate that one more stop.

Almost over.

Almost there.

After completing one exposure, repeat.
Don't give the voices in your head a break.
Prove them wrong.
Will yourself to do what is normal.

It was working. I was expanding my life again. Not perfectly. Not my complete cure. But it sure seemed like I had found a way out. And while I was doing all of this, life was moving on. I was getting more responsibility at work, now managing of a team of thirteen. My team's new technology was now considered business critical. With scale came stress and growing office politics.

~

Sally and I created a wedding ceremony that we both could love. We would get married in Mt. Tabor Park. Ziggy would be part of the ceremony. We decided not to invite everyone to the actual wedding. It would be family and our closest friends. After, we would host a blow-out reception for everyone at Melody Ballroom, a favorite blues music haunt. Sal and I wrote our own vows and found a giant white oak tree, one big enough for everyone to stand under. Her bridesmaid would be her sister. My best man? John, of course.

For John, being honorable was important. When I asked him to be my best man he seemed a little overwhelmed, as if I had bestowed upon him a sacred trust. Before the wedding I found a gift for him. I got a gold money clip and had DUDE engraved on it. His combination of childlike glee and solemnity was a joy.

Two days before the wedding, my family arrived. I was worried no one would show, but Sally kept telling me, "Honey, people are going to come." I figured my parents and my brother, but not anyone else. I mean, why? I was too old for that. Too distant. Too isolated. But Sally was right. Parents, brother, wives, husbands, aunts, uncles, cousins, nieces, nephew ... they all came. I was overwhelmed. We had the rehearsal dinner the night before at a tavern. I moved from table to table talking to everyone. It was exhausting, but I was so happy and honored that all these people cared about me and my wife-to-be.

On the day, Sally and the women disappeared up the hill to the wedding site for pictures. I was alone at home, getting dressed and getting worried, not just about the day but wondering where John was. I tried all the usual contact technology and he didn't respond. I did have one distraction. My San Francisco Giants were in the playoffs and on television. I joked with everyone that if they went into extra innings the ceremony would have to be delayed. Was I serious? I'll never tell.

Thankfully, the game ended in nine innings and John showed up. He brought me the biggest green Tupperware bowl I had ever seen. He opened the lid and revealed a tidal wave of rotini pasta in red sauce. "I'm Italian," he said. "You have to have pasta or you will have bad luck."

Even though I had doubled up on my Ativan and my mouth was as dry as Indio in August, I took out a fork and dug in for a few bites. "Dude, this great," I said. "Now, let's go get me married."

The ceremony was just like Sally and I had dreamed it. Under our tree, we exchanged our vows. Ziggy was released to be with us as soon as we turned to the crowd. Not having a religion of choice, the officiate was a distant friend of Sally's, some sort of Druid as I recall. We walked over to sign the wedding certificate on the hood of a car. Like the flaw in a Navajo weaving, because only the gods can be perfect, she had misspelled our last name. I had to cross out Blackwell to make it Blackwood.

Neither Sally nor I wanted a big cake. Sally put herself in my hands. I don't like frosting. Never have. I loved my mom's chocolate cupcakes with no frosting. So, I ordered 100 frosting free cupcakes, then arranged them into a tower. In an exercise of love and tolerance and fun, my new wife let me ask Bob, my DC baseball buddy, to lead the crowd in singing "Take Me Out to The Ballgame" while Sally and I threw out the first cupcakes.

John was nervous. I had asked him to deliver the first toast. After I directed the attention to him, he pulled a sheet of paper from his coat and began reading it. I remember it began with, "Everyone raise a glass ..." but recall nothing after. It was so John. He hadn't allowed time for anyone but him to actually fill their glasses. He marched ahead, raised his glass to Sally and me, and took a long drink. I looked out and maybe a handful of other people had a glass in their hand. Mostly, they were confused. John didn't realize. I didn't care. I just gave my best friend a hug and told him he did a great job.

We didn't have a honeymoon. Practically, our family was still in town, so running off seemed silly. I mean, they had all come so far to see us. And ... we were exhausted. Nobody does the wedding for you when you are forty-two. We did all the work and said we would take a trip later, but there was an underlying truth. Where would we go? I didn't fly and even long-distance car travel was not yet a reality. Sally knew that adding the anticipation of trip to everything else would just make me miserable in an already challenging situation. She didn't want to risk the wedding for the honeymoon.

Sally was now working in community mental health. Her expertise still amazes me. She specialized in childhood sexual abuse and trauma. Yeah ... that. She actually spends her days helping kids manage and recover from the unimaginable. When I had a good day at my corporate job, I made the world a better place for an insurance company. On her good days, she saves someone's life. That's one hell of a day.

With two stable incomes, we had talked about getting a slightly bigger house. The neighborhood was being discovered and it was clear that was not going to stop. Every morning, Sally and Ziggy headed out for a long walk up to the park. One day she came back with a flyer for a house on sale just two blocks farther up Mt. Tabor. Our little house sold as fast as we put it on the market. This slightly bigger house, with ample room for my dahlia obsession, is our home still.

Chapter 24

Back in the Left Field Box Seats

BASEBALL is more than a game for me. It's a constant in my life. Maybe it's the fact that there is no clock. The game is deliberate and must resolve within itself. The Zen of the game is that when you think nothing is happening, everything is happening. Playing the game is so hard that success is rare. To love the game, you must accept human fallibility. Some of my most cherished memories from childhood and beyond have a baseball park in the background. When I was poor those first years in Portland, my one true luxury was a ten-game pack of general admission tickets to the AAA Portland Beavers. I usually went alone, got a beer and a dog, and always wore my San Francisco Giants hat.

For a time, Portland lost its AAA franchise and the downtown park stood empty. Then a terrific owner of a short season A ball team moved his franchise there. My fortunes increased. My work buddy Don and I bought two season seats, three rows back, even with third base. I got VIP parking across the street from the stadium. I had gone to the park on the day ticket sales opened in February. I met the owner and we walked down in a snow shower so I could try seats until I found the ones I liked. Even with all that, I was in still in deep pain about baseball. I had not seen a major league game since that awful day in Baltimore almost 20 years before.

Less than three hours away in Seattle, the Mariners had a wonderful new stadium I had never seen. There had always been an invisible barrier on Interstate 5, north of Portland, somewhere just across the Columbia River. Safeco Field might as well have been on the moon. I followed the Mariners, watched the games on TV, and even looked at hotels in downtown Seattle. I often did that little ritual of hope, pain, and anger. Anger at my disease. Anger at myself for not being able to do such a simple thing. At work, when my team members went to major league games, they brought me souvenirs. I smiled and thanked them, then displayed them in my office. Somehow, they avoided the topic of why I didn't go by simply saying, "You should go."

I was ready. I had chosen a game on September 12, 1999 against the Baltimore Orioles. I was going to see my old east coast team, and finally see the new Iron Man, Cal Ripkin. So many birds to kill with one stone. Sally and I loaded up my new Ford pickup and headed north. The drive was a relay race of freeway rest stops. In Tacoma, I was wavering. Sally got out of the truck and told me, "You can do this. You are going to see a major league baseball game."

Just outside of Seattle Interstate 5 makes a sweeping left turn revealing all of downtown. I teared up when I saw the city and kept saying to myself, *I did it. I did it.* I almost broke down completely when, for the first time, I saw the roof of Safeco Field. "The roof ... there's the roof!" I yelled.

"I know, honey. I can see it, too," Sally responded, touching my shoulder. We dropped off the freeway to find our hotel. Not knowing the city, I had gotten a place near the Space Needle. I doubt the D-day invasion had the level of planning I put into this trip. I wanted to control every moment to get me to that game. Except ...

We couldn't get to the hotel. Unbeknownst to me, I had chosen the same weekend as the biggest event in Seattle, the week-long Sea Fair. I tried street after street to get to our hotel. I just wanted to get there and settle down, take some more drugs, eat something out of my carefully prepared cooler. We kept getting close enough to see the hotel, but streets were blocked for a marathon and a huge parade that all started at ... you guessed it ... the Space Needle.

I was burning through my carefully marshalled mental reserves. Panic attacks rolled through me. I was yelling, pointlessly, "How can they do this to me!" Thoughts of my last attempt to fly with days of fog delays crept in. At another dead end, Sally jumped out to talk to a policeman. He relented and let us get to the hotel parking lot. In the room at last, I fell onto the bed and yelled, "Don't they understand how hard this is?"

We turned on the television. The night parade was about to begin. I was exhausted. I realized that until the parade ended, and people cleared out I couldn't leave at all. No exit. I was hemmed in. My recovery tool kit seemed pointless. Sally tried so hard to talk me down. I washed my face and worked with my breathing. I stretched and tried to eat a few bites. The drugs weren't helping. I was fully into my fright/flight mode and it was time to run. I gave up. The voices inside my head and the city itself had won. Without checking out, near midnight, we left.

I had my map to the stadium and told Sally I had to at least see it and touch it. We drove the now empty streets. I parked right in front of the stadium. We got out and I walked up to lay my hand on the brick facade.

"Isn't it beautiful?" I said through tears. "I wish I could see the field from here."

Sal said, "You can still do this, honey. Look at where you are. You did it."

As I walked along the darkened side of the park, I was sad and tired. I didn't have the energy to keep fighting the voices in my head, the hundred scenarios where I would be in the crowd the next day in danger and couldn't escape.

We left. After an hour, my vision was getting blurry. Sally drove the rest of the way home. At work, I had told them about going to the game. I lied and told them a sad tale of food poisoning. I'm a pretty good liar to hide my reality. Lots of practice.

But here's the thing. When I went to see Gets It, she made it about my success and convinced me that I had merely fallen into circumstances beyond my control. I could still do this. Sally told me the same thing. I believed them. I still wanted this so badly and I'm hillbilly stubborn.

I had been so close. I was sad I didn't get to see Cal Ripkin but maybe trying to fix DC by seeing the Orioles wasn't a thing. Maybe it was just a bridge too far. I went back to the Mariners' schedule and found an Angels game on Saturday, September 25th. The first trip had told me I needed a different hotel, closer to Safeco Field. I found one near Pioneer Square. I took everything I learned on the first trip about myself, my tools, the logistics, and created a new plan.

There's a unique feature of Safeco Field. Outside gates, beyond the outfield, there are places that allow little glimpses into the ballpark. Not the field, but just above the bullpens. As we walked with the crowd, I heard this familiar sound. *Whack!* Wait for it. *Whack!* And again. It was the sound of a pitched ball hitting the catcher's glove. I turned to Sal overcome with excitement.

"I know what that is! That's the starting pitchers warming up. Oh my god, Sal, that's the starters!"

Once through the turnstiles, we walked up a huge set of stairs to the field level seats. I discovered there are no tunnels in the new stadiums. At the top of the stairs is the field, so green, the beautiful brown clay infield, and then there they were, major league players. Sally held me while I cried. I stopped caring about what other people thought. She had seen the worst and now she was the only person in the world sharing the absolute best.

In our little upstairs library, on a shelf above the books, is a framed photo Sally gave me that Christmas. I'm standing at the top of the left field box seats. Behind me is the field. I'm wearing my Portland Rockies hat. Over each of my shoulders, perfectly spaced, are shining banks of lights. I seem to be floating there surrounded in an angelic glow. I look at that picture often. It reminds me of what is possible. But mostly, I look at my face because it is what I have worked so hard to achieve in my life. I am content.

Chapter 25

How Work Really Worked

I WORKED for Standard Insurance Company in downtown Portland for almost 24 years. Nothing about that career was planned. So many people around me had constructed careers with meticulous attention to the education and training. My career was mostly a combination of hard work, intellect, and guile. I have often said that an expert is someone who knows just one more thing than you do. People smiled when I said that. But the truth was I always searching for that one thing. It was how I created my career.

I was managing a team of senior systems and network engineers. I was also constantly scheming to adjust the people and practices around me to do my job with panic disorder (PD). When I became a manager, I got subsidized parking in the garage across the street. Transportation problem solved. My teams had erratic hours. Computers never sleep and the perfectionist types I managed worked all the time.

Hours and locations in the IT systems world can be almost completely virtualized.

The anxiety and doubt every work day morning meant I would take a small dose of Ativan every day before I got into the shower. It took the edge off. As I ate my toast and drank my orange juice, I could feel the little dip in energy as the drug came on. After that, I was ready to go to work.

Well, 'go to work' was kind of a silly idea. I woke up with my Blackberry in hand. They called me 'virtual Jim.' I was almost never in my office when the work day was supposed to begin. My teams had a network prototyping lab next to the company's data center. The entire floor was behind two security carded doors. Only my team had keys to the lab. It was quiet there. I could ease into the day. It was my hideout. If my guys were using it, I headed out to the data center and used one of the consoles there.

I loved the data center. Row after row of computers and network gear in racks. The floors were raised with massive cooling systems that generated a wonderful white noise, my primal stress relief sound. It was even better than the air conditioner noise of my childhood. Some days, when my anxiety was especially high, I disappeared to the back of the data center to work.

In the evenings, I was a student who retreated to our small upstairs home library to do the things that sustained my soul in ways my accidental career never would. I journaled and read and studied. I spent over a year reading and understanding first century Christianity ... for fun. I dove deep into Jungian psychology, binged authors, and studied Buddhism. I built an extensive library of self-help books about anxiety and the medications used to treat it. Searching for that cure, always searching. With my favorite mechanical pencil in hand, I underlined, marked up pages, wrote questions, and marginalia. I was fully myself, an intellectual and a student.

If you are going to live with a mental illness in the workplace, it helps to develop a reputation as an eccentric. Without my PD, I'm pretty sure I would still be an oddball, but with it, eccentricity becomes a cover for all sorts of self-care.

For most of my adult life I avoided dining out. I'd go to a bar or a club or a pub. If in the process of drinking I had something to eat that was fine. A dog and a beer at the ballpark? Sure. But if someone said let's go to lunch or let's go to dinner, my anticipatory anxiety kicked in. My nervous system is wired to my gut. Once at a table with others, there is no subtle way to simply disappear. I suppose a memory of that Chinese restaurant always lingered in my nervous system. I had a downtown job where going to lunch or dinner was how people commonly did business. It was how you met friends at noon. It was normal and I wasn't having any part of it. I can't begin to add up how many sack lunches of peanut butter or ham sandwiches I have eaten at my desk.

But I was now the manager of a technical

department that made deals for millions of dollars of equipment and services. I met with vendors and sales people and every one of them wanted to take me to lunch. My trick? I never went to lunch ... with anyone. *Never.* Odd at first, everyone soon wrote it off as just one of my eccentricities. It got to the point that my team members laughed when vendors asked me out. They became the ones to volunteer, "Good luck on that; Jim doesn't go to lunch." And when you have fears you are trying to cover, double down. I would say things like, "I'm not here to be entertained. I'm here to do business." Now I was the hard-ass negotiator who couldn't be swayed by perks. Like I said, I know how to manipulate most realities to cover my disease. I am very good at it.

The flip side of this was that after work, even leaving a couple hours early, I would often take my entire team out to our favorite old school bar, The Lotus Cardroom. I had no problem abusing my corporate credit card for my team. I really enjoyed that time. Why? Drink first ... liquid calm onboard. Food optional. Lots of storytelling. And ... I could come and go as I pleased.

A sad fact of my work life is that I never travelled. In the course of my 24-year career, I could have traveled to conferences in every major city in America, all expenses paid. And for the cost of air fare, Sally could have joined me. Never happened. For a long time, I dodged my way around travel with excuses about more important needs. Eventually, I had to tell a couple of my bosses about my 'fear for flying.'

I was a voracious reader who expensed books and magazine subscriptions to virtualize my knowledge.

My career existed in the crease in time when a smart generalist could manage high tech teams. I rode the wave of new technology where we were making up the rules as we went. With my project leader skills, I designed and ran our technology implementation projects. I loved complex, high risk changes to the company's infrastructure. The planning and prototyping went on for months. The changes had to be made in 24-36-hour windows on weekends or holidays. We would work around the clock, food delivered to the data center, updates on the hour from me to the company executives. You would think this sort of stress would be a complete mismatch for my nervous system, and yes, I took some meds, but something about that need to focus overrode my usual fears.

At the end of the 20th century my corporate world started to change. New management rotated in with an obsession for structure and methods. I had thrived in a more entrepreneurial world. I found myself in corporate nonsense training more and more. Also, information technology was changing. Increasingly there was an emphasis on credentialing. That wasn't me. I became embroiled in defending new technology and turf, turf that my teams had actually created. I was spending more and more time on office politics. The fun was draining away.

The real breaking point for me was that some of

my team members were opposing tough hiring decisions I had to make. (Those hires? Still the technical leadership at the company. I wasn't wrong.) I was especially hurt that people I considered close were now actively undermining me with the new management team. Given my psyche, I interpreted that as being bullied. I began to feel the nervous child reemerge in ways that became destructive. One of the first signs of trouble was that I began to take my little half pills of Ativan both in the morning and at lunch. My journaling is full of long, work related rants. And to sleep? Maybe a bit more Ativan.

I knew I was in trouble psychologically. I didn't seem to have a way to fight back against the bullies. I tried to take more care of myself. I again expanded my circle of activities to manage my stress and anxiety. I took a Tai Chi class. I added days to my exercise routine. And I started attending a mindfulness meditation class at the Unitarian church one night a week.

From my earliest attempt as a child to learn self-hypnosis, I instinctively knew there must be some way to slow down my thoughts. I consumed the works of the Buddhist Monk Thich Nhat Hanh. I read books on the history of Buddhism and its various schools and founding teachers. Something about Zen Buddhism moved me. I liked the combination of simplicity and mystery. I happened upon an intersection between punk rock and Zen in Brad Warner's book, *Sit Down and Shut Up: Punk Rock Commentaries on Buddha, God, Truth, Sex, Death,* and Dogen's *Treasury of the Right*

Dharma Eye. And I read books of ancient Zen Koans, the strange little stories of enlightenment and learned that Zen also had a wonderful, ironic sense of humor. In the darkness that was becoming my daily work life, I retreated to my little library to breathe, meditate, and study Zen.

Then I made a big mistake. This is a little wonky but stay with me. The company was deploying its network to its growing number of national offices. This was at the point where national Internet providers were beginning to build what we now call "the Cloud." Much of what we do now on the Internet now is in the Cloud. It is how you stream Netflix, or use your word processor, or share files and pictures. I was excited by the new technology. It had always been my job to be part of the teams looking out over the technical horizon. I spent a lot of time studying what the new network providers were doing with this pre-cloud technology. As a team, we would say it was okay to be on the cutting edge, with its assumable risks; just don't be on the bleeding edge because that is where companies go to die. I was stumbling toward that bleeding edge.

I was having an internal war with staff, former friends, who disagreed with me. I'm stubborn and was hurt by their actions, so I kept pushing this new way to do our national networks. I saw it was the future. I got the new chief technology officer (CTO) in a room and drew it all on a whiteboard for her. She didn't say much. I knew I was struggling, not at my best, but I was sure this would be the future. Trouble was, I was wrong. I was about ten years too early. I had chosen the wrong way to fight with my perceived bullies.

A few days later, my boss came to get me. He said the CTO wanted to see us in the executive suite. That required taking one bank of elevators up 12 floors, then switching to a smaller executive elevator. As we started to get onto the small elevator all the blood went out of my face.

"Hold it. Am I being fired?" I asked.

"No ... But it's going to feel like it."

I had a full-on panic attack and said I wasn't going. I couldn't go. I left my boss standing there and was in full flight. I almost ran down 12 flights of stairs, got my bag, kept going to my car, and drove home. Soon I got a call from the CTO; the director of human resources and my boss where on the call. She told me my team was being broken up. A guy I had hired long ago and mentored was taking over and I would be left with a much smaller team of three people. Yeah, like my boss said, it was like being fired. I was devastated. And most importantly, in my heart and mind, the bullies had won.

Things were coming unglued. In ways I could have never imagined, life was about to become harder than I thought possible.

Chapter 26

What Goes Up

BEGINNING IN 2000, scrawled in my almost illegible printing with a very specific model of mechanical pencil loaded with extra hard lead, I journaled for almost 17 years. I sometimes found my sanity in those college composition books. The first entry reads:

10/18/00 I woke up in a long tunnel of depression. Depression and anxiety. Sally helped me drill down to the source. I have been bullied and betrayed. These are deep, dark threads. I was in the 'I don't know' place.

Can you imagine what it felt like to sit in a darkened living room with my dying friend and listen to him joyfully, wistfully tell our story from the very first network we worked on to the ones we designed today? In that room, at my elbow, was the newly installed hospital bed that he would die on four days later. I didn't tell him what happened. He didn't need that information. I sat there drenched in the irony and so happy he would die with the world as he had known it.

My new little team of three people managed the company's UNIX computers and most importantly the Internet security. John, Colette, and Bob. My management assignment had been scaled way down, a remnant of my original team. At least I still had a job and a team.

Bob was a stocky guy with a big bushy beard and long pony tail. He was also a programmer genius. Before most companies had one, he created our first email system from scratch. Between smoking breaks outside, he was affable and much loved by those who worked with him. His desk was covered with little pewter statues of Tolkien characters from the *Lord of the Rings*. All of his system and code names were based on those characters' names. Bob could also be unintentionally scary. In design meetings, especially with outside vendors, if he whiffed the slightest bit of bullshit, he would shift about in his seat. *Here it comes*, I would think. When he couldn't take it anymore, he would rise in his chair, thunder at the offending person, brush his chair aside, and go to the whiteboard, slamming the markers as he drew why his target was an idiot. He was our enforcer.

For a couple of months, Bob had been dealing with a bad back. He was a big believer in chiropractors. The day before I left on vacation, Bob asked to go home early. "My back is just killing me."

"Of course," I said, "Go now." As the sun poured down on him through our windows, I remember thinking Bob looked kind of yellow. It was a strange thought.

When I returned from a ten-day vacation, Bob still hadn't come back to work. I called to check on him. His wife, Judy, told me Bob had been diagnosed with Stage 4 liver cancer. He was dying. My team member and friend for the last 12 years, one-third of my team, was dying. Judy asked that I become the contact at work for Bob. We all sent cards and encouraging emails. I didn't tell others what I knew.

Home on a sunny day in October, I got a call from Judy. Bob wanted to talk to me, just me, no one else.

"Now?" I asked.

"Yes."

I was desperate to collect myself. "Can I come over tomorrow?"

"You could, but no longer. He won't be here long. Jim, he needs to see you."

"Let me call you right back."

I went for a walk on the grounds of the little religious seminary at the end of our block. I was trying to catch my breath. I took my drugs. Standing in the plaza, I called Judy and said I would come now. I asked if Sally could come with me. Judy said that was fine.

Bob was jaundiced. His eyes were yellow. He was smiling through the pain. It was clear he was taking some sort of opiate. He would brighten, then fade, as we talked. Judy and Sally disappeared. At first, Bob and I sat outside in the sunshine. He told me details about his life with Judy, things I didn't know. There was something both natural and deeply unnatural about our conversation. He took me to his bedroom. He had put all of the cards he received on the wall. I had written him a long note that he put close to his pillow so he could see it. He pointed to my card and said thank you.

We came inside and he relived all we had done over the last 12 years. I was trying to conceal my deep calming breaths. Then, with some urgency, he told me what he planned to do next to improve our security systems and network. I so wanted him to be the guy to do those things. I lived inside his fantasy with him. He started to fade in and out more. He was done. He had bravely held himself together for over an hour. On our way out, Bob and I stood on the landing looking at each other. Still a big bear of a man, he put his arms around me and whispered in my ear, "It will be okay."

We both teared up. As he turned away, I put my hand on my heart and said," You will always be here." I don't think he heard that.

A few days later Judy called. Now it was my job to tell everyone that Bob had died. My job.

This was the first time I had been so intimate with death. I wasn't sure what to do. I am no more lost than when I'm in what I call my 'I don't know' place. I feel frozen, mind spinning, every action doubted, every thought questioned. I tried to take care of myself. I kept my appointments with Gets It. I helped organize the work memorial for Bob. He didn't want a service.

John, Colette, and I had to dismantle Bob's cubicle, a space frozen since the day I told him to go home. Judy told each of us to pick one of Bob's little Tolkien statues. I never read the trilogy and picked a guy with an orb. Turned out I picked Gandalf.

~

I began an unbreakable ritual I called 'Read, Write, and Meditate' every night. I hoped my discipline would keep me safe. But on top of my mental state I was now having serious problems with sinus infections. It kept me physically tired and sometimes caused me to feel a little unstable as it worked on my inner ear. This compounded my anxiety. A specialist put me on a course of steroids. It was a disaster.

Even as I was sinking, I was still going to work and trying to maintain normal with all the energy I had. This is the story of mental illness sufferers. We do everything we can to keep moving forward with our lives. I used the sinus infection, a disease people could understand, as my excuse to leave work early. I didn't know it but I was having what some call a mental break down.

I was having more night terrors. I had had them since I was a kid, but now it was happening several times a week. I would wake up at night, sure I was being attacked. In that state between sleep and consciousness, I would sit up punching and kicking at something I saw, except my eyes were still closed. (Thankfully, I have never hit Sally.) Fully adrenalized, when I did actually open my eyes, I was sweating, heart pounding and confused. And then my thoughts rushed to believe I was having a heart attack. It sometimes took hours to calm down and fall back asleep, only to wake sleep deprived for another work day.

Heart disease is big in my family. Grandparents, uncles, Dad, my younger brother. Now on top of everything else, I began to obsess about my heart. I used a little phone app to take my pulse and I got a home blood pressure monitor. I love my data. I thought more data was how you kill doubt. Mostly, I was just reinforcing a new fear.

At the Unitarian church meditation class, we had a visitor, a 6' 4" tall, brown-robed Soto Zen monk from the local Shasta Abbey priory. Reverend Kensai had come to teach us the meditation practice of his order. Sometimes it's hard to know when your life has changed in a moment. This time I knew.

Soto Zen monks are sometimes called 'wall sitters.' They place their zabuton (meditation mat) and zafu (pillow) about an arm's length from a wall and then face the wall seated in a lotus or half-lotus posture. I asked Rev Kensai, "How do you do your style of meditation?" thinking he would give us a method.

His answer was wonderfully Zen — "Just sit." He bowed to the wall, spun, and bowed to the world, then spun and bowed to the wall once more. Rocking on the zafu to settle, he said to take two deep breaths and breathe normally. Facing the wall assures that you are not 'getting busy' with your eyes.

Rev Kensai said, "Think of yourself as a hitchhiker next to a freeway. The cars and trucks are rolling by. Those are your thoughts. You simply choose not to stick out your thumb for a ride." Now I had consistent approach to my new meditation practice.

In the constantly cascading fear and obsessive thoughts that enveloped me, the simplicity of this school of meditation was an oasis. Zen Buddhism seemed more like a special psychology that could exist wholly apart from any religious trappings. And most importantly for my nature, it didn't evangelize. You came to it or you didn't. Your choice. No one was selling it. I had begun what has become a life-long practice and what would become an essential pillar to manage my PD.

My grief was constant. I found myself breaking down in tears over little things. At work, I was increasingly thinking about my safe people. Where was Sally? Could I get to her? Where was John? Where was my other friend, Brian? My father-in-law lived downtown. Would he help me? As the trust in my ability to take care of myself collapsed, I fortified my imaginary support network.

I was deep into a world of catastrophic thinking. My people, the panic people, know this well. Every ache in my body. Each time an elevator door hesitated. Every time I got caught in traffic. All of these common events triggered little baths of adrenaline. My amygdala was working overtime, slapping around my big brain with one fight/flight response after another. Most of the time, this relentless turmoil was invisible to everyone around me. All they saw were curious actions that I successfully explained away. Sometimes in meetings, I would lay my sweating palm down on the table and raise it to see the moisture pattern it created. I was using my body's reactions to fear to distract me for a second or two. I was living two lives: one visible, the other invisible. Entire days, I was using my tools to suppress the invisible world. It was a losing battle.

One of the new tools in my kit was writing my way through panic attacks. My journals are full of long entries where I recorded the sensations and thoughts of panic attacks in real time. I wrote affirmations, reminders of all the training I had taken or of the Buddhist thoughts I was learning. I could see my shaking handwriting start to smooth as I weathered blasts of adrenaline and my parasympathetic nervous system took control again. Recovery from a big panic attack is never a straight line. In some entries I could see my mind's distress rise and fall. I kept writing until the act of holding my mechanical pencil and scraping the lead across the paper became an end in itself. Pages later, my body settled, my mind finally cleared, and exhausted, the words stopped.

I made it to the Thanksgiving break, then took a week off. I still thought I could keep going, somehow get on the other side of the bullying, betrayal, grief, and depression. On my birthday, November 27, Sally went with me to see Linda, the psychiatric nurse practitioner. Upon hearing my tale, she was direct. I was clinically depressed. I needed to take a disability leave to recover. She even broached the idea of inpatient care. Far from this news freaking me out, it was a relief. Her lack of hesitation took me out of my 'I don't know' place.

I was taking a low dose of my antidepressant. She said we would increase the dosage until it was at a therapeutic level for depression. I hated the idea of riding through side effects, but I had no choice. She said increasing the Elavil would help me sleep. She also said I needed to break the anxiety cycle with regular doses of Ativan. No choice. Just take it. I had to slow everything down. I was in a dangerous place. I slowly increased the anti-depressant in 10 mg bumps to minimize the side effects. I needed to sleep. The thing you don't know about clinical depression until it strikes is that it is a physical illness. The exhaustion is real. The muscle pain is real. It isn't all in your head.

I filed the paperwork to go on short-term disability. I would not return full-time for almost six months. Gets It suggested the book, *Feeling Good*, by David D. Burns. It became my study guide for overcoming depression. I had a plan.

Sally still had to work. I knew my neediness and this disease were incredibly hard for her. My dependence was stifling. I could see the effects on her but couldn't change anything. I think because they were worried about me, and to give Sally a break, my parents flew up for ten days. It was a relief.

While they were here, I went out to mow the front yard. Halfway through, I collapsed to my knees behind the mower. I came in the house crying and angry that I couldn't even mow my yard. My dad's reaction was perfect. He got me a glass of water and a cookie, told me to eat and drink and when I had recovered go back out and finish mowing my yard. I did. Hillbilly stubbornness is useful sometimes. I was so proud of myself. Cookie therapy was a thing. I set a goal to walk around the block by myself. I didn't make it at first but every time I got my coat, Dad came over and handed me a cookie. Blackwood men sometimes have to find different ways to say I love you.

I began to reclaim territory. I drove my truck on the freeway, for one exit only, then two. I tried going to stores by myself. But the Willamette River, something I had crossed several times a day for years, now seemed like a gator-filled moat. Late at night, I drove to a parking lot a block from the east ramps to the Hawthorne Bridge. I got out of my truck and looked at the bridge trying to visualize what was once common. I did that a couple of times and then I went for it. I turned up some loud rock and roll, gripped the wheel hard, and made it across the bridge. I went to my office building, drove around the block it occupied and headed back across the bridge. Then I did it again.

Finally, at night, I asked Sally to go with me to actually enter my office building. We parked across the street. Sally held my hand on the elevator. I had a panic attack on the way up. I went around to my corner office cube and sat down. I actually logged into my computer but didn't look at any email. I wrote funny, mysterious notes on the whiteboards of my two remaining team members and fought back tears looking at Bob's empty cube. Then we left and headed back across the bridge. I still marvel at the love, patience, and faith of my wife. It fills me with the deepest compassion for my people, fellow sufferers, who don't have a Sally in their lives.

As the year ended, I put a stop to what felt like the doctor's experiments with my chronic sinus problems. Specialists, antibiotics, antihistamines, decongestants, nasal probes, CT Scans. Enough! I took control again. No more drugs. Just more water and a handy saline spray. If this was a new normal, then I would just deal with it. My chronic sinuses would remain a convenient excuse to leave work on demand.

Sally and I needed a ritual to end what was an awful year. We gathered up little pieces of 2000: letters, notes, work objects, doctors' instructions. We toasted with wine and burned them in the fireplace. 2001 would be better ....

Chapter 27

So That's What It Is

SO MUCH FOR OUR RITUAL. On the third day of the new year I lost my beautiful, custom wedding ring. When I saw it was gone, I took a flashlight and revisited every place I had been for the last two days. It was gone. The symbolism was especially cruel. I felt naked without it. I was inconsolable. Finally, Sally drove me down to a department store and I bought a basic gold band. Sally created a little ritual as we sat in the parking lot. She put it on my finger, and we embraced. It was, at least, something.

Sally did something else that I didn't know about until years later. I had begun to suspect that once I was back to work, I would be fired. They had almost done that before. Sally sent a secret letter to my boss, Bill, telling him that having that job to come back to was absolutely critical to my being able to recover. Sally was right. Showing them I could come back was a big part of what got me moving every day. I didn't learn about the letter until a few years later when Bill pulled me aside and told me at his retirement party.

The immediate challenge was getting through each day alone in our house. I needed a job. Too cold to work outside, I cooked up the idea of creating a little home network. Not a technician, I turned an old PC into Red Hat Linux server. I emailed my team that I needed some long ethernet cables, then picked them up one night in my office cube. I ran cables through the heating ducts. My team thought it hilarious that I was teaching myself Linux. It somehow made me feel closer to them.

The strain of always being available was eating at Sally. She wore a pager I had forced on her. I grilled her on what she was doing that day and where she would be. I wished I could make it different for her. All I could do was keep working hard to change myself, to recover. She began to see her own therapist to help her survive me.

Our dog, Ziggy, the wonder border collie, was my constant companion. Ziggy was getting old. She still wanted to chase the ball but the distance she could run was getting shorter and shorter. She was having problems with a progressive nerve condition in her rear legs. Having her to hold, pet, and talk to kept me sane during days when I was counting the hours until Sally got home. The radio theme music at 4:00 for the business report was a daily celebration. I had made it another day without calling anyone.

More nighttime trips to the office. I began to

stay longer and read my email or look at papers that had been tossed on my desk. My team liked my funny little notes, so I kept writing them on their whiteboards. The cloud was lifting. I had more energy and willingness to tackle new things. I was confident enough to drive to the suburbs alone to see Linda, the PHP. At the end of January, she shocked me. "Jim, you no longer have the symptoms of depression. Stay on the medications at this level and focus on the panic disorder setback." You would think I would have been overjoyed. I was confused.

What happened next was a shock. I don't remember why I was so upset. We were in our little library space. Sally and I were talking. She was burnt out and I think we may have been arguing. I began to cry, then my emotions changed. I felt myself being pulled toward something indescribable but clearly dangerous. I fell into a different kind of waking terror. Time stopped. Reflexively, my body curled up. My fists, especially my right hand, rose to my face in a defensive posture. I was gasping, crying, and could not stop. I don't know how long it lasted. Sally stood a bit away from me.

"Jim, I'm here. I know what this is."

She ran downstairs and carried up Ziggy. Ziggy couldn't walk upstairs anymore.

"Jim, take Ziggy. Just take your hands down from your face and pet her."

I did. As I petted her, the room came back into focus. I caught my breath. Sally came closer and touched me for the first time.

"You're okay now, honey. Just keep petting Ziggy. It's over now. I know what happened. We can help you."

Even Jim the empiricist can't believe my life is entirely random. I had married a woman who became a respected childhood trauma therapist and educator. She was exactly ... exactly ... who I needed in that awful moment. I had had what is called a dissociative event. Essentially, something in that moment triggered a trauma from my past to such an extent that I disconnected from reality and tried to relive the event or events. My reaction was to protect myself. Sally knew it would be the exactly wrong thing for a person to touch or embrace me in that moment. Ziggy was a safe way for me to reconnect with reality, to regain my cognitive skills. Sally knew.

The emergence of trauma in relation to my lifelong anxiety was a turning point. I had always wondered, why me? I had the family history. A genetic predisposition. But now, for the first time, I knew there was something deeper going on, maybe, at long last, a cause. Sally put out queries to her professional friends. I needed to find a therapist who specialized in trauma.

Epiphanies don't stop the clock. I spent Valentine's Day hiding little messages and gifts for Sally all over the house. I wanted to bring her just a little joy because it was clear that Ziggy was fading fast. We strike a hard bargain when we choose to bring animals into our lives. They offer unfiltered love and companionship over awfully short lifetimes. We in return tell them we will not let them suffer when life has run its course.

Ziggy's legs were giving out. Her herding bark was now a rasp. We still played a little game with the ball where she was the goalie and I took slow shots at her so she could stop the ball. Just a few feet apart, she still begged to play the game and proudly brought me the ball. But one day she went outside, fell over, and I had to help her up. I looked into her eyes. The sparkle was gone.

We arranged for the vet to come in the evening. Ziggy slept most of the day between us on the floor. At one point, her legs began paddling. She was having a dream of running. Maybe it was with Sally on Mt. Tabor. Maybe she was back on the street with me after a show at 2 a.m. chasing the frisbee. Sally said she had stayed here as long as she could for me. I knew that. That evening, warm on our living room floor, we said goodbye to our flying girl.

~

Out of the blue, John came by to visit me during the day. I was so happy to see him. He had gotten engaged to his girlfriend, Susan, and they bought a house just over the top of Mt Tabor from us. He talked about work and music and rambled in ways I always loved. Funny thing was, he didn't want to come into the house. I don't know why. With John I just played the moments as they laid.

Working remotely, I had helped add someone

to replace Bob on my team. Years before, I had spotted Wendy working as a typesetter in the company's printing plant. In the background, I had been promoting her career in IT. A woman on a systems administration or engineering team was a rarity. It was going to be a bit of a stretch for her, but I knew she could handle it.

In anticipation of my returning to work half-time, I asked Gets It to have a talk with my boss, Bill, about my return. Afterwards, she told me, "You're right. He is clueless." That is how it is with mental illness. The law protects us. Businesses now have to accommodate us, but individuals, unless they have been touched by these illnesses, remain adrift. I think mental illness scares people in some fundamental way. Maybe because it is mostly invisible and still all around us.

When I started working 28 hours a week, I needed to do basic things like have a staff meeting. I emailed my team that I wanted to have our Monday staff meeting, but in the little conference room next to the lab. I got there early, closed the door to the lab, and psyched up. Unknown to me, my team was waiting in the conference room. I walked in and saw that they had all dressed up for the day. John in a coat and tie, the two women in formal black outfits. They all sat at the table, hands folded, upright posture. The tension bubble burst immediately in laughter. They nailed it … just what I needed.

Sally used her connections in trauma therapy to

find two candidates for me to meet. I was now looking for someone to treat panic disorder with an underlying basis in post-traumatic stress disorder (PTSD). For the first time in my life I had a fuller picture of what I had been up against all along.

    The first woman had a proper office in a nice building. She seemed competent and professional. I liked her. The second woman was completely different. Her office was in a converted, rough wood paneled attic. The room smelled vaguely of incense. She had varied credentials and was also a massage therapist. Her dark eyes consumed me as I talked to her. My punk rock alarm went off because she was damn close to the dreaded hippies. But something else caught my attention. On one side of the room on a cabinet was a sitting Buddha statue. Behind her on a book shelf was Quan Yin, the Buddhist Bodhisattva of mercy and compassion. I had recently acquired a sitting Buddha statue at home and created a little meditation altar. Unlike the first woman, who showed me a workbook, this therapist talked about methods for healing trauma that seemed a little mystical. Sally assured me they were methods widely practiced. A couple of days later I wrote in my journal:

    I am going with the little, freaky lady with the beady eyes. She is a very earthy, fringe type. Not a type I favor as a rule. Though I have never told her this, I think of her as The Gnome.

    A week later, we began working with my latest flashback.

The Gnome, well versed in PTSD therapies, uses a method called Somatic Experiencing (SE). The theory is that trauma gets stuck in the body as much as the mind. There were clearly body postures and movements that repeated when I had flashbacks. The process involves deconstructing those movements with the help of a therapist and recreating them in tiny pieces, each time creating a new context of safety for the movements. Deeply held emotions come tumbling out. The Gnome helped me not fall back into a full dissociative state. When that did happen, she was able to help me through it and use the experience in the moment to cultivate recovery.

Therapist Peter A. Levine created the method. He saw that when other animals experience fear/trauma they have ways to release that in real time. Ever see a dog shake after getting scared? Yeah, that. It's tough. I didn't fully understand it but I gave myself over to the process and, unlike much of my life, I decided to just trust what I didn't fully understand. One time, after an especially hard and draining session, The Gnome went over to her shelf and handed me the Quan Yin statue. "Take this. You will know when you are ready to return it."

~

In the midst of my recovery, John celebrated his 40th birthday with a big party at the new home he and Susan shared. I was still pretty shaky. No one had seen me for months. He met me at the door. "Dude, you're here!" We hugged and I made tentative steps into the living room. I felt like a wobbly baby zebra fresh to the world. I greeted a few people, then saw a nice chair against the wall at the dividing line between the dining room and living room. I grabbed a beer and sat down. John and Susan were in the kitchen. Suddenly, he grabbed her arm and pulled her my way.

"You see! I told you he would come and that would be his chair. Dude, I put that chair there for you. It's right where you like to be, keeping an eye on everything. See, Susan?"

"Good job, Dude," I said. "I like it here."

Spring came and Sally said she thought it was time for us to choose life. We were ready for a new dog. We rescued Luna, a two-year-old female, mostly black with brown Chow mix. She was Sally's choice and mostly her dog. Luna didn't have much chase instinct, which I missed. Like all of our dogs, she was a bit of a project. Someone had been unkind to her and she was very cautious. We had to help her learn to trust us, Sally first, and very slowly, tentatively me. It was clear a man had hurt her.

Then my Grandma Blackwood died. Sweetness is what I think about when it comes to Pearl. Even when she went into a care home, I sent her regular updates and letters. I always ended the letters asking her to say hello to the roadrunners and coyotes. She kept asking when I would come see her. My disease stole my grandparents from me. I wrote another eulogy.

Soon after she died, I got two family heirlooms:

my grandpa's working bible, worn out from use, and my grandmother's clock. From a distance it looks like a fancy fireplace mantle clock. Closer, you see it's plastic, fake wood. It is so out of place in our 1932 living room. But I keep it on the mantle, both to remind me of my grandparents and to remember where I come from, a place where a nice-looking plastic clock was a luxury, something to keep until the day you die.

I was back at work full time and not happy. Both my therapists told me I should, for my mental health, just quit. That scared me. I didn't have a clue what job I could do next. We had cars and a house to pay for. Sally's job in community mental health didn't pay that well. My Great Depression survivor parents always counseled stability. I wasn't so sure. I was desperate to be happy again. I wanted Sally to be happy, too. The office politics were still brutal. My boss was forced out.

I set a secret date to quit my job. I was done. I had no idea what I was going to do next. I just had to get out. But on that day, I didn't pull the trigger. Sally was wise. She said, "If you leave now, you will lose your confidence. It will feel like you left a failure and the bullies will have won."

Chapter 28

Wings of Desire

BESIDES TEACHING ME PUNK ROCK, John had a stockpile of guitars and amps he was forever picking up at pawn shops. Sometimes I would hang with him in his basement while he hammered away on his bass guitar. His prize possession was a 1984 pink Gibson Flying V. He let me strum along with it. I had taken classical guitar as a kid but only remembered enough cords to make slightly organized noise. Finally, he said, "Dude, get a guitar." I obeyed John's orders. He escorted me to his favorite music store and I bought a blue Fender Strat and a little Peavy amp. He said the strap I bought was dumb. At work one day he gave me a leather strap he had hand studded. So punk.

But something wasn't right with my friend. He was nodding off at work and sometimes disappeared during the day. I knew drugs and booze and didn't think I saw the effects of either. He was getting fat, unkempt, and grew his thinning hair into a straggly pony tail. One day, I followed him for a ways as he roamed away from the office. I stopped when he turned into one of his favorite second-hand stores.

People noticed his decay. I got on him about his work habits, but I sometimes covered for him because I loved him. He still had his moments of technical brilliance. His future oriented designs were amazing. But he also still lived like a twenty-year-old. Staying up all hours on computers, eating horribly. He and his fiancé Susan shared a strange, conspiracy theory world where health problems had mystical origins and cures were just as odd.

I had to do something. I finally convinced John to see a doctor. I wrote him and Susan a personal letter telling them how worried I was and how much I loved John. I had to come down hard on him. His health was affecting how people saw him and me. My other team members couldn't trust him. He responded by sharing his blood work from his physical. I pushed him to do what the doctor told him. He said he would, but I saw no difference. He would get caught up in other ideas and forget to take his medications. Almost in tears, I had to go to Human Resources and officially threaten him. In my journal I wrote:

I can't save him but I have to show him love.

In the HR note I wrote, "John has a huge heart and a chaotic mind."

And yet, when I was in a panic episode and making my little 'who's there'? lists, it was always John at the top of my list.

~

On September 6, 2001, John and I both worked late. I came over from my office and found him at a console in the Data Center.

"Dude, how goes?" he said with the clipped greeting he often used with me.

We adjourned to the quiet of the lab and he then regaled me with a series of wonderfully crazy observations. He then handed me a crumpled section of the *NY Times* with a story he wanted me to read. It was getting on toward 7 p.m.

"You about done?" I asked.

"Yeah, just checking something on the firewall."

"Okay, see you tomorrow."

"Later," he said.

The next morning, I was standing in the hallway talking to Wendy and Collette. It was late in the morning and I was both annoyed and disappointed that John was still not in. He had been warned. Why was he still fucking up like this? My phone rang. I could have run and gotten it before went to voicemail, but I was sure it was John with another excuse and I really didn't want to hear it. I finished talking to my team and went to my desk and punched up voicemail.

"Jim, this is Susan. Something has happened. Please call me at home."

I knew. I knew it was bad. My heart raced. With one last deep inhale and slow release, I dialed. Susan answered.

"Jim, John died. We had and argument last night and I slept on the couch. I knew he didn't want to be late but when I went to wake him he didn't move. He was so cold, Jim. He was cold."

All the blood rushed out of my head. I couldn't breathe. I turned my chair and looked out the window. Susan was worried about telling people. I told her not to worry; I would do that. She said the coroner suspected he had died in his sleep of a cerebral hemorrhage. *Fuck*, I thought, *he didn't get a chance to fight*. I stumbled back around the corner to Wendy and Collette's cubes. I somehow told them everything. They were both in tears. I wanted to be the one who told everyone else, but that wasn't going to happen. Shock and panic were kicking in, wave after wave.

"I need help," I said. "I need to get out of here now. I need to go."

Wendy came and put her arm around me. I think Colette said, "Just go." Wendy grabbed my bag and with her arm around me walked me across the street to the garage and my pickup. It was one of the kindest things anyone has ever done for me. In a haze, numb, I somehow made it home. I pulled the truck into the driveway and called Sally. She wanted to know where I was. I told her and she said she would be there right away. I broke down, convulsively, almost a dissociative event. I was still in the truck when Sally got home.

We quickly learned from the autopsy that John had been very ill. He had a rare blood disease, an enlarged heart, and cirrhosis of the liver. Enlarged heart? Of course. Ironic.

I was tired of writing eulogies. Now, I had to write one that I had never imagined. John and I had joked about being two old retired dudes sitting on his porch. Until that point, it was the only time I had ever really thought about getting old. It occurred to me that my father had also lost his best man at a young age. What a terrible thing to share.

It turned out my friend was a Catholic. We had talked about many religions but never his religion. I wondered if he was the Catholic or if for some strange reason his family now needed him, in death, to be one. He had always seemed too universal to be dropped into one religious bin.

There would be a viewing. A viewing? Susan was going to have him wearing his favorite t-shirt from the New Orleans Jazz and Heritage Festival. I didn't want to see my friend like that. Later Susan told me it was good I didn't. "It was fucked up," she said. "Not him." I occupied time making a cassette tape with Black Flag on one side and Social Distortion on the other. Susan said he would like that. She slipped it into the coffin.

That evening, Sally and I went to the office so that I could send an email with all the funeral information. I stood staring into his cubicle. Everything frozen in a moment waiting for him to return. Open notebooks, stacks of papers, systems manuals, and probably most haunting, his white board with notes to himself and much rubbed-out designs for network changes. He could have just walked away to get coffee. I asked Sally to take a walk while I composed the email. Then I heard noises just over the wall in John's cube. Susan was there, looking for his address book. I felt a sense of relief that she, not one of us, had broken the frozen time of John's cube. It was selfish, but my little team would have enough to handle to take it apart without being the first to disturb it.

My journal is full of long sections where I worked on the eulogy. I mowed the yard and practiced it in my head. So many of the raw notes are exactly as I ended up giving it. Somehow, I made it into the office for a half-day. Grief zombies, there we sat. Folks came by. Others, the bullies and grotesque new management team, made no effort whatsoever. I was fine with that. Fuck 'em.

I wasn't sleeping. I kept replaying times with John in my head. I was so angry that he didn't have a chance to fight. It was like a robber had creeped in during the night and stolen his life. Sleep deprived; I woke up late on the morning of 9/11/01. Still in bed, I turned on the clock radio and heard some confusing news about people running away from the White House. I turned on the television and saw replays of the jets hitting the towers. I had used up my shock a few days before and my grief already surrounded me like an impermeable fog. I still can't separate the two events in my mind. In some ways, it was a relief to have something to watch on television hour after hour. A national tragedy as a distraction. Sickening. I simply couldn't summon any emotion about the events of that day. I had a eulogy to finish and my friend's funeral to attend. I was a pall bearer. I had to summon the courage to overcome my mental illness and make the day all about my best friend.

Eventually, seeking some sort of energy from outside of myself, I sat down and listened to a cassette my parents gave me after my grandfather's death. Someone had recorded him giving a sermon at his Trinity Baptist Church. The story was that there were warring factions in the church. No politics like church politics. He was a deacon and took the pulpit to preach on reconciliation. I had seen him in the pulpit. His voice could rumble, and hints of his southern accent jumped to the fore. Uncharacteristically, he seemed nervous at the start of the tape but once rolling brought the word of God to life. He was scolding with verses from the New Testament, then offering a soft place to land from the same chapters. I felt filled with the power of my grandpa. I was ready for the next day.

September 12 was warm with a bright blue sky. With all air traffic grounded, the sky was empty, something none of us had ever seen. The service was in a small Catholic church. Outside, I met the other five pall bearers. They were old friends of John's from his childhood. I couldn't remember their names, but I had met them all at John's 40th birthday just months before. I had doubled up on my Ativan. I had also sent Sally out to get those little 6-ounce water bottles. I had one in each coat pocket and the rest in a cooler in the car.

Sally, wisely, had made me a ham sandwich and put it in the cooler, too. She knew she would have to prompt me to eat.

The funeral director was more like a master sergeant giving us orders. He knew his business and that we were just six lost boys. He pinned a white rose on each of our lapels and lined us up at the back of the hearse. We pulled out the coffin and put it on a cart that we rolled into the church as a priest swung an incense orb in front of us. This was all foreign territory for me. Because I could never travel, this was my first funeral. I kept looking at the coffin thinking, *what the fuck is John doing in there?*

The rituals were strange. I shifted and sweat in my seat. I snuck drinks of water. We were seated in the front row, so there was no place to hide. It felt to me that the priests and other celebrants were only there to make sure they got their hands on John's soul. They didn't know him. The endless mass pissed me off. I was shocked when they said it was time for communion and most people lined up to share germs from a goblet and eat wafers. I used the commotion to sneak to the back of the church to the restroom. I urinated, washed my face, took a long drink of water, and looked at my two sheets of paper. As the last people drank and ate, I slipped back in my seat. One of John's buddies gave me a pat on my leg.

The priest read eulogies from John's mom and his utterly crazy and exploitive sister. He then asked if anyone else would like to speak. No one moved. I thought I would be one of many. As I stood, I realized I *was* the eulogist. I was now riding a wave of love for my friend. I looked out from the pulpit, thought of my grandfather, and in a nervous voice began to read.

Late last Thursday, I went over to the Data Center to check in with John. The two of us adjourned to the lab. For those who have never seen our network lab, think of those old submarine movies. Our lab is pretty much like the inside of a U-boat, with fiber optics and only slightly better lighting.

People laughed. Not loudly but just enough relief came into the room that for a second the grief bubble was punctured. Then something truly surreal happened. Portland is home to the Air Force fighter wing that protects the entire northern west coast. Pairs of F14 fighters had been flying Combat Air Patrol over the city since the attack on 9/11. From a distance the sound of those fighters got closer, then roared right over the church, rattling the windows. I shook my head and thought John would have loved that.

In just over an hour we covered at least 20 topics. We started with John's current theory on the location of two secret helicopter gunships somewhere in Clackamas County. I countered with a review of his projects for the next week. And knowing that I, too, am an aficionado of Korean owned mini-marts, John told me how the tacky little glass vials that held fake roses, the ones always near the counter, were actually crack pipes and he had finally badgered a clerk into admitting it.

More laughs, especially from the people who knew John. *Okay*, I thought, *I am actually doing this*. But

I was also beginning to fade. The adrenaline was wearing off and the emotion was squeezing my voice. I only saw John's coffin in front of me.

I got lucky. 16 years ago, I saw a guy at an insurance company with purple spiked hair and said to myself, 'Now we're getting somewhere.'

If fate smiles on us, we will meet just a couple of John Allens in a lifetime. You will know them mostly by your essential discomfort. That is our problem, not theirs. Our challenge is to love the curious, the silly, the innocent, and the extreme. If you open your mind and your heart, you, too, can glimpse the world as an endless array of possibilities. And if you can let go of your anchors for long enough, you will once again hear John.

See ya later, Dude.

I started to break down as I finished, but I had done it. I had honored my friend. I caught Sally's eyes. She was in tears. My comrades with the white roses and I were called forward to take the coffin back out to the hearse for the drive to the cemetery. People walked up to me for hugs and handshakes. They said I had really captured John. But the one comment that meant the most was from John's childhood friend, "You seem so much like John. I can see why you were friends."

Now, I was once again the panic disorder guy. Sally got into the car and handed me a water and the sandwich. I suddenly realized that I couldn't just drive to the cemetery on my own. I had to join a caravan. The cemetery was miles away. Strange how the nervous mind works. I had just done the hardest thing in my life but was ramping up with panic at driving in a group I could not escape.

At the cemetery, my new crew lined up at the back of the hearse. John was to be buried at a beautiful site at the top of a ridge under a big tree. But the six of us were looking at each other because we realized we had to carry that ornate monster of a coffin with John up that hill. We struggled through the grave yard, stepping on grave markers to keep going on a straight line. The thing about shared weight is you don't want to let your crew down so you keep all the tension in your arms you can. We were all breathing hard and sweating. It was brutal. About 15 yards from where everyone was gathered, I looked around and saw we were all fading. Then I said out loud so we all could hear, "Damn it, I told John to lay off the pasta!" Everyone laughed, a laugh that got us to the top of the hill. I'm sure people standing above us were confused but in that moment, it was just what we needed. We smiled at each other after we placed John over the grave. The drill sergeant took off our roses and laid them on the coffin. We had done it.

Afterwards, everyone went to The Lotus Card Room for a wake. It was where we always celebrated big events. I don't remember much about the toasts and long table of people. I was done. I had done my friend proud. I walked away. Sally took me home for a long sleep.

A couple of days later, Sally and I went to John and Susan's house. Good lord, John had accumulated so much stuff. His inner sanctum, a room I had never seen, was long and skinny, about three bowling lanes wide. At one end was a cache of computers, samples of every computer we had used: Macintosh, PC, AT&T 3B2 with a console, a Sun Microsystems workstation. All were networked together. And on the wall, book shelves full of generations of technical manuals. This was where John spent his time at home, in a museum to his entire career, a time capsule.

Then there were boxes and boxes of carefully catalogued comic books in rows on the floor. Susan took us to the guitar section of the room, offered a box of guitar effects switches and said she had no idea what they did, that I should take what I want. She then walked me over to his guitars. "Go ahead, open that big blue case."

Carefully packed inside the custom Anvil case was his most prized pink Gibson Flying V.

Susan walked closer and said, "He would want you to have his guitar." I teared up and picked it up. The fret board was stained with the oil from his fingers.

Over the next few weeks, I was often over at Susan's place, helping her slowly dismantle John's stuff. On one of the visits, Susan picked up a small hinged box.

"I found this hidden away in the back of a closet. John was really funny about this box. He called it his treasure box."

From the box she pulled out the gold money clip engraved with DUDE I had given him as my best man.

"He was so proud of this that he couldn't use it. He hid it away so he would never lose it. You should take it now."

I said, "This is something I never wanted back."

She then pulled out one more thing for me. When I went to my first major league game in Seattle, I brought back goofy souvenirs for my team. I gave John a silver plastic Mariners bat that was a pen. Long and odd, it would hang out of his pocket. One day he lost it and went berserk tearing the lab apart to find it. I guess he finally decided that it, too, was too precious to use, and it ended up with his treasures. You never knew what would touch a guy with a heart that big. The baseball pen still sits on my desk.

It took the three of us weeks to take apart John's cubicle. I took all of his notebooks home with me and a couple of albums — Poison Idea and the New York Dolls. When we were done, no one had the heart to erase his whiteboard. I came in at night, took a picture of it, then erased it so it was done before my team came in the next day.

Susan brought by his lanyard and ID and his cell phone. The lanyard smelled of his aftershave. I turned on the phone and a text message said, "This device will self-destruct … NOW!" I spent the day turning it on for people so we could laugh together. A couple of weeks later, I finally had the courage to listen to his voicemail greeting one more time, then hit the delete button.

Sally called to check-in on Susan who oddly

asked if Sally had any plans to drive to Ashland to see her sister. Sally said not for a while.

Susan explained, "John liked it when Jim put him on call for your trips out of town. He was so happy that someone trusted him."

Years before his death, John and I went to see the Wim Wenders' German film *Wings of Desire*. From that night on we made endless references to that movie. The film is set in West Berlin where invisible angels are everywhere watching the mortals, some longing for mortality. That night John told me he believed in angels.

He said, "They're right there at the edge of your peripheral vision. You just can't turn your head fast enough to see them."

Looking back, I think John was telling me how to find him when I needed him. Every time I'm at a rock show, the driving bass notes slamming the air in my chest, I look up to the rafters and try to move my head fast enough to see him. He is there somewhere.

Chapter 29

Getting Back

2001 WASN'T THROUGH WITH US YET. When my dad called me with bad news, he always asked me to sit down. My Grandfather Blackwood would say, "Get something against your back."

My Aunt Joy, the youngest of my dad's siblings, had taken Uncle Phil's work van and driven to a place with a view of the ocean at Pebble Beach. She shot herself. She was 60. Somewhere during my own troubled time, I had heard she was having problems with anxiety and depression. The parallels shook me. It's in the genes. Sally, wisely, told me to imagine what it must have been like for her to have mental illness suddenly appear at fifty-eight.

I know it's ego, but I wondered if I could have done something. After Dad's heart attack, he recovered physically, but as is often the case, he began to have anxiety symptoms, panic attacks, and hints of avoidance. He didn't understand it. I immediately knew what it was and sent him a book I had called *Don't Panic*. My life experience meant that I was able to recognize his problem and quickly intervene. He recovered completely. My illness had yielded something helpful. I wonder if I had been feeling better, if I might have been able to help Aunt Joy. I'll never know.

And then ... Julie. I mostly remembered my second cousin as a cute blond little girl I saw at family occasions. She was still a kid when I left the desert. I didn't know the specifics. I was told she suffered from depression, turned to drugs for relief for years, and was found dead days after she had overdosed. Suicide. The line between flourishing and falling in a life with a mental illness is stark. I had to look no farther than my own family to know that.

Having seen me in the worst of it, my parents came to visit us for Christmas. It had been many years since I had shared Christmas with members of my side of the family. Sally's family is local. Arriving home after my last day of work before the holiday, Mom greeted me in the kitchen. With my briefcase still in my hand she stopped me and held my face in her hands. She looked deeply into my eyes.

"That's what I wanted to see. You are back. That's all I really wanted for Christmas."

I teared up a little and agreed but I knew I wasn't completely back just yet.

~

The work with The Gnome intensified. Using

my stories from childhood and the present-day experience of bullying at work, The Gnome watched my body movements as I told the stories. She was looking for what my body wanted to do. This type of therapy was so against my highly intellectual nature. So not me. But I was slowly letting go of that part of myself to heal. I had chosen the right person. My trust was complete.

I can't emphasize enough how important this is for anyone suffering from a mental illness. The connection to your therapist and their methods has to be total, otherwise you will hold back at the precise moment healing requires you to let go. The science of healing trauma actually shows that your brain is creating new pathways. My throw-everything-at-the-problem approach was working on several levels. Two years into my meditation practice and SE work, my resting heart rate was lower. I was actually rewiring my brain.

Sally and I were pushing my territorial boundaries. To be back, I needed to break the safety bubble. And Sally desperately needed to get away to recharge herself. The toll on the people close to you when you are consumed by a battle with a mental illness is deep. We took a day trip down the Columbia River to Astoria. On the way home we stopped to get eggs and bread. By the front door of the store was a young man in a heavy coat and watch cap. Between his legs were two puppies. Like any dog person, I reached down to pet the pups. In a low voice he said, "Do you want one?"

His stories didn't connect. But one thing was clear, he was getting rid of the little Aussie puppies that night. Sally and I talked to him about the Humane Society, but he was leaving ... no time. We took our groceries to the car and talked. I loved Luna but really missed my flying dog Ziggy. An Aussie could fly.

I went back to the young man and said okay. Both puppies were female; one was active, the other afraid and hiding between his legs. I knew fear so I pointed at the grey and white one he called Baby. We were now a family of four with a cautious puppy I renamed to Bodhi. Of course, I did.

On the last day of March, I was welcoming spring, scraping winter off the patio and gardens. Our patio has two small sunken places for the basement windows. As I was scooping leaves from one of the sinks, I saw something shiny a couple of inches from the open water drain hole. I froze and stared at my missing wedding ring. Somehow, though I had regularly washed the patio down the previous summer, my ring had been hiding there for 14 months. I would never have created such a trite and improbable metaphor for the beginning and end of hard times.

When Sally came home, I met her in the driveway and held the ring aloft for her to see. She screamed and broke into a dance. We held each other. She said, "Is the bad part really over?" I pulled my substitute ring from my finger and she put my ring, our ring, back where it belonged.

Then a breakthrough. After months working

with The Gnome, I found a partial answer to what happened to that eight-year-old little Jimmy my folks found pounding his head against the bathroom wall. My PTSD orbits a lifetime of bullying but the earliest one I discovered with The Gnome would frighten anyone. Across the street from our pink house on Adobe Road lived two older boys. They built a plywood box that all the kids used as a car or a small house or whatever our imagination could conjure. What it conjured for them was a prison. In the summer desert heat, they had sealed me in that dark box. My recovered memory was of them laughing outside and pounding on the box. Not unlike what the CIA did to break prisoners at black sites after 9/11, in my eighth year, I experienced torture. I had written that fear deep into my brain and body. Now, at last, I could begin the work to release it.

Like an alcoholic who has to hit bottom to recover, I guess my mind needed to finally run out of psychic work-arounds to begin to fully discover and work with the PTSD. Years before the box incident, I was the little kid who balked at going to kindergarten, the nervous child. My child's mind, my genetic inheritance, was already fertile ground for such a traumatic event. Maybe how long it took for this to emerge is actually a tribute to how hard I always worked to hold the darkness in check. I like to believe that is its own kind of strength.

~

Work offered another chance to see just how

back I was. My little team was at the core of a completely new design of the company's networks. The plan was immensely complex. We prototyped and tested for months. Over a two-day change I had the authority to judge several go/no-go points I had put into the plan and to do what everyone dreaded: 'call a back-out.' Kind of a big deal for a guy who the current bosses wanted to fire. On the second day of the changes, we got hung up for two hours on a tricky problem. I let the clock roll to the very end of our time window. I believed my team and they nailed it. Professionally, this was simply as good as it could ever get. When you have a crack-up, doubt sticks to your psyche like English Ivy. Driving home that night I knew I that as far as work was concerned, I was back.

Soon after the success of the project, management gathered us in a room to celebrate. My new boss gave a nice, pointless speech. Because she didn't even know the names of the team members, she asked me to hand out the bonus checks. I handed checks to several of the guys who had undermined and bullied me. Then my friend, the lead architect, came in the room with a little flag that was handed from employee to employee, a peer reward for excellence. As he talked about the recipient, I kept scanning the room to figure out who was getting the award. Then I realized it was me.

~

In September, I wanted all of our family together for my folks' 50th anniversary but I still hadn't figured out a way to get on a jet. So instead, Sally and I decided our gift to everyone was renting a huge house on the side of Mt. Hood for three days so we could all be together. Sally had collected information about my parents' lives. She sent them a questionnaire and assembled over 100 pictures of them and our family. She turned it all into hand-crafted memory books, a picture collage, and even made cards for a trivia game about their lives. My wife plays the craft game at a very high level. Me ... I was going to film it all on my new digital camera, then make a movie of the three days that I would give to each family member.

Everyone gathered at our home. When Mike walked into the kitchen, Mom squealed and yelled, "My boys!" Mike and I both hugged her at the same time. I have never seen her so happy. It is hard for people with a 'normal' family life to understand how badly my not being able to travel distorted the bonds in our family. It had been years since Mom's two boys had been in the same room with her.

Once up on the mountain, we hung out, ate too much, and enjoyed each other. We had a grand family dinner where Dad and Mom made heartfelt speeches. I kept my camera on a tripod running the whole time. (Another admission; the way I overcame my natural tendency to disappear was to create a job.) When I got nervous and wanted to slip away, I moved behind the camera, making myself less of a participant and more of an observer. Sally told me once that I was more comfortable with strangers than family and friends.

Maybe so, but this was one time I found a way to be present.

Sally's memory book had quotes she had gotten from my parents; one in particular my mother called her greatest lesson in life, her credo.

Today is today, yesterday is gone.

There is no time to hate.

Hardly enough time to love.

She told Sally a young man had once told her that. Sally assumed it was my father. But when everyone was off playing cards and watching movies, Mom came to me and asked if I knew who had given her that credo.

I said, "Dad."

"No," she said, "it was you, that night I had the gun in my hand and Dad called you in DC."

What I did not know was that she had taken what I said and used it as her way to work through the pain Dad had caused. What I told her to write down had become a guide for the rest of her life.

After everyone had gone home, Sally and I were still at a painful crossroads. At 38, having never wanted children because of her beliefs about the environment and our planet, Sally confronted what some women do. She realized she would never be a mom. Her commitments in her youth had caught up to her. She spent so much of her professional and personal life caring for others but never as a mother. Eight years older than Sally, I had long ago moved on from the idea of being a father. I tried to be compassionate, as she had been so many times for me. I felt inadequate to the task and could only be with her in her grief.

While the immediacy of the pain has receded, there is still a hole in her life she will never be able to fill. It's a loss we will never completely share.

Somewhere in the midst of all our trips, I bought a little statue of the Hotai, the traveling happy Buddha. The fat little guy has a smile and a bag tossed over his back. I tucked it into the glove compartment of my car. One day, looking at the statue, almost out of the blue, I told Sally, "I want to get on a jet and go somewhere."

Hands sweaty on my computer keyboard, 23 years since I had last been on a plane, I bought round trip tickets for two to Seattle. If I was going to be back, I needed to be all the way back.

Chapter 30

It's Okay to Close the Door

POST-TRAUMATIC STRESS DISORDER with panic disorder and generalized anxiety disorder. That's the full diagnosis. Unlike a broken arm, which heals with time, my illness became a lifestyle with a hierarchy of fears. I had actually written down my fear hierarchy early in my treatment with Gets It. At the top: flying. The sad irony of choosing to live 1,000 miles from my family is that I had no idea I wouldn't be able fly home any time. Now I was ready to put a check mark at the top of my fear list.

The one thing that ultimately got me on a plane was love. It was Sally. She had ridden out the worst and shared the joys. Her life was altered by my illness but she chose to stay.

I had 23 years to plan my return to the air. I needed the experience of both leaving and returning in the same day. Alaska Air has a constant loop of turboprop planes flying between Portland and Seattle.

After not flying for so long, some might think it crazy that my first flight would be on a 36-seat turboprop plane. That's the thing about my flying, it was always about the process, the letting go of control of my ability to come and go when I pleased. It was about them closing that damn door.

Through security, heart pounding, I had filled my little back pack with mixed nuts, power bars, a ham sandwich, a magazine, my copy of the Barlow workbook, my copy of *Don't Panic*, my medications, Buddha statue, and a bottle of water. Always ... always ... the killer for me is the anticipatory anxiety, the demons my busy mind summons to chase me away from any forward motion. In the waiting area, I could not sit down. I paced and made one trip after another to the restroom to pee, to not pee, to sit in the stall and practice mindful meditation, and most importantly, remind myself that I had already decided how this day would go. Decide, plan, and act.

There was also another reason I needed to fly. For my entire life, I had lived in fear of 'The Call,' that inescapable emergency with my family that meant I had no choice but to get on a plane. I had disappointed them so many times and bathed in the cold bath of regret enough. I needed to fly on my terms, so I could be there with them when it was essential. I needed not to flinch every time the phone rang and I saw it was a call from my folks.

My plan then was, and still is, to be the last one on the plane. The shorter amount of time I have to sit staring at the open door, the better. This habit still drives Sally absolutely mad. I have boarded only after the last call of my name.

We walked hand in hand out into the cold air and up the portable ramp. Our seats were in the front. Yeah, I had picked ones close to the door. The plane was tiny and not completely full. I pulled my little traveling Buddha from my pocket and held it in my hand. I busied my mind looking into the open cockpit door, out the window at the propellers, fiddling with the air vents, both of which I aimed at my face.

"You can do this," Sally said for the last of many times that morning.

And then the door was closed and the engines fired up. I was okay, not thrilled, but okay. I never had the urge to bolt for the door. I was ready to fly.

The plane taxied out. I paid no attention to the safety lecture. First in the line-up now, then up … up. I was flying again. The little plane banked and buffeted to altitude. I was kind of glad. It was the full experience of flight, not the mitigated, smooth sameness of a larger jet. I gave Sally a hug and put the Buddha in my shirt pocket. Only 30 minutes in the air. I took a drink from my water bottle and looked at the volcanoes of the Cascade Range out the window. Then we were down.

At Seattle's airport, SeaTac, I felt strangely normal, like this was something I did all the time. Sally's smile was a direct pipeline to joy. We held each other, then roamed about. Not much to see. Ha, our return flight would be delayed. Good, I thought, experience it all. I had set up a web camera that looked down on our dogs in the basement at home. The LunaCam was something I shared with friends. After figuring out how to connect a Microsoft PDA (remember those) to the airport network, we checked in on Bodhi and Luna; the Girls, as we called them, were sleeping.

Before we left, I bought two of the tackiest SeaTac souvenirs I could find: Space Needle snow globes. I would mail them to both The Gnome and Gets It. Gets It still has my globe in a honored place in her office. Only now, it is joined with a collection of other tacky airport globes and gifts. I started a thing. I like that. My people, we know how to celebrate the big ones.

On the flight home, on a larger turbo prop plane, I was a commuter dude and enjoyed the free IPA beer in a can, a thousand monkeys off my back. Back on the ground, in the car, I broke down, exhausted and happy, tears of joy and freedom. Having said nothing of this attempt to fly to my family, lest I risk disappointing them again, I called my folks.

~

I changed my appointments with The Gnome to once a month; still work to do, but now at a calmer pace. I was studying American history and the Constitution at night for fun, went to lots of live music shows, and two different baseball games in Seattle. We took the girls to the mountains and coast. On a cold 4th of July, my folks visited, and we blew up a mound of illegal fireworks in front of the house. I love blowing things up. Mom sat wrapped in my big winter coat on our front lawn clapping at the explosions.

At work, my team expanded back up to eight senior staff. Work was relatively easy but dull. I was done, thinking constantly about an exit, but my health insurance covered Sally, too, as she was then in private practice, so there were practical considerations. I wanted a different job. I had adapted a lucrative job to my innate skills and made it work with my illness for more than 20 years. It had bought us a home and a good life, but I still wanted to do something new, something I had actually chosen.

~

In October, I got one of those calls. My brother, Mike, had had a heart attack at 44. He had survived the 'widow maker.' My brother, the deputy sheriff, was an adrenaline junkie. He smoked, ate like a teenager, and went on almost no sleep for days. His real fun was sneaking up on Mexican gang meth labs or hopping out of helicopters to take down giant marijuana farms. He had come home off of three days doing just that — living on coffee, donuts, and no sleep —and had heart attack symptoms in his back yard. His second wife was a nurse, so he immediately got lifesaving care. When my doctor heard the story, he handed me a prescription for a statin to lower cholesterol and said to take a baby aspirin daily.

I began to check out local master's degree

programs. Sally had an MA. Almost all of my friends from college were lawyers, MBAs, or had other graduate degrees. When I thought about it, there was something strange about my not having done graduate work. I was a perpetual student. I tackled challenging subjects for fun. Lord only knows how many times I rushed down the stairs excited to tell Sally about some new discovery. Truly, to be patient enough to stand smiling while being bombarded by an obscure academic tangent, the woman is a saint. Finally, I ran across a program at a small school, Marylhurst University, that offered a Master of Arts in Interdisciplinary Studies (MAIS). A liberal arts MA where I could finally have peers to kick my recluse little academic ass? I was excited.

For my 47th birthday, I got my first carry-on luggage. It was time to fly home for Christmas. I hadn't been down to Southern California since 1985 when I drove down with Peg. This wouldn't be a test flight. We would be spending time in my parents' new home in Hemet and then Sally and I would drive down to visit my brother and family in Indio. There was other family in the desert I wanted to see — my Great Uncle Jake, Aunt Jo and Uncle Dick — but as I made plans, I realized there was no way to make up for missing a couple of decades. Mostly, I wanted Sally to finally see the desert she had heard so much about.

We flew into Ontario. Seems strange to have it all that happen in just four words. I duplicated what had worked before. My head was on a swivel during the flight as I welcomed a bourbon on the rocks to join my usual tranquilizer. I was reminded that many people need a little chemical help to fly so I stopped kicking myself about that. Ontario is a relatively small airport. My parents were standing at the bottom of the escalator. I hugged them both. Mom had tears in her eyes. I was having a hard time blending the mundane and miraculous, so I stayed mostly within myself. We talked traffic and trivialities on the hour trip to Hemet.

My folks went all in for Christmas. Mom baked for days, special spice cakes I loved and that she gave away to all the neighbors. I had received holiday care packages from Mom for years; now I was eating her spice cake and ice cream in her kitchen. I was restless and needed to take a walk, get my legs under me, breathe the air, and realize where I was. As I went out the door, my dad said, "Uh, with that black leather jacket, you best be careful and don't get shot." Yeah, there it was, fear all around. They lived in an achingly neat over-55 community with all the amenities. The motion detector front lights on the houses all flicked on to mark my path in the night. "Very good neighborhood," Dad said. "Secure." I stood on the sidewalk, staring at the stars and soaking in what I had just accomplished.

The next day, we got to meet *all* my parents' friends. It was then that I realized I was a bit of a mystery. It hadn't occurred to me how all these years my parents had explained their missing oldest son. There were pictures of me and Sally all over the walls. Baby and childhood pictures of Mike and me. Every time Dad introduced me the same way, "This is my oldest son, the one from Portland. He and his wife flew down to see us." There was pride in the way he made each introduction.

After everyone was asleep and the house was quiet, I pulled out my little traveling Buddha and a small candle. Sitting on pillows from the couch, I meditated at my makeshift coffee table shrine.

Dad loaned Sally and me his Volkswagen Bug and we drove to the desert. I was on home turf I hadn't seen for a very long time. I took Sally to the house where I grew up and the remnants of downtown Indio where they were having a yummy Tamale Festival. We found my grandparents' former home. To my horror, my beautiful giant white sand dune desert had all but disappeared, covered by over 100 golf courses. In order to show Sally what *my* desert had looked like, I had to take her to a "desert preserve." Growing up, probably the only thing I really loved about the desert was the actual desert and now that was gone.

We stayed at my brother's house. Based on our fundamental differences, my brother and I have an eternal tension. My journals are full of the same note: *Mike didn't call.* Throughout our lives, I'm the one who has to initiate contact. It's like he doesn't have a thought about me when I'm not around. But when I do make contact, we can talk for an hour like we saw each other yesterday. The dynamic has never made sense to me.

Talking between the two of us that night, he said, "People were betting you wouldn't come." I get it. I really do. But something about that statement means he didn't get it, the long desperate work I had undertaken to be there with them. This is a constant dynamic for people who suffer from mental illness. At some point, we just want to be understood, the manifestations of our illness somehow forgiven, or even embraced. He had no idea how much it would have meant if he had said, "I knew you could do it."

I needed to visit my grandparents' graves. At the cemetery, Mike had to find the markers. I asked to be alone. At my grandfather's marker, I thanked him for our little house. At my Grandma Pearl's marker, I broke down and said I was sorry for not coming to see her. I thanked her for praying for me. I then bowed to the graves, making gasho. It all felt a little hollow as the truth was stark. I was too late.

As I was falling into regret and grief, a van pulled up next to a huge Mexican family who had been visiting their dead. Not in a sad way. They were eating and talking, and the kids were running among the stones. Out of the van popped a full Mariachi band. I love Mariachi music. They played songs happy and sad. It was wonderful. Sally had never seen such a thing. "Pretty cool, huh?" I said. "That is just what I needed."

We flew in a week early as the idea of the heavy crush of travelers seemed a little bit much for my first flight home, so everyone came to the folks' house for an early Christmas. This day was about Mom. She got the Christmas she had always been dreaming about.

Her entire family, food, gifts, her Dickens village all lit up … this is what I wanted to give my parents for Christmas.

In the new year, I went to an introductory meeting for the graduate program. In order not to be so nervous, I had taken several trips out to the school, which was about 12 miles up the Willamette River. I tried different times of day, including rush hour, when I would have to go out for classes. I played tag with the school until I could lower my anticipatory anxiety.

I made a commitment to take the program's introductory class before I signed up for the full program. I was excited. More importantly, I let myself feel the excitement.

Chapter 31

It Feels Like Home

IT HAD BEEN 27 YEARS since I walked into a university classroom. The line between excitement and anxiety was invisible. I got to the campus early and took my little white half Ativan. I hid out in a bathroom stall going through the same routine that got me on jets, and like the jets, I got to the room just in time to begin my graduate school career.

The Master of Interdisciplinary Studies (MAIS) program had been designed by Dr. Debrah Bokowski to get every participant to the MA finish line. A practical political scientist from the Midwest, she had seen too many people put in years of work and not get the hood and diploma. She screened all the applicants for success. We were all older, thirsty for the experience, and blowing up a big part of our established lives to be in the program. There were no slackers. That alone made the experience remarkable. The program was designed for two classes a term but like everyone else who had real-world jobs, I was doing it year-around, one class at a time for three-and-a-half years.

The first class was a compressed version of everything one had to do to succeed in graduate school. We could choose our research topics. Sitting alone in my reading chair at home, I had spent years studying the separation between church and state. I would walk around wondering how Thomas Jefferson, the Deist, could have put those references to God in the Declaration of Independence. Seriously, I thought about this stuff all the time. Now, I set out to answer my question.

With my big dog, Bodhi, sleeping at my feet, I dug into stacks of books on the Declaration of Independence. I found one that had reproduced an actual size copy of the rough draft of the document. Soon, I could easily read Jefferson's original hand and the writing of his editors, like Benjamin Franklin. Everything about the work was thrilling. I got an A on my first graduate school paper.

There was a new flame burning inside me. I hated my job and had to get out. I was a different person in so many ways. I had cut my visits to The Gnome back again. When I told her I was worried I wasn't journaling as much she smiled and said that was actually a good thing.

After the introductory class, I wrote an official application to the program. In an act of excited overkill, I wrote an introduction letter twice as long as needed. I met with Dr. Bokowski. She had copy of my first paper. *Strange*, I thought. She said I should submit my paper to an academic journal. I don't think I understood what she was saying and had no idea how to do what she had suggested. I mean, here I was, this almost 50-year-old guy doing this academic work mostly for fun. To have someone think I was good at this based on the first paper was crazy talk. When I got home that night I wrote in my journal:

I feel like I'm home at last. It took so long and though I have always believed I'd get here, down in the core of my being was a black doubt that I would not.

At work, I tried hard to apply my new Buddhist principles. Some days I succeeded, breaking the attachments and staying in the moment. But I'm a barely recovered perfectionist, drilled with a familial obligation to give my all to what I do for a living. Those cross currents constantly buffeted me.

I began my next class and ran headlong into David Denny, a PhD in post-modern philosophy. Every concept was new. I was a nervous wreck getting to school for that class and fought to settle down. I think one of the strangest things about my illness is that I remain most anxious, shifting in my chair, tapping my feet, and fighting for control until I can say something. It was true at work, and especially in these new classes. My anxiety mounts and mounts until I engage. Once I could argue with David, I was in the moment, calm and happy.

Every class was about my Zen beginner's mind.

I was a blank slate eager to learn. Baffled by the philosophical material, my first paper was a hot mess. I got a C+. I panicked and talked to David. He only said, "Talk to your colleagues. Jan is a good writer." This is how I met my first new friend in the program. She generously emailed me two of her papers. Oh man, she *was* good. I studied them to understand the form and approach. My entire life, if I can see a writing style, I can mimic it. Once, early in my corporate career, an assistant vice-president asked me to write a memo to the company. I asked, "What style do you need it in?"

She stopped, cocked her head and said, "You have more than one style?" It hadn't occurred to me that that was odd.

I had to tackle the French icon of post-modernism, Michael Foucault. Bodhi and I locked ourselves away in my room. The night David returned our papers, I was bouncing off the walls. This seemed like make or break to me. Could I do this work? I had taken a chance on a quirky approach comparing a floor of office cubicles to a prison in lock-down. David offered little critiques as he handed each person his or her paper. His criticism was biting and he had saved my paper for last. All I could think was, *I am so fucked.*

Holding my paper, he looked at me and said, "This paper has a take on Foucault's 'On Discipline' I have never seen. I want to do something different. I think everyone would benefit from hearing this paper. Jim, would you please read your paper to the class."

I thought my heart, pounding in my chest, was

going to explode. Public speaking was the part I dreaded the most. I have trouble reading aloud. I'm a fast reader and inevitably my eyes get ahead of my mouth. I had no choice. Stumbling at times, I read my paper. At the end, the professor led the applause. I was embarrassed and proud at the same time. On the last page, I looked at the grade: A+. David wrote, "If you increase the length a little this paper is publishable." What in the world was happening?

My freaky discipline took hold. I only allowed myself breaks one night a week and half-day on the weekends. I loved the work and it didn't feel to me like I was sacrificing anything. One Thanksgiving when I was researching my thesis, having fed the family, I got up, thanked everyone and disappeared into my office. It got so predicable than on my one night off my dog Bo would stand in the doorway to my office staring at me because it was time to go to work. For Sally, even knowing what it meant to me, the separation wasn't easy. She began to call my nightly migration to my office, 'going behind the door.'

My breaks between terms were actual breaks. We flew to California again for Christmas. At the dinner table with my entire family, I mostly stayed quiet. There's a thing about my family. They almost never ask me what is going on in my life. Not work, and now, especially not graduate school. I would offer that I loved it and the conversation ended there.

On that visit, Sally and I went to the desert to see my Uncle Dick and Aunt Jo, my dad's older sister, who had been an actual beatnik. Acerbic, funny, and an intellectual, her second husband, Dick, was a deeply intellectual Hindu/Buddhist truck driver. I had not seen Jo since my brother's wedding. Their joy at having Jimmy and his new wife in their home was overwhelming. She had health issues but held court, vodka in hand. Dick showed me his lovely garden full of brightly painted Buddha and Shiva statues. As we parted, he slipped a Buddhist book into my hands. I was sad as we drove away. I knew this part of my family, too, had been stolen by my illness. I marveled that I could be loved by people who had not seen me in decades.

At work, I saw my network architect friend, Steven, overwhelmed by stress and falling into a depression. Now, I knew all the signs and was able to get him the immediate help he needed to survive and recover. My brush with the illness gave me new, compassionate eyes. My emerging Buddha nature encouraged me to act.

~

Marylhurst was founded by nuns. I had no idea about PhD nuns until I took a religion class from two small elderly nuns. When the sisters introduced themselves, the most elderly and tiny of the two, Sister Frances, said she had done some work at the university in the past. Her tag team partner, Sister Cecelia said, "Sister is being too modest. She was president of the university for two decades." *What?*

In this class I came up with two ways to address

my fear of public speaking. Yeah, after several classes, it wasn't getting better. For one presentation, I handed out tangerines just so I could move about the room. Quoting the Buddhist monk, Thich Nhat Hanh, I said, "When eating a tangerine, eat a tangerine." And ... *pay no attention to the nervous guy now pacing around the room.* For the second presentation, I made a short film. Just press play. It happened again. The Sisters gave me an A+ and asked me if I had ever considered getting a PhD. I was 50. *Is that a thing?*

As I became more of who I am, I separated from the friends I had made when I moved to Portland. I didn't have time to read the book for the monthly book club, but showed up to say hello and have a beer. I was much more interested in the friendships I was making at school. Purposeful, not accidental.

I took a very difficult class from Debrah. Social justice with a heavy dose of the sometimes-impenetrable John Rawls. Of course, I knew nothing about him. Intellectual ignorance is bliss. At the end of the class, Debrah, whom I now considered my academic mentor, took me aside and said I was her first student to truly understand Rawls and write so clearly about him. She then moved a little closer; the tiny, intimidating woman looked up at me, "You really should get a PhD." I think I said thanks and that I would look into it. Later, I told my colleagues Jan and Kermit what she had said. I was looking for some sign that this was simply crazy talk. Jan said, "Kermit and I have been telling you that for a long time. Don't you believe us?"

I took a serious look at PhD programs. I saw that we would have to move to a university somewhere. Ultimately, I saw that I was 25 years too late. I became sad and angry at the cards I had been dealt. I had been an academic all my life. I know my professors were being honest in their appraisals, but among the things my illness had taken was this path in my life. I had a long list of losses in my life, but until that moment I had not contemplated that I may have missed an entirely different life.

~

I couldn't stay in that place of melancholy. Too much fun to be had. Sally and I went to see the last ever show by one of our favorite bands, Sleater-Kinney. Halfway through the show, the band began huddling between songs. Sally looked up at me, eyes wide, and yelled over the din, "They're off the set list!" Something about Sally's ability to tap into innocent joy and her sudden rock and roll fan savvy sent a cool shiver through me. I yelled back, "I will remember this moment for the rest of my life!" There it was. The great life I have.

We were supposed to fly down for Christmas again that year. I was deep into my thesis research and had been sick for two weeks. At the airport, I didn't have any energy to do my usual tricks. My past disappointments for my family were haunting me. My training as a Blackwood said you push through, no matter what. Finally, Sally sat me down and explained that it was okay.

She said, "Jim, you fly now. Remember? People get sick. It's okay to be sick. There is no reason to be ashamed. Jim, people cancel flights all the time for good reasons. This isn't a setback."

We walked to the garage. I stood looking out at planes taking off and landing for a bit. She was right. I made the call. Three months later, research in hand and feeling well, we flew down to see my folks.

~

I was having too much fun in graduate school to keep up the work charade any longer. I decided to leave after the first of the year in 2007. For my thesis, I had chosen to tackle political polarization and needed big blocks of time to hide out and write. I came up with a way to get paid to write. I negotiated 'writing Fridays.' I would use my vacation time to take every Friday off. I had lots of vacation time. The writing was so damn much fun. Work now had a point. I lived for those three-day weekends.

To present my thesis, I had finally come up with a trick that worked. I wrote my presentations, then stood and gave them to the window shade in front of my home desk. I used a digital recorder so I could time them and listen to how I sounded. I did this over and over until the actual content was more like an out-of-body experience. I heard my voice coming out of my mouth and had to keep my body still enough not to disrupt what I was saying. It worked!

My folks came up for the hooding ceremony. I loved being in the robe and mortarboard. Our hoods were white and Debrah hooded each of us. I was especially happy for my peers. The biggest surprise of the day was that when I walked outside, my brother and his new girlfriend were there. My little brother ... always a bit of a mystery but there when I need him.

I was my usual anxious self for the full school graduation. The ceremony was in a huge theater downtown. As I stood in line next to the stage to get my diploma I looked for my family out in the audience. I found Sally and locked in on her eyes. For a few seconds, we were the only ones in the room. Everything in that moment was because of her love and support. Across the space of that hall, I wanted to her to know that.

Five days after graduation, I quit my job. I gathered my team in a conference room for a staff meeting. I told them how much my time with this current version of my team had meant to me. Some had been there from the old days with John and Bob. When I said the words, "After 24 years, I'm leaving Standard," they actually gasped. It is the single most gratifying gasp I have ever experienced. Everyone ... I mean everyone ... assumed after so much time I would retire from that company. As word filtered out, I came to realize just how many people I had touched. Telling my team had been damn hard, but once I did, a calm settled over me. I didn't allow any of that conference room 'sheet cake' bullshit. We went to the Lotus for beers and shots. This time everyone else paid for my drinks.

I had yet to figure out what I was going to do next. With one more class to take, I wanted to finish my graduate school career with straight A's. Taking a class without working was luxurious.

It was our tenth wedding anniversary. I was a flyer again and we wanted to do something special. We decided to go to the Californian wine country. Flying into Oakland we drove up to a lovely bed and breakfast in Sonoma. Some of the country was an old haunt for me from my days in Santa Rosa. I gave Sally the tour. We headed down the Russian River to sample wines, enjoyed actual fine dining and even saw my old apartment in Santa Rosa. This was the honeymoon we never had.

We drove to San Francisco for the anniversary day. Dinner in a lovely restaurant looking out at the Golden Gate Bridge. I was so happy to give this to my wife. On our last day in the city we went to AT&T Park and saw my Giants. Because of my illness, I had never seen my boys play a home game. But on a warm night, the last home game of the season, and Barry Bonds' last game ever, there we were. It was simply our most perfect vacation ever.

In my journal:

No, Jim, this is not just a vacation. It's the rest of your life.

Chapter 32

Bold Moves and Second Chapters

F. SCOTT FITZGERALD WAS WRONG. There *are* second chapters in American lives.

Beyond the limits imposed by my illness, I'm a ninja level introvert. In order to redefine my work life, I pushed all of my boundaries. The sane people in my life told me that no one my age just drops out of a successful career and heads off into the unknown. I was cognizant of the fact that for a guy whose life was bounded by fear this was both crazy and fearless. But Sally now had a job with good healthcare. As a couple, we were always frugal. There was a healthy cushion in the bank we could stretch. One minor miscalculation, though; the stock market crashed and America fell into the Great Recession. Uh ... nice timing.

From 1980, there was a gaping hole in my professional life. When the panic disorder struck, I was on the cusp of realizing a childhood dream to be that guy on the inside of the political world. I had spent my adult life wondering how I would have done at that job; more importantly, I was sure I would have been good at it. Now, when I described my goal for this life change, I said I wanted to work in politics and public policy. Pretty bold for someone with no professional credentials in either.

I started to network. I wrote an op-ed about the demise of the polling places. *The Oregonian* published it. I joined the Portland City Club, the city's oldest civic engagement club and volunteered for one of their issue research committees. I ambushed people on street corners after events and cold-called City Hall staffers, lobbyists, and executive directors of non-profits. I was doing everything I didn't know how to do long ago in Salem. Who was this version of Jim?

Most importantly, I came up with a pitch, a very good pitch. I had one precious commodity to offer: time. I had heard that my younger competition came to people in power with demands. I decided the best way to differentiate myself was to ask people what they needed with no expectations. My pitch was: 24 for three. I said, "I will give you 24 hours a week, three days a week for free. How can I help you?" Turned out that even if the people I met had nothing, they were amazed at the offer and reached for their address book with suggestions and introductions. I have never sold anything, but it turns out I could sell myself.

At one of those meetings, I was asked, "Do you know Nick Fish? You should meet him." I filed that idea away.

In the networking hopscotch, I cold-called Arnold Cogan. He and his wife, Elaine, ran a boutique planning and public engagement firm. As state planner to legendary Governor Tom McCall, Arnold had championed policy and places that are now seen as quintessentially Oregon. Arnold loved my pitch and my story. He told me his life had been devoted to transformation. I met with the partners. They offered me a volunteer position, joining them at planning meetings.

Arnold was getting ready to write a book about his life in planning. He needed someone to interview him to create the book outline and draft a first chapter. Once a week for two hours, I spent time learning at the knee of one of the great figures in Oregon public policy. He jokingly called our weekly meetings 'the seance.' I am grateful for what Arnold and Elaine did for a complete stranger.

Arnold offered me a little cubicle space at his firm, a downtown base where I could work with him and any other projects. My desk was at one end of a long office occupied by a senior planner. One day, my cell phone rang. I had forgotten to silence it. My ringtone was the Ramones' "I Wanna Be Sedated." I was a little embarrassed. When I finished the call, a small, older man with a big smile tapped me on the shoulder and said, "You are not going to believe this, I have the same ringtone."

On the other side of the cubicle wall, unknown to me, was his chart of the punk rock universe with The

Clash at the center. As he spoke, it hit me, *Oh my god. It's him.* For years, when I went to see live rock shows, I looked around to confirm I was the oldest person in the room. Several times, there was this even older guy in a Mao hat. All I had to do was upend my life to finally meet the Buddhist, baseball fan, aging punk rocker, and my new best friend Bob.

~

At a weekend advocacy training, I looked at the leadership lunch sign-up and saw the name Nick Fish. I still didn't like lunching but ended up sitting next to Nick. He had lost a close campaign for city council a few years before. We hit it off and he took my card. A few weeks later, a sitting city council member resigned. Nick called me and asked if I would like to work on his campaign. I had been scoping out other candidates, but this was the ground floor of a new push. *Absolutely!*

In my journal I wrote a line from a Buddhist text:

The person who wakes up in the morning is different from the one who went to sleep.

The campaign was an insurgency. Driven by a short window to the special election, the team was small. The core team consisted of Nick and three others. I was *the* policy guy. Wherever my laptop was, there was the campaign. I researched issues and wrote with Nick to answer the endless endorsement questionnaires that are the mark of Portland politics.

Nick did his first head-to-head forum with the

other six candidates. I showed up to see how it went. I took many notes and after offered Nick a critique. This was audacious for a complete outsider. But Nick was delighted and asked me to have sushi to go through my notes. Barely able to eat, I went for it and gave him some critical notes. He loved it. From that point on, we wrote all the major speeches together. Between the campaign and my work with Cogan, I was putting in some long days and could not have been happier. Nick called me for advice day and night. By the end of the campaign, he asked me to coordinate the entire show as we really never had a campaign manager. I was doing it, actually doing it.

Nick's first political job had been on Congressman Barney Frank's first campaign and as a DC staffer after Frank won. In the midst of the economic crisis, in an act of remarkable loyalty, the congressman flew out for our fundraiser, as well as a former governor and movie director Gus Van Sant. I brought Sally along for fun. I got to see Barney work a living room for money. Later, he came up to me, offered his hand, and said, "So you are the famous four-in-one guy people tell me about." The story was that in Nick's previous campaign, four people had done the job I now did alone. Star struck and amazed at the political skill to keep that little fact in his head, I have no idea what I said in return. Mostly, I thought, *how is this possible?*

Nothing ends so suddenly as a political campaign. On election night, we demolished our opponent. I got a thank you in Nick's speech. I helped write his swearing-in speech. Everyone told me that now I would be going to City Hall with Nick. That is, everyone but Nick. No mention of a job. Nick thought he had to have experienced insiders on his city hall staff. I was crushed. Yet somehow, Nick compartmentalized what he had done to me and still called for advice.

I kept working with Cogan and delivered his book outline and draft first chapter. I became active in neighborhood issues and did some work creating a non-profit, but now Sally said, "Buddy, you have six more months before you have to call your old IT buddies. Despair is not an option."

Out of the blue, they called me. The economy in shambles, one of my old bosses called about a project leader consulting gig. I hated the job description, but the money was way too good to turn down. The work environment was awful. I kept cashing the checks and actually went out and bought a brand-new Mini Cooper S, my first real geek car since my high school muscle car was totaled. Have I mentioned how great my wife is yet?

I was still meeting with The Gnome and practicing meditation. My confidence was sky high. In a moment of pure craziness, I decided to do some track days with my Mini Cooper at Portland International Raceway. Peeking out from my helmet visor, driving the car at its limits is the most Zen thing I have ever done. If you make a mistake you can destroy your car. No insurance on a race track. A 20-minute session leaves you both adrenalized and exhausted. Afraid of getting on a bus but thrilled to drive my car on a race track. Go figure.

I had been at the IT work for nine miserable months when I had lunch with a friend on Nick's staff. Hannah confirmed that the office was a mess. Left to his own devices, Nick went full speed in nine directions at once. He had a weak chief of staff and no one person on the team could contain him. It was showing.

Getting close to the end of 2008, Nick called again and asked me to meet with his new chief of staff, Betsy. I heard Betsy was a heavyweight. She had worked for a mayor, was a deputy director of a city bureau, and was one of the big four policy wonks in his first campaign. I didn't know her.

I was very nervous waiting for Betsy. I held off ordering a drink. We met outside at the little bar beneath the office tower where I worked. She peddled up on her bike, shook my hand, and hung her helmet from the back of a spindly chair.

"Hi Jim, I'm Betsy," she said. "IPAs?"

The first beer calmed me. I told the already tiresome-to-me tale of why I had abandoned a 24-year career. She told me stories from the first Fish campaign and about her jobs at the city. We both shared an obsessive love for our dogs. That night, Betsy was funny in a curiously restrained way. Her face turned deep red when she shared insider stories. No poker player she. But one beer in we were already a team.

Just two kind of political nerds hanging out.

Finally, empty bottles crowding the table, the fourth round on the way, I was getting a little tipsy. I said, "So ... Betsy ... what are we doing here?"

Her laugh boomed and she turned red again.

"Oh! Oh, I forgot to ask you. Do you want to come to City Hall with me and work for Nick?"

"I was hoping that was what we were doing. Yes."

She offered me a touch over one-third of what I had made in IT. I didn't care. I had done it. Two years and two months from walking away from a different life and career, I was in.

~

Inside the east portico of Portland City Hall is a small brass plaque that simply says City Hall. Never a day passed that I didn't look up at that plaque and smile as I came to work. As a policy director, the work was hard and rewarding. Betsy and I were a team. Both systems thinkers by approach, we became what was the most intimate working partnership of my entire professional career. And most importantly, we had both been on campaigns with Nick and knew how to help focus his energy.

There is no slow start in small political office. I was given liaison to the Parks Bureau, one of the largest and most complex in the city. In the crashing economy our job was to lay people off and preserve as many services as possible. I was doing media, staffing the commissioner, writing speeches and talking points. Every day was long, and the challenges came at high speed. For a person who is easily bored by repetition, the job was perfect.

Nick, son of a congressman, always made a big deal about being a public servant. In the depths of the recession, I got frustrated that my Parks Bureau was all about bad stories. I spent a day driving around looking at the barren parks in the poorest parts of the city. At one, I saw what looked like a grandmother holding hands with a toddler. They came to the empty park, looked around and left. That gave me an idea.

Parks had been used to creating giant master plans for new parks but on a shelf, I had spotted some low-cost improvement projects, projects our demoralized Parks team could do with existing resources. Even in lean times I knew I could get all five council votes to do something for overlooked neighborhoods. All of the worst parks were east of the I-205 freeway.

I called my plan E205. Everything we did had to be east of the freeway. We built children's playgrounds, paths, installed drinking fountains next to resurfaced basketball courts, and fixed broken picnic tables. Near the end of the project I went to the opening of a children's playground at the park where I had seen the grandma and child walk away. I watched kids playing on the new equipment and turned to a long time Parks employee. "Isn't this great?"

He looked at me and smiled. "You know what's

really cool? Twenty years from now you can come back and still see kids playing." It was then I understood that I, too, was now a public servant.

~

In 2010, I was in a crowded meeting and felt this thumping in my chest. It seemed to have a pattern. It concerned me. I obsessively watched my pulse on my phone app. Then, as Sally and I were getting dressed to go to a rock show one evening, I felt the same wave of the pulses. I showed her on my phone app that my heart actually seemed to stop. We diverted to the ER.

Ever want fast service at a hospital? Just say the words, "I think something is wrong with my heart." Whisked into a room, surrounded by nurses and a cardiologist, I was hooked to monitors, blood drawn. They said I had unifocal PVCs and something called Quadrigeminy. Everyone's heart skips beats. It isn't dangerous but my heart's electrical pattern was anomalous and my resting pulse way too high. I had an echocardiogram and other follow-up tests. I never did see that band.

Given the history of heart disease in my family, I was kind of screwed. I was handed a beta blocker to lower my heart rate. Then the kicker … the cardiologist said it was entirely possible that the Elavil I took every night could cause both the fast heart rate and electrical problems. I was told I had to get off that drug. I was now going to be a subjected to psychopharmacological roulette.

In rapid succession, tinkering with my baseline

drugs and the new stress of constantly monitoring my heart tossed grenades in to my life. I was sneaking an Ativan during the day, something I hadn't done for years. And yet, I also did another track day, this time in the rain, even more scary fun. My family wasn't helping my heart obsession. My Great Uncle Jake died of a heart attack. Uncle Jim had a heart attack and my brother had to get three heart stints. *Really?*

I worked with another psychiatric nurse practitioner to replace my trusty Elavil with a new generation drug that didn't affect the heart. The side-effect laden transitions can take months. For almost two years I tried a myriad of drugs. Depending on the change, I felt more anxious, hammered, stoned, had memory loss, balance issues, insomnia, or profusely sweating hands. I kept meticulous records of all the changes in my journals. I was hopeful when we thought we had reached the right combination of medications, only to fall into despair when a new side effect appeared. For a lifetime, I have not trusted my body. Little changes get misinterpreted as 'something is wrong … red alert!' My underlying anxiety was higher and my sleep erratic. Every day I went to work in my high stress, high visibility job. I had to tell Nick and Betsy some version of what was going on. I kept the version they heard simple and far less scary than what I was enduring each day.

But once again, my hillbilly tenacity was coupled with my desire to do something with Sally. We made a trip in the Mini Cooper to Canada. We went to Vancouver, played tourists, and even went to a terrific Arcade Fire show. I wasn't completely engaged all the time. I was worried about the next leg of trip, a ferry ride up to Victoria. Me, my car, and Sally on a boat with no escape. It was a larger version of my fear of the closed jet door. In the line-up waiting for the ferry, I went for a walk. Well, I actually went to the restroom and called The Gnome for a pep talk.

Once on the big ferry, I loved it. I was all over the boat looking at the sea and scenery. Do the thing you fear. It's the anticipation that is the killer. We had great fun in Victoria. I was just curious old me. Our hotel balcony looked out at the bay and Parliament building beyond. Twice a day, I saw the Redball ferry to Port Angeles, Washington come and go. I felt like a veteran when we got on it, and Titanic style, I stood in the bow feeling the cold, salt air and waving to Sally warming inside. It was terrific.

At the end of the year we flew south again for my niece's wedding. The desert in winter is a warm relief from the northwest cold. Mom had clearly lost more ground. No denying it now. Early stage dementia.

~

Nick and I were a good team when on the same page on tough issues. He is naturally a consensus builder and I was more aggressive, looking for a win. Between the two of us we landed in the right place. I was having an effect, a long-term effect, on how the city was run. As a staffer, I got to bring my experience to the table and sometimes move my elected official to a position he had never considered. There is this curious alchemy when the commissioner takes complete ownership and credit for an idea he never would have had. I never stopped marveling at what it was like to hear my words come out of his mouth in front of audiences. And yes, almost every week during the city council meetings, I was that guy leaning in to whisper something in the elected official's ear, just like I always wanted to be.

Our office also managed the Portland Fire Bureau. One day, suffering mightily from the effects of yet another drug change, I was sitting alone with Nick in his office. Suddenly, I felt faint, my heart raced, and I had a panic attack. I tried to hide it but I must have looked awful because Nick asked if something was wrong. I said I wasn't feeling well and was having heart palpitations. Big mistake. I should have gotten up and gone to my office for an Ativan. Before I could move, the commissioner was on his cell phone to the Portland Fire Chief. Nick was just trying to help in his BIG way but I knew that I was now just a passenger on a hurtling rocket to absurdity.

"Chief, one of my people isn't feeling well. Maybe something with his heart. What would you recommend? Oh … good … thanks."

"Nick, what are you doing?" I asked.

"Don't worry, Jim, the Chief said he would send someone over to check you out."

In minutes, I heard sirens, then four firemen and two EMTs came through the door. Nick yelled to them from his corner office. There was no escape. I was hooked up to monitors and of course my blood pressure and pulse skyrocketed. I knew what was going on, and I expect the EMTs did, too, but they were now in the office of their big boss, the commissioner-in-charge. The chief sent them at the commissioner's request so I was getting the full treatment.

"What should we do?" Nick asked.

"Oh, probably a good idea to go to the ER and get checked out," the EMT said, as I watched four firemen, bored, looking at posters on Nick's walls.

As they loaded their gear to leave, Nick called in our community liaison, a gentle former preacher, and had him take me to the ER. Again, walk in, say heart, rinse, wash, and repeat. After a couple of hours of monitoring they handed me a valium and sent me home. Just another day in the commissioner's office.

Chapter 33

Too Much Loss

I WAS SITTING in the Multnomah County Commission Auditorium when my cell phone buzzed. Nick was rolling out a new Parks budget to a big crowd. As Parks liaison, it was a big deal for me, too. Sally knew I would be late that night, so I wondered why she was calling. Sitting down front, I found a pause to sneak out.

Sally left a voicemail; "There's something very wrong with Bodhi. Call me now."

Bodhi, my big dog? No, she meant Luna, who had been diagnosed with mouth cancer. We had cancelled a trip to California after the diagnosis so we could have one last, long beach vacation with both girls. I called Sally. She was at the veterinarian emergency room.

"You have to come her now. Bodhi might be dying."

Not possible. That morning, Sally left before me.

I opened the front door so Bodhi and Luna and I could all say goodbye through the screen. It was a ritual they loved. I basked in Sally's smile every time we did it.

"No," I argued, "You mean Luna."

"It's Bodhi. Something happened. You need to come now."

I sped to the hospital. One look at Sally's face told me it was bad. Bodhi had jumped off the back porch as usual to chase a squirrel and yelped so loudly that Sally ran to see what had happened. Bodhi was in pain. Always the athlete Aussie, Bodhi was forever straining muscles in her legs. Sal gave her an anti-inflammatory but soon after Bodhi began to crash. Sally carried her to the car and took her to the ER. Bless her, Sally thought she had done something wrong. I went to the counter and they said I had to wait. I wasn't having it.

"My dog could be dying and I have to see her!"

Ushered into the ER, there was my big dog, Bo. I had even put her in the dedication of my thesis. Bodhi was laying on a table, an IV in one leg. A tech stood over her directing oxygen toward her nose. Bo spotted me, raised her head and wagged her tail. I scratched her ears and told her, "Big dog, we need to get you out of here."

The doctor took us to a screen to show us an X-ray of her gut. He pointed to fluid in her body cavity. It was blood. A cancer. The spleen had burst. Sally was asking more questions, but I got it immediately.

"She's bleeding out internally, isn't she?"

We knew she was dying and we had to ease that for her. They had moved her to a floor level crate. I sat down on the floor talking to her and stroking her ears. Luna and Bodhi were inseparable. Sally and I had heard that when one dog in a pair dies, it is better to have its mate there to understand what happened. I still don't know if that is true but we decided to go get Luna.

This is the moment I wish I had back. I was in shock and feeling the hum of panic. This was a slow-motion emergency and I had too much time to think. Sally could have gone to get Luna by herself. I just didn't want to be alone. As I got up to go, Bodhi, fading, rose on her front legs, raised her head, wagged her tail, and tried to come with me. As I always did when parting I said, "No, you have to stay, I'll be back."

When we got back with Luna, they took us into a room with a big couch. The tech carried Bodhi in and laid her on a rug. She was unconscious. I had always told her I would be there when this time came. She began writhing. I yelled for a vet to take her now. Luna walked round and round the room, barely noticing Bodhi.

It's simple. I should have never left Bo. I think of all the times my illness intervened in my life and this may be the one I want back most. Somehow, because I couldn't explain it to her, I still feel like it's Bodhi I let down the most.

We took the next few days off. When I picked

up Bodhi's collar to put away, Luna came running at the sound of the jingling tags. A week after losing Bo, I woke up to find Luna panting and alone in the middle of the floor. We took her to the vet, the same damned vet. She was kind of mean in the way she said Luna was dying. We said goodbye to Luna in our living room. I will always believe she died of a broken heart. She had borrowed the big energy of her mate for months and with Bo gone, she gave up. Now the house was quiet, awful, ghost dogs everywhere.

In the spring, we decided we needed a new dog in our lives. Luna had been Sally's great solace. The new dog would be hers. We found a beautiful — everyone has to tell us she is so beautiful — collie mix and named her Mozy. She had been removed from a drug house at two-years-old. Clearly abused by men, it took years of work for her to trust me completely but for Sally, the healing and bond was instantaneous. The unqualified love of a gentle dog at home was transformative.

Chapter 34

Finding My Higher Purpose

I WAS STILL IN A HAZE from continued drug experiments and desperately needed to reassert my control. I advocated to get back to the drugs I knew worked, take the beta blocker to lower my heart rate, and call it good. Sally was insistent. I would take my chances with Elavil in exchange for getting off the dizzying drug carousel. My cardiologist said that would be okay. *What? Hold it!* Why in the world didn't he say that before the two years of experiments? So much suffering for nothing? Like so many patients, I had deferred to the expert against my own self-interest. Lesson learned.

I was still doing my job at a high level. Some days were unqualified fun. Fun with a purpose. I took over as chief of staff for two weeks while Betsy was on vacation. It was very cool. I loved being 'the man.' Another check on the list of things I always wanted to do. However, I still didn't want to return to being a boss. Been there ... done that. I liked sitting on the side of the conference room table now, being the advisor and subject matter expert managing ideas and not people.

I had paid a serious price for the daily instability caused by transitioning from one side-effect laden drug to another. As in the past, I was masterful at concealing what was going on in my head and body. But each day required parallel efforts to deal with my side-effect symptoms and then address how my anxious mind was interpreting that chaos. Like water slowly eroding away a canyon wall, the strain began to show. I was having more night terrors and was up to my old work tricks, adjusting my work environment to manage my disorder. It was exhausting. And in now bi-weekly meetings, the trauma work with The Gnome intensified.

Having delayed one California trip because of the dogs, in the spring of 2013, I aborted a second flight to California. That wasn't good. I did it because I was afraid, caught in the old bad habits of my mind. It was time to reconnect with Gets It. Both Sally and I were afraid I was heading toward a setback. Mental illness is like that. While no one's life is a straight line, these illnesses can oscillate up and down. A good life depends on what you do when the downs come. And ... they will come.

When Sally and I met with Gets It, they both agreed on one fact. Gets It said, "You don't move fast enough to eliminate suffering." Suffering. Duh. The most fundamental teaching of the Buddha is: "Life is suffering and the end of suffering." They were right. This damn hillbilly stubbornness also gets me into trouble. As I kid, I was often told to just, 'gut it out.' I turned that into a life lesson, a sometimes self-destructive one. Because so much of my life has been about will power over my mind's tricks, I sometimes forget to be kind to myself. I don't have superpowers. The life I have comes with flaws I need to accept.

The behavioral treatment of PTSD and panic disorder had shifted since I last worked with Gets It. She was now using something called Acceptance and Commitment Therapy (ACT). Created by a psychotherapist named Steven Hayes, the therapy brings together many of the pieces I had accidentally assembled over the years of my search for a cure. It included the behavioral work of exposures combined with the mindfulness I had discovered in Buddhism. The difference between ACT and earlier behavioral work is that instead of fighting or trying to mitigate the feelings, thoughts, and sensations of panic disorder, the key is to accept all that icky stuff as something that cannot hurt you. By refusing to fight the disease, you rob it of its power. All my life I had been fighting.

This isn't an easy transition, so ACT is structured to slowly challenge existing thinking and coping tools. I began to see this new approach as a circuit breaker for my nervous system. New thoughts replacing old ones. And most importantly, ACT insisted that I use actual evidence to make my decisions. For example: my mind is constantly telling me I can't take care of myself. Gets It would walk me through my latest panic attack or avoidance behavior moment by moment. She proved to me that at every point I was, in reality, very good at taking care of myself. Think of what I was doing every day at work. Bombarded with drug side-effects, I still did my job. ACT opened up the choice to either be a victim of my thoughts or a detached interested observer. This is precisely the same state one seeks in meditation, what a Buddhist monk had taught me, choose not to take a ride on the passing thoughts.

The part of ACT that startled me was, like most enlightenment, obvious once made clear. I was challenged to consciously guide my actions with a higher purpose. This is the spiritual element I had been seeking all the way back to my experiment in Jungian psychology. ACT asks that you step back from the immediate goal — like taking a long drive out into the countryside — and ask yourself why are you willing to risk creating the dreaded anxiety symptoms? What is really important beyond the immediacy of your illness? What is more important than merely enduring the sensations? In the case of the drive, the higher purpose is about the joy I feel steering around winding country roads. Leaving the city is about feeding my soul with the beauty of mountains, trees, or steams. And the trip was really about my relationship, spending time with Sally. A higher purpose is almost always more powerful than the passing anxiety symptoms. When my muscles ached or I fell into old ways of thinking, my new job was turn to the real reason I was doing something.

Always the good student, my new guide would be a book by one of Hayes's colleagues, Russ Harris', *The Happiness Trap: How to Stop Struggling and Start Living*. He has the rare ability to take an approach to therapy and make it interesting, even funny. And like Gets It, he is a fellow sufferer. He knows the sensations and thoughts and sees through the carefully constructed fabric of avoidance. My copy of his book is marked up, dog-eared, and almost worn out. It's even on my phone. I don't hesitate to reread sections as little reminders. Inevitably, I return to passages reminding me how to approach the parts of my illness I find most vexing. I don't judge my need to remind myself how to live better. How many times does a baseball player throw and catch a ball or a NBA star practice free throws? Each refresh from the text was practicing the fundamentals. I finally felt as though all the pieces had come together, and I could be cured. Not quite … I was still an idiot about the true meaning of *cure.*

~

Sally and I needed to recharge. On a cold spring weekend, we made a trip to the coast. Mozy was starting to get good off leash, though she still only came when Sally called. Her golden coat waved beautifully as she ran wild on the beach in widening circles. Not understanding moving water, she ran into a flood level creek on the beach and suddenly stopped in the middle. Sally called her. She didn't come. When I got there, I saw she couldn't come. The swift current had wedged her back legs into a hole. Hypothermia was setting in. I thought, *well shit, I need to go get her.* I wedged my downstream leg against the current, fighting to keep my balance, and worked my way to mid-stream. Leaning to her, water up to my pockets, I grabbed neck fur and collar and gave her one huge pull, almost falling in myself. It was enough to dislodge her, and she bounded for shore and Sally. I saved her but now I was shaking and needed to get to warmth fast. Jogging back up the beach I yelled to Mozy, "So, can you come to me now that I saved your life, you silly dog?" She didn't.

Finally, I couldn't take it anymore and had to have a dog that chased things, my dog. I'm a total pushover for the neurotic herding breeds. At the Oregon Humane Society, we found a little boy dog. I had always had girl dogs. He was a rail thin recently rescued stray. A whippet/border collie cross, nine-months-old, and only 32 pounds. In the greeting pen he was all about the tennis ball. I said, "Dude, we are out of here." I named him Zoom after my favorite punk guitarist from the band X, Billy Zoom. We fed the little guy an astounding 5,000 calories a day to get some bulk on his hyperactive little body. Our home has stairs everywhere. It was clear he had never been up and down stairs. They terrified him. I spent two days working with the nervous, shaking little guy until he could go up and down our stairs by himself. There is boundless satisfaction in helping another creature heal.

~

ACT tool kit in hand, I started taking MAX rides again and did a repeat performance of the same day Portland to Seattle flights. Recovery is sometimes about humility. If I had to start over, so be it. This time, I had a higher purpose. It wasn't about me; it was about Dad and Mom. When I hesitated to get on a train, I pulled my new circuit breaker and thought of the look on my parents' faces. Two weeks later, we flew down to their new home in Redlands. That's right, of all places, Redlands, my undergraduate home. My folks had moved to a tiered-care community. The Great Depression kids had worked hard and were frugal. Now they could afford the best when they needed it the most.

My best work partner ever, Betsy, moved back to a senior position in a city bureau. She was ready for change, but the truth was that Nick had worn her out. He is never malicious, just a big old handful of a politician. Hannah was the new chief. Like Betsy, she was another of the original big four from his first campaign. She was a different kind of partner, but still a good one. We won a good battle to keep the city safe in the post 9/11 world. At lunch, nights and weekends, we got to do one of my favorite things, run and win a ballot measure campaign. For a guy who used to run campaigns in his head for fun, nothing was better than again being part of the real thing. I was now the senior policy director dreaming up ideas for new ordinances that would go into the city code with my name as the author. More checks on my political do-over list.

But in my journal a new idea appeared:

I think I could retire tomorrow and not give it a second thought.

I traded my Mini Cooper track car for my ultimate car dude extravagance, a BMW sport coupe. Living what ACT had taught me, Sally and I took our first real road trip down the Oregon and Northern California coast. We roamed the giant Redwoods, sat staring out into oncoming fog banks, explored cute little Northern California towns, and I got to play on lots of winding roads with my new toy. I hadn't done so much driving since my last drive back from California almost two decades before. It was glorious.

In November of 2014, we flew down to see my folks. When we had visited in 2009, it was clear something was wrong with Mom. I found her staring at her laptop typing passwords over and over. Now Mom was in a memory care facility. She no longer knew who I was. Dementia is cruel. I was now going down for my dad and brother. When you tell people you have the disease in your family, a broad community of shared experience appears. People who know precisely what you are enduring. For me, now Mom was gone. That wasn't the case with my dad. As a couple, they had traveled the world together, now he rarely left Redlands so he could be with Mom every day for lunch and dinner. After 62 years, she was still his great love. Every time I saw him with Mom, an old-fashioned word came to mind: steadfastness.

My brother has always been the one who stayed, the guy who was there, on demand for each family crisis. He retired after 20 years as a deputy sheriff, and appropriately, lives in the mountains actually looking down watchfully on the valley where our parents live. As the one who lives away, my role is to be supportive and only intervene when necessary or asked. Being up close and far away are different ways to live the hard parts of life. Mike is naturally a caretaker, a servant to others in ways I have never been. That was the nature of his entire law enforcement career. I think my family got the better part of the deal with him close by. I mean, I can't imagine me putting on the giant bunny costume for Easter at the memory care facility. He does those things with great joy and equanimity. He has that gift.

In quick sequence, two of my uncles and Aunt Jo died. The roots of the family tree were fading. A natural generational transition was underway. I'm the oldest of the next generation of Blackwoods.

~

Baseball being my one true religion, there was a pilgrimage I had yet to make: spring training. I had fallen in love with the Giants at spring training as child. In DC, all my baseball buddies went to spring training. My mental illness had made the idea of going to Arizona for spring training like a desert mirage. Over the years, I would look at the schedule, make plane and hotel reservations I didn't complete, then walk away from my computer with a sigh, sure it would never happen. But I was a different Jim now. On the evening of March 8, 2015, Sally and I stepped off a plane in Phoenix, picked up our rental car, and drove to our fancy resort hotel. In the hotel bar, I was surrounded with a different set of my people. Scottsdale is the home of the Giants. Everyone was wearing their Giants gear. My people. Baseball people. *Is this heaven?*

The next day, we posed for pictures in front of the stadium sign. I couldn't stop smiling and kept telling Sally, "Sal, look where I am. Look where I am."

Patiently, she looked at me and smiled. "I know honey, I know."

We took pictures in front of the white boards where they write that day's starting line-ups. I took pictures for other fans, just as giddy as I was. It was different than a regular season major league ballpark. Smaller, more human scale. Everyone just seemed happier. Maybe it was the fact that so many of us had escaped winter for a few days. Perhaps it was the recognition that we all were baseball nuts and that here that was more than okay, it was an expectation.

Then we started up the walkway to the field. I had that wonderful moment where I would finally see the field. This was different. The sight of the field hit me like a punch to my chest. I made it halfway up the walk, then collapsed against the wall in tears. Decades of disappointment flowed out in tears. Sally hugged me. All I could choke out between breaths was, "I'm here. I'm actually here. Look, Sally, it's the field." She knew. Sally understood. Every piece of the trip — the jet, the rental car, the hotel, the ride to the stadium —

was a series of tiny victories over the past. Knowing my higher purpose was sharing all of this, I took Sally's hand and we walked all the way up. And there they were, under an achingly blue desert sky, standing next to a World Series Champion logo chalked behind home plate, my team.

I saw three games in three days. Sal has a baseball limit. The second day I went by myself. Pause on that one. I went to a Giants spring training game by myself. Yeah, it was heaven.

Chapter 35

Knowing When

SOME DAYS, I was actually bored at work. Always dangerous for my restless mind. I was stuck on a project that would take a year. Worse yet, I was creating a new oversight body that I didn't think the city needed. That made all my effort seem not only tedious but pointless. In my entire work life, the longest project I had done was six months. Then, in a surprise, Hannah quit. She and her husband, lifetime world travelers, were moving to Europe. I was once again in transition at work. Yet another set of work relationship changes made me even more restless. I began to seriously consider a next chapter.

Original Fish staffer, Sonia became the new chief of staff. I had been her mentor and pushed her to take the job. While I am a lifelong political geek, love thinking and talking about the ins and outs of politics and governing, she isn't political by nature. Mostly, she loved Nick and saw herself as his defender. Where

I had had two partners interested in pushing Nick out of his comfort zone, challenging his limits, this was no longer the case. Sonia couldn't be the kind of partner I enjoyed most. I became conscious that I was at a time in life where I got to choose to be happy at work.

As 2016 began, something new, a dull ache in my stomach. I tried everything but couldn't shake it. A dear friend had recently died from colon cancer. I remembered her talking about the same kind of gut pain before she was diagnosed. Something new to worry about. In yet another reminder of mortality, my brother survived a second heart attack. Life just keeps coming at you.

Portland City Hall was becoming a very different place. On the days that city council met, I always kept the TV in my office tuned in, listening to the testimony and interplay between the elected officials. There is something sacred about how any group of people comes together to govern itself. I believe in the process and the rules that unify us. Now, weekly council sessions were a mess under the new mayor. He had removed most of the security from the building in a pandering call for 'openness.' There were angry, screaming interruptions at almost every council meeting. Sessions formerly done in hours now took most of the day. People coming to make their case before their government were treated with disrespect by a few individuals behaving badly. The illness of our entire democracy had infected city government. It was heartbreaking. Now when I looked up at that little brass City Hall sign, I felt dread.

After the election of Trump, Portland became a hotbed of protest with City Hall as ground zero. Our internal offices and even the entire building was often in lockdown for the safety of the staff. On Council meeting days, squads of police were secretly stashed in a conference room in case we needed them. The drama seemed endless. At times, the entire city council was moved to an isolated room and proceedings streamed on television so they could be in session. This wasn't any sort of government I anticipated or wanted.

In an age where every public building in the city needed prudent security, ours was wide open. Our offices were surrounded by glass, without safe rooms. Many of the people working in City Hall began to feel it was a dangerous place to work. The genuine lack of personal safety began to gnaw on me. I began to calculate how I would escape in an active shooter situation. It baffled me that there was no organized effort for all staff to practice that contingency. I slipped a box cutter in my desk drawer and a small container of pepper spray into my briefcase with no idea what I thought I was going to do with it. I was arming myself to try to feel better. I tried to address my own fear by being powerful, personally challenging the rowdy disrupters in the hallways, lobbying my boss and city officials for better security and organizing staff in the building to do the same. The bureaucracy moved very slowly. At first gradually, then rapidly, my sense of being unsafe activated my PTSD. I was losing my battle with my demons.

~

Sally took a ten-day trip to Spain by herself. In her professional and personal life, Sally has been a caretaker. She deserved to have an adventure by herself. I was good with her leaving for that long. I wanted that for her. While I travel more now, I am a bit of a boat anchor for the types of trips she wants to take. Even if I was the go-to-Europe guy, I think she will always need to take these solo breaks from the rest of her world. She had a great trip and I had a good two weeks at home with the critters.

~

As winter fell, we made another hard trip to California. My mom was in hospice care. Always stubborn, her mind had failed but her body would not give up.

~

I began a series of tests to determine what was going on with my gut. Upper and lower GI tests and finally a CT scan. They found nothing. What was going on? Only after I had left City Hall did it occur to me that my gut was trying to protect me. The sensations I was feeling were the same as when I was a child holding my belly and begging not to go. My unfocused gut pain was actually an old friend returned to warn me.

Finally, the powers decided to do something to protect the employees in the building. A plastic cover was put on the inside of all the windows so at least someone breaking them couldn't walk right in. A safe room was being installed, someplace we could shelter in case of an active shooter. The logical place was our kitchen and supply room. My office door faced into that room. Every day, I monitored the progress as workers installed ballistic sheeting on the walls so that shots fired at the walls couldn't reach us. Looking out of my office door, every day I was reminded that I wasn't really safe.

My PTSD was fully unleashed during an actual riot in City Hall. Not the first one we had seen but the worst. People pounded on our locked doors. Police were released from the conference room. More came from all directions, deployed in a battle with anarchists and protesters to clear the building. Pepper spray. Some staff were roughed up. Everyone was filming everyone else. I was just glad the cops were there to protect us. It went on for hours inside and outside of city hall.

The four corner council offices looked out into a central room and atrium in City Hall. It is a majestic space with tall pillars and marble floors. The front of each office is all windows so we could see the pushing and shoving and hear the bullhorns, yelling, and screaming.

I stood at the front of the office, vaguely aware that one of our interns was somewhere behind me, over my shoulder. When I looked out the windows I only saw bullies, every bully I had ever known. Then, coming out of my mouth, just above a whisper, I heard something that scared the hell out of me: "They should just hit them, kill the motherfuckers." If he heard it, it must have shocked him coming from the senior advisor to the commissioner, the older guy who told him his first day to ask any question, any time, so he could learn. The intern didn't say anything. I knew I was tapping into some scary ancient stuff; for a few seconds I had lost control and was fighting old battles from deep in my psyche. All the things I was afraid of actually seemed to be happening in front of me. I backed away and went to my office, shaking, muscles tensed for action, fighting the urge to raise my fists to my face in a defensive posture. This is what my PTSD was like.

As the melee continued, I paced in my office, monitoring the fight, when we were issued a new order. No one could enter or leave the building. My trauma broke through. Primal reaction. I couldn't fight. Now I wasn't being allowed flight. I grabbed my bag and ran down the stairs. I shoved my way by police and protestors to get out the door. I ran to my garage, got in my car, and drove across the Hawthorne Bridge before I pulled over to the side of the road and broke down. I called Sally. She came, got me, and took me to see The Gnome.

Everyone ... family, friends, doctors, told me that for my physical and mental health I had to get out of City Hall. I had wanted to stay one more year, until Nick's reelection. Stubborn, against my best interests as usual, I felt I owed him something. But that wasn't rational. I had completed my public service dream. I had worked hard over a couple of careers and didn't have to go to any job if I didn't want to. Sally and I had another trip planned to Arizona spring training. Exhausted, reflective, sitting in my office the day before for I left on vacation, I told Sonia I was ready to retire.

My mental state made the second trip to see the Giants a little less joyful, but it was still good to be away from Portland with Sally doing something fun. Even depleted, I still used my ACT skills to fly to Arizona. A ballpark in the sun was the perfect place to find perspective. I loved the game and roaming around Scottsdale, but it was also time for Sally and me to decide. After watching the first game, it was clear to both of us that I had reached the end of my second career, accomplished all of my goals, and laid to rest some ancient ghosts. Why not have more fun? Why not see more baseball? Why not do other things I loved, like write for myself and not for a politician? And why not be a better person for Sally?

I came home and wrote my resignation letter. On the day I was supposed to return to work from vacation, and deliver my letter, there was another little riot in City Hall. I couldn't be in that building anymore. It wasn't safe for me. I didn't return to my one-time dream job and I was happy about it.

My last day was April 1, 2017. April Fools.

Chapter 36

The Good Work is Never Done

THIS MEMOIR BEGAN with the most basic question. Over a year ago, I sat down for lunch with my first college girlfriend, Megan. As we talked about our time together and the impact of my mental illness on our lives, she looked me and asked, "What happened?"

I muddled through an answer with the stories I told myself for years, but I don't think what I said was satisfying to either of us. Later, I thought, *Yeah, what did happen?*

Buddhism tells me that life is often suffering and that compassion, both for oneself and for others, is a way to create and compound joy in one's life. Everyone ... *everyone* ... has secret and public burdens in their lives. My life has been partly defined by mental illness. You have heard the estimates. According to the Anxiety and Depression Association of America (ADAA), 40 million Americans over the age of 18 are affected by anxiety. Anxiety is a normal human condition that can manifest itself in a variety of mental illnesses. This means that mental illness is not exceptional. It's normal. When I have finally spoken to people about my illness a common response is for them to reveal that they, or someone they love, have, or have had, a mental illness.

To this day, I continue to medicate, meditate, and work with a mental health professional. Read, write, and meditate. That is what my normal looks like. In the course of writing this book, I catalogued over 20 different things I did to try to cure my illness. My innate stubbornness, a trait for both good and bad, pushed me to keep trying. Part of my path was that my panic disorder manifested at a time when there simply were no good options for recovery. One of the things I was able to tell Megan was that, in many ways, we were both doomed by the times we lived in. What happened to me and how it affected our love was not our fault. We did our best.

It was only in writing this memoir that I discovered the greatest fallacy in my view of my own illness. My definition of 'cure' from the those first awful days in Washington, DC was that I would one day not have this illness. More specifically, I would find a way to stop having the thoughts that made me anxious. I would fully trust my body, stop having panic attacks, not be afraid to travel, let go of my fear of bullies, and live a 'normal' life like everyone around me. Sounds wonderful as I write it … but it is ridiculous.

I was looking for the golden chalice, The Holy Grail. I was on a quest for unicorns and The Maltese Falcon. Given my genetics and childhood, what I sought was never going to happen. But the good news is that in writing this book I came to the conclusion that I am cured. I am cured. What I so desperately wanted, I already had. With hard work, love and compassion, I have a good life. While I'm often frustrated and anger flares at my fate, I now understand that acceptance is the actual cure. Now I can put away my treasure maps to the fool's gold.

This memoir became another path to healing. My dissociative events have always been marked by a physical expression. I pull my closed right fist to my face in a protective posture. Using Somatic Experiencing I worked on this motion with The Gnome. She asked, "What does that hand want to do?" For a week, I kept moving my fist around to see what it wanted to do. One night, I stumbled on a television documentary on east coast punk bands. The film made a big deal about skanking and the circle pit. I watched the dancer's hands and suddenly recalled my friend John teaching me how to stand when in a circle pit. There it was. John told me. My hands wanted to be swinging wildly in front of me, fists held tight. I wanted to claim my space. I repeated the motion over and over. My closed fist was now not just protective. Away from my body, it was powerful.

At the next session with The Gnome, I told this story. She said it was amazing and thought we would have needed to work a long time to find what that fist wanted to do. Then she said, "Have you had any night terrors since you discovered this?"

I thought, *No. I haven't*. She shook her head and said, "You are done with those now." She was right. My sleep hasn't been shaken by a night terror since. Healing is a continual process. It is possible to be curing yourself every day. I finally understood one of the most important riddles of my PTSD but still live with the disease every day.

In November 2017, my mother died. We flew down, on my birthday, and I delivered her eulogy while touching her casket. I was fully present with my family and myself. That's what being cured looks like.

In many ways, this book allowed me to rediscover Mom. Like many boys, I was on a long quest to find my missing father. Even now, missing his wife of 62 years, my father says it is Mom who really raised my brother and me. I rediscovered just how present my mother was for me. It's her face I remember most at the bottom of the escalator as we arrived from my first flight home in over two decades. In discovering the pain and confusion of my early childhood troubles, I found wells of compassion for how she must have suffered to see her first born in a pain she could not contain for him. The sound of her voice, when, as adults, Mike and I could surround her with hugs for that first time in years rings in my head with absolute clarity.

I write a lot about dogs and baseball. Too much and not enough. I'm on my fifth generation of dogs. In the worst times, the warm coat and boundless love of my dogs have helped me beyond measure. So many of our dogs were damaged when we got them that helping them recover has taught me patience with my own bumps and dents. And when joy seemed out of reach, the simple sight of a dog running for a ball reminded me that happiness could still be simple and lasting. Having never had the joy of children, I still think everyone needs to be owned by a dog, or a cat, if you must.

I was a gangly, uncoordinated kid who could never play baseball but loved it, nonetheless. I know … I know … old men get all gushy and strange about baseball. Guilty. For me the timelessness of the game wraps around my Zen Buddhism like a warm embrace. Watching baseball on television, in my darkest times, was where I could not be me for a few hours. When I was poor in Portland, minor league baseball was the one luxury I allowed myself. Losing major league baseball in DC was one of my deepest pains. Getting back to that ballpark in Seattle for that first major league baseball game in 20 years gave me a motivation beyond myself. Seeing spring training brought me both joy and closure. It was a restoration of something importantly normal in my life. The road to my getting back on a jet started when I pulled out of the driveway on that first trip to Seattle to see the Mariners.

In the midst of writing this book, my friend and former boss, Betsy, died of the cancer she had lived with for almost three years. It is the truth of time that you can begin to measure the days in the number of passings you must endure. To compound the loss, my last boss, and the guy who helped me live a long-lost dream, Commissioner Nick Fish, was diagnosed with cancer. He lives with it at full speed today, still deeply committed to public service. In life, and death, fairness is not a thing.

I have worked hard on my recovery, but it should be absolutely clear to you now that my wife, Sally, is my second beating heart. So many times, she has reached down into the inky pit of my despair and grabbed my hand to pull me out. We pledged that we would always do that for each other. There are an endless number of things she hasn't done and places she hasn't seen to both love and stay with me. I take some solace in the heights of the joys we have shared when together we reached new goals. For many of those moments, what I see first and most is her smile. I live for that smile, that pure, loving smile and those sparkling blue eyes. Only she really knows how hard I have worked. Our minds and hearts are joined in this journey.

I have had the unique opportunity to create some huge do-overs in my life. I owe some of that to my hillbilly roots and the 'don't fuck with me' stubbornness of the hill people who populate my family tree. I fought my way back from death and the depths to, in the end, leave my long IT career at the top of my game. I went to graduate school and succeeded in ways I didn't think possible. Almost insanely, I left one professional life to see if I could have done that political job in Washington, DC. Turns out I was pretty good at that, too. And that's the thing; if my life had been linear, if I had naturally gone from one thing to another, my life would have been full but I don't think I would have valued accomplishments in the same way. I got to do what had seemed impossible, over and over. That is the gift of my life with mental illness.

Just as importantly, my hyper vigilant mind is the source of many of the things I most cherish in myself. I see little details all around me that pass most people by. I appreciate the hills more because I didn't just have to climb up from the valley, I had to first climb out of a deep hole to get to the valley. For my people, the invisibly mentally ill, I want you to know I see you. I know what is possible. There is a cure out there and it may not be what you think it is. It may be better.

~

Early in my time in City Hall, I had to be in the room for the negotiations that drove AAA baseball out of Portland. After over 100 years, my city would not have a team. It was heartbreaking and left me angry because my dream was to be one of those retired guys I saw in the stadium, scorecard on their laps, beer in their hand, watching a day game on a lovely day. After watching the last Portland Beavers game, and taking home a handful of the soil from around home plate, I swore I would do all I could to bring baseball back to Portland.

One day, I was in my office and got a call from a guy named Ken who was a dreamer. He wanted to bring baseball to Portland and was looking for someone in City Hall who gave a damn. He found the right guy. He came in and pitched a wooden bat-college players league in one of the city parks in East Portland. I was all in. Baseball in one of the most underserved parts of the city. Yeah, I could help make that happen. I coached the ownership group on how to maneuver city politics and help cut bureaucratic red tape, and a deal was made. I didn't do it alone, but because Ken found the right guy to be his champion, the Portland Pickles came to East Portland. Baseball was back and I now have season tickets three rows behind home plate.

The first summer after I retired, I was always at the ballpark. Dad loved the idea of a team called The Pickles. I sent him a hat. Soon after Mom died, he finally was able to get knee replacement surgery. He always said he wanted to come up to see a Pickles game, so eight weeks after his surgery, my 85-year-old dad said he was driving up to see us. My brother and I were worried about the 1,000-mile trip but my stubbornness didn't come from nowhere. I told him the timing wouldn't work to see a game as the season would be almost done. He didn't care. "I just want to go see that ballpark you keep talking about."

What I didn't tell Dad was that it was possible he could arrive on the last day of the Pickles season. I didn't want him to do anything stupid to get here to see the game. Stubborn indeed. If it happened, it happened.

And so, it did. He arrived in Portland early afternoon on a sunny Saturday, game day. He was using both a walker and a cane to get around. When he got here, I fed him and told him to take a nap. We were going to a baseball game. He got a huge smile and went right to sleep as ordered.

I bundled him and his cane into my car and timed our arrival for the second inning so I could drop him at the front gate and then park on the other side of the park. Still moving very slowly, I helped him up the stairs to the seats behind home plate. I got us beers and dogs. While I was out getting the food, I ran into one of the owners.

"Hey, Bill, my old man just drove 1,000 miles to see his first Pickles game. He had a knee replacement, but he made it up here. You think you could drop by my seats and say hello?"

Bill said, "Oh yeah, I'll be down as soon as I can."

I came back and sat down. The next inning Bill came down. I know, I was being kind of a big shot and showing off for Dad but what the hell, it was my dad and he loved it. Bill sat on the steps and talked to Dad for the inning. Dad was beaming.

"What a nice guy!" Dad said.

Bill wasn't done. Before the next inning there was an announcement on the PA.

"Ladies and gentlemen, tonight we have a special guest at the ballpark. Down in the box seats is Jim Blackwood who helped get the Pickles off the ground here. His dad, Jim Sr., who is 85-years-old, just drove 1,000 miles to see his first Pickles game. How about we give him a hand!"

My old man pushed up on the seat and stood, no cane, to take the ovation from the crowd. He smiled and waved. Some folks rose to give a standing ovation. Behind his back, I looked up to Bill, mouthed thank you, and gave him a thumbs up. But Bill still wasn't done. The mascot, a giant walking pickle, came down and got between us for a picture. I think it was my most perfect night at the ballpark.

By the seventh inning, I could see Dad was getting tired.

"You okay? Ready to call it a night?"

"Yeah, but I could stay for one more inning."

And there it was, that thing I got from Dad: striving for the dream, even when you are out of gas, staying for just one more inning.

Chapter 37

My Cure

THE COMMON SENSE DISCLAIMER: Your mileage may vary. I can offer a lifetime of experimentation that led to my cure. My illness appeared in the relative dark ages of treatment; today, the number of resources available are diverse and effective. While you can't have my wife, the good news is that current treatments come with support groups. The Internet? I tried message boards, but ultimately found them unhelpful. The individual suffering can be overwhelming and counterproductive to your own recovery. Use those resources with great care. Pause to ask: How is this helping me?

- It feels like anxiety resides in the body. Early on I found that **physical activity** helped me feel better. Truth is, every bit of time you spend exercising pays off in better health and longevity. The picture in my mind was that I was actually burning through all that stored nervous energy. If you can, connect vigorous activity to the outdoors. A power walk, even in miserable weather, can be a revelation.

- Science has shown that **meditation** lowers anxiety. For me, that means Zen meditation. I sit every night. The method, or even religion, isn't as important as taking time to simply be with your breath. So many of the natural reactions to fear in your body begin with your breath. Learning how to change your breathing is a tool you can do anywhere. I have managed panic attacks in crowded conference rooms by being conscious of how I was breathing and slowly changing it. No one had a clue I was doing it. Learn to breathe.

- Even as an introvert, I have tried to cultivate a few important **relationships**. When I have honestly shared about my life with people, I have discovered wells of compassion. To be sure, I have also found confusion but having someone who knows who you are and how you live is a relief. Suddenly, you are not alone. That is a good thing.

- I have almost always had my dogs. **A pet** doesn't care how awful you feel or why. They will still curl up in your lap or chase a toy. Sometimes just seeing the goofy face of a pet will pull you out of yourself and back into the world of simple pleasures.

- **Know your joys** and cultivate them. Even in some of my worst moments I found joy watching baseball, listening to live music, reading a good book, or puttering in my garden. These are things that ground us in life and offer respite from our busy minds.

- Before turning to therapy options, it is important to understand what you are willing to devote to finding your cure. It is going to take **discipline**. Recovering from a mental illness is hard work that sometimes doesn't have immediate rewards. There are still times when my most important act is putting one foot in front of the other; just doing the next thing ... and the next thing. The **willingness** to keep at it is a reward in itself. You begin to trust your own tenacity. Coupled with that is **patience**. Give yourself a break. It is so easy to get discouraged. Break your effort into small pieces. **Celebrate** every single accomplishment. I mean it. If your goal is to walk to the corner and back, celebrate it like winning the Super Bowl. Patience is sustained in constant flow of small victories.

- Approach your illness with **humility**. There are no straight lines in nature. Anxiety and depression ebbs and flows, rises and falls. Hold the good times close and revel in them, but know nothing in life is permanent. Try to be as understanding when the effort is hard because that, too, is a passing moment.

- If you have been advised that **medication** is a good idea, then follow your prescriber's recommendation, but be your own advocate. Ask questions and learn about why you are taking a medication. If you can't do that for yourself, ask someone to help you with those questions. I resisted using medication because I thought it showed weakness. I was wrong. I take a low dose every day and supplement as needed, all under a doctor's care.

I'm skeptical that any drug is a silver bullet, but medication can be an important tool.

- Later in life, I discovered that one root of my panic disorder was long-term post-traumatic stress disorder (PTSD). That discovery was a relief. I chose a therapist who specialized in **trauma diagnosis and treatment**. Among the many good therapies, I chose Somatic Experiencing. I found that approach worked for me. The good news is that many clinics now specialize in PTSD. The illness has been largely demystified. If your path includes trauma, find the therapist and method that feels right to you. And if in the midst of a treatment you have questions, ask your therapist. I tried a couple of approaches until I felt comfortable and a good therapist always follows your lead.

- **Cognitive Behavior Therapy** (CBT) is the roll-up-your-sleeves, blue-collar work of managing anxiety. It is hard because you have to face the fears and by doing so rob them of the power in your life. For me it was about getting out of the house, getting in a car by myself, and adding one freeway stop after another. It was time on a street car without my cell phone. It was time alone or time in a crowd. This work is still my daily challenge, but nothing feels better than reclaiming territory or adding something new to my life. For this work, after many different tries, I landed on **Acceptance and Commitment Therapy (ACT).** ACT finally combined all the different pieces I had tried over decades into a consistent and easily understood approach. It blends meditation with finding the higher purpose for my actions. The therapists, books, and materials for ACT are available worldwide. I simply haven't found a better overall approach.

That's my cure. Each part of it is an ongoing practice that sustains me. It is where I have landed after more than 40 years living with my illness. I'm not writing a prescription as much as I want you to know that to create the best life with a mental illness, I have discovered you need a diverse tool kit. The most important thing is to gather those tools and techniques that work for you and carry them wherever you go.

Resources

I FOUND THESE BOOKS most helpful and they now occupy honored places on my book shelf:

The Happiness Trap: How to Stop Struggling and Start Living: A Guide to ACT, by Russ Harris

~ This is the book I use most often. It travels with me on my phone.

ACT Made Simple: An Easy-To-Read Primer on Acceptance and Commitment Therapy, by Russ Harris

~ When there are courses on ACT, this is the text.

Get Out of Your Mind and Into Your Life: The New Acceptance and Commitment Therapy (A New Harbinger Self-Help Workbook) by Steven C. Hayes and Spencer Smith

~ I liked having an orderly way to learn ACT. This workbook helped.

Waking the Tiger: Healing Trauma, by Peter A. Levine and Ann Frederick

~ This text is the key text to understand Somatic Experiencing.

The Body Keeps Score: Brain, Mind, and Body in the Healing of Trauma, by Bessel van der Kolk M.D.

~ This book on the treatment of PTSD lives on the bestseller lists. It's a great survey.

Feeling Good: The New Mood Therapy, by David Burns M.D.

~ I found this book most helpful when recovering from depression.

The Miracle of Mindfulness: An Introduction to the Practice of Meditation, by Thich Nhat Hanh

~ Meditation is simple and hard. I always recommend this book as a starting point.

Fear: Essential Wisdom for Getting Through the Storm, by Thich Nhat Hanh

~ Finding a different way to understand fear was very helpful.

Zen Flesh, Zen Bones: A Collection of Zen and Pre-Zen Writings, by Paul Reps and Nyogen Senzaki

~ These ancient texts are short, explosive and funny. Who knew Zen was funny?

Sit Down and Shut Up: Punk Rock Commentaries on Buddha, God, Truth, Sex, Death, and Dogen's Treasury of the Right Dharma Eye, by Brad Warner

~ This is a funny and powerful book on the logical intersection of punk and Zen.

Acknowledgments

THANKS to my early readers, Hannah Kuhn and Bob Wise. My provocative and patient editor, Jami Carpenter. Megan asked the question that lit the fuse. For cutting the early trail, Carl. For the second act, Commissioner Nick Fish. My academic mentor, Debra Bokowski, PhD. My helpful grad school and writer colleague, Jan Wilson. My indispensable humans, Linda Zahavi, M.A., L.P.C. and Mary Englert, M.S., MA., L.P.C. All the mental health professionals along the way. And my many work professional team members in all their guises.

My family: Jim Blackwood Sr., Dorothy Blackwood, and Mike Blackwood. All of the great grandparents, grandparents, aunts, and uncles whose stories I absorbed along the way.

Dobbsie, Ziggy, Luna, Bodhi, Mozy, Zoom, and the hundred lost tennis balls.

Baseball ... just because.

Then there is one. Sally Jo Blackwood, my wife.

About the Author

JIM BLACKWOOD, JR. grew up in the Southern California desert and lived on both sides of the country before settling in Portland, Oregon. He was a successful information systems manager and senior policy director for a Portland city commissioner. In 2017, he embarked on his third career as a fulltime writer.

Jim has a Master of Arts in Interdisciplinary Studies focused on political science and religion. He is a student of Zen Buddhism and baseball, which he feels are pretty much the same thing. When not at his keyboard, he can be found in his garden, at local rock clubs, or in his third-row seats watching the Portland Pickles baseball team.

Jim and his wife, Sally, live high atop Mt. Tabor with their dogs and too many baseball hats.

~

To contact Jim, learn about future projects, or read his blog, please visit www.jimblackwoodjr.com.

www.ingramcontent.com/pod-product-compliance
Lightning Source LLC
Chambersburg PA
CBHW051348290426
44108CB00015B/1927